The Gospels of Jesus Unplugged

The New Wine with Less of the Old Wine

Christopher John Joseph

Published by Christopher John Joseph

Cover Images by Vecteezy.com

Design by Christopher John Joseph

Published by Christopher John Joseph

ISBN 9781763770331

Printed by Ingram Spark

Second edition

Available from: Book Retailers

Other books by author. The Teachings of Jesus Unplugged

Contact Author: jcinfocus@gmail.com

Gospel texts compiled from, The Gospels of Jesus Unplugged, Assorted Bibles, Interlinear Greek Translations and the Author's own Understanding of Jesus as Seen Through His Words.

Contents

Introduction

The following is a single reading, combining the main early Christian Gospels of Matthew, Mark, Luke, John and Thomas, which give us a Spiritual path to follow, that leads us to a Spiritual awakening and transformation. Jesus of Nazareth taught this path, which comes from a Divine Source of Eternal Spiritual Love in a Heavenly Spiritual World. He states it is this Divine Spiritual Being's Life-force of pure Love that gives us our True Life as Spiritual children of a Loving Creator. We all have a Soul mind and Spiritual body empowered only by a Loving Spiritual Life-force placed within us, to find and become at one with. This is the one great pearl, the one great and good fish, the yeast in the bread and the treasure in the field. Once we are born again into our True Spiritual identity, then we must manifest this Divine Love in our Spiritual body and Soul through our temporary body of flesh while here on the Earth. It is the ultimate medicine we can apply to all suffering in this world.

This is done through our own actions and words that spring forth from an Eternal wellspring of Loving Spiritual Life-force, or Living water as Jesus called it, in our Soul mind and Spirit. We must Love all other children equally, sharing this gift of Light and inner Spiritual Love with everyone we meet during our life. Sharing it especially with those in great need, as Jesus taught us to do. The purpose and heart essence of the Teachings of Jesus are to awaken and transform us from a life lived out of the temporary dualistic mind and flesh body and help us arise into a new experience of our Spiritual Soul mind and Eternal Spiritual body. These are empowered only by the singularity of Divine Love and the Loving Spiritual Life-force of our Loving Spiritual Creator, who gives us Life Eternal in a Heavenly Spiritual world if we wish to accept it. The choice is ours to accept or reject.

To understand the Spiritual message that Jesus taught, the Gospels contain profound insights through His Spiritual Teachings and Way of Life. They can transform anybody into a Spiritual child if we immerse our Souls and Spirits in them and allow them to open us up to experience a new Spiritual identity and Life. As Jesus Himself said, "My words they are Spirit and they are Life." The Gospel translations in this book do not contain superfluous accounts or misleading translations concerning Jesus.

Over time, after Jesus died to the flesh and rose in Spirit, the early authors of the Gospels, influenced by their sacrificial religion, felt they needed to implant various links and Jewish overlays. Their overlays emphasised Jesus as being the promised Messiah of the Old Testament, a sacrificial lamb who died for our sins and was the only son of the dualistic God of the Jews Yahweh.

They did this to try and legitimise Jesus to the Jews, so they would follow Him out of their distorted understanding of a dualistic two-headed God of War and Love and bring them into the One True Loving Spiritual Creator. But they created a problem. They set up a view of Jesus that sees Him mainly through an Old Testament Jewish lens, instead of being an awakened Universal Spiritual child of the One True Loving Spiritual Creator.

Jesus was like a gold panner searching for golden nuggets of Love amongst the river of dualistic words describing the two very different opposing Godheads of the Jews on one body called Yahweh. It had a brutal Godhead of war, murder, revenge and thieving intention along with another Godhead developing towards only Love and Peace on the one body called Yahweh. He found all the gold nuggets of Limited Love and put them together to discover a pure circle of Golden Spiritual Love, with no evil war God in it at all. Our Loving Spiritual Creator in the Heavenly Spiritual World.

Once He discovered this, He underwent a transformation and awoke to His True inner Spiritual identity as a Spiritual child on Earth empowered only by the Loving Life-force of our Loving Creator in Heaven. This is what He called, "The Treasure hidden in the field of our flesh," that we must all find before our death. He became Spiritually enlightened to the Truth of who our Loving Creator really is and realised we must all become at one with Her perfect Love to be Her Spiritual children. For as Jesus said, "Our Spiritual Creator's Love rises and shines on both the good and the evil."

Jesus taught we can all become children of our Loving Spiritual Creator just as He did. He is initially our Teacher, guide and great friend, until we awaken to the Spiritual Truth of who we really are. Then we become his brothers and sisters equal in every way with Him. He should be seen correctly as one who awoke to His True identity as a fully enlightened Soul in Spirit and Spiritual child of our Loving Spiritual Creator in the Heavenly Spiritual World, while still here on Earth. A Spiritual Teacher who dedicated His life to help us all find what He had found within Himself and is in all of us. He awakens us to become Spiritual children of the Loving Spiritual Creator while here on Earth and guides us home to the Eternal Heavenly Spiritual World.

The following Gospel accounts are focused on the main, essential Teachings Jesus gave to awaken our Spirits to True Eternal Life and on important events involving Him. All superfluous, redundant and inaccurate accounts are not included so as to clarify His Spiritual Way and Teachings of Love and the One True Loving Spiritual Creator accurately.

Daily Prayer to Center Your Spirit

I use the female pronoun She. Traditional Christians use He.
Our Loving Spiritual Creator is beyond gender.

As I rest upon this Earth
the Holy One She will give birth
to who I really am.
Awakening me from clay and sand,
a Spiritual child of the Divine
with only Her Love that fills my mind.
To every creature I will be kind,
in every single land.
For this is truly who I am.
A Spiritual child
of the Loving Spiritual Creator
in the Heavenly Spiritual World.
Born out of the Earth
to bring Her Love to children in need
and help guide them home to Heaven
as She has guided me.
Through the Spiritual Way and Teachings
that Jesus gave us to be, just as He.
A Spiritual child of Love on Earth.

Chapter 1

Our Loving Spiritual Creator

Our Loving Spiritual Creator is Only Love

Matthew 5:38-39, 43-48, Luke 6:27-36 Jesus describes our Loving Spiritual Creator and Her perfect, Loving mind and nature when He taught, "You have been wrongly taught of old, 'You shall Love your neighbour and hate your enemy. An eye for an eye and a tooth for a tooth.' But I say to you, Love your enemies, do not retaliate in kind to an evil person but to him who strikes you on the one cheek offer the other to him also, bless those who curse you, do good to those who hate you, pray for those who spitefully use you and persecute you, so that you may be Spiritual children of our Loving Creator in the Heavenly Spiritual World. For She causes Her sun to rise on the evil and the good and sends rain on the just and the unjust. She is kind to the ungrateful and the evil and forgiving to all who come to Her in Truth and in Spirit. Therefore, you must be as merciful as She is to be Her Spiritual children.

If you only love them who love you, what degree of Spiritual Life is that? Do not even sinners, thieves and tax collectors do the same? And if you greet your fellow brethren only with respect, what more are you doing than others who are little in Spirit? And if you only do good to those who do good to you, what Spiritual merit is in that? But I say to you,

Love your enemies do good and lend, hoping for nothing in return and your Spiritual Life will increase.

And from him who takes away your cloak do not withhold your tunic from him either. Give to everyone who asks of you. And from him who takes away your material possessions do not ask for them back. And if you only lend to those whom you expect to give back, what Spiritual motivation is that? Even sinners do the same. In everything treat others the same way you want them to treat you. Therefore, if you wish to be Her Spiritual child on Earth and later enter the Heavenly Spiritual World, your Love now must be as perfect as Her Love towards all of Her children on Earth."

Author: Our Loving Spiritual Creator's identity and very existence is only formed from a Loving Heavenly Spiritual Life-force and mind of Pure Love. She can harm no one. She Loves and cares for every living thing. She is the giver of True Spiritual Life and only heals, restores and uplifts our Spirits to Heaven. And She has created a Spiritual world of Love for us to come to if we just choose to be Her Spiritual children of Love on Earth now. It is a free will decision we must all make by ourselves.

Jesus clearly states throughout His Teachings that the source of our Spiritual Life comes forth from this Divine Spiritual Being of Perfect Love from another Heavenly Spiritual World. Jesus gives us a very clear and precise understanding of who our Loving Spiritual Creator really is by describing Her character in detail. She is merciful, generous, peaceful, non-violent, seeks no revenge, forgives and Loves all of Her children equally the good and the bad and She is Spiritual not material so material things have no hold on Her. There is no mention of murder, thieving, revenge or infanticide as seen in the description of the two headed God Yahweh of the Jews.

So, for us to awaken and be Her Spiritual children on Earth we must also have these same characteristics of Love as She has and live out of them now as pacifists. Jewish/Christians go to war and kill other children just like the Jews with their two headed God Yahweh. True Christians who understand the Spiritual Way to Heaven of Jesus do not.

Our Loving Creator is Spirit

John 4:23-24 Jesus said, "The hour is coming and now is when the True children of our Loving Spiritual Creator will adore Her in Spirit and in Truth; for such are those who our Loving Creator seeks to be Her children in Heaven. Our Loving Creator is Spiritual and those who wish to be with Her must come to Her in their Spirit and in Truth."

Author: Jesus clearly states our Loving Spiritual Creator who creates our Spiritual bodies to come to Heaven in is not a material being but Truly Spiritual. And we can only enter Heaven in our True Spiritual body that we must become at one with now, not our dead body of flesh.

Jewish/Christians wrongly teach that our dead body of decomposed flesh comes back to life at the end of the world at the Apocalypse. Jesus never said any of this. They are all false Jewish overlays put onto Him to distort the Truth of what He really taught. Jesus taught our Spiritual body leaves our body of flesh at the time of death and is taken to be near to our Loving Spiritual Creator to reap as we have sown.

She is Wholly Good and Only Gives Good Things

Mark 10:18 Jesus said, "Only our Loving Spiritual Creator is Truly and wholly good."

Matthew 7: 7-11 Jesus said, "Ask and it will be given to you, seek and you will find, knock and it will be opened to you. For everyone who asks receives and he who seeks finds and to him who knocks it will be opened to him. For what man among you if his son asks for bread would give him a stone? Or if he asks for a fish, will he give him a snake?

If you being imperfect know how to give good things to your earthly children, how much more will your perfect Loving Creator in Heaven give Her Loving Spiritual Life-force to all Her Spiritual children who ask Her."

Author: She is pure Love like pure Gold that cannot be tarnished by any evil and She can only do good and give good things to us all if we just ask Her for Her help. And the ultimate gift She offers us is to become Her Spiritual children of Light in Heaven if we wish to accept it.

She Never Harms Her Children

Matthew 18:14 At the end of the Lost Sheep parable Jesus says this regarding those children lost in sin. "Just as a man rejoices over finding a lost sheep so also it is the will and intention of our Loving Spiritual Creator that not even one of the least in Spirit that has gone astray into sin should ever perish or be destroyed."

Luke 12:32 Jesus said, "Do not be afraid little flock about your earthly life, for it is your Loving Spiritual Creator's great pleasure to give you all Spiritual Life in the Heavenly Spiritual World."

Author: Neither Jesus nor our Loving Spiritual Creator can ever harm us. They constantly strive to help and guide us all to Heaven. We may harm ourselves or others through sin and get lost in darkness and have to reap the suffering we have sown but their Love still shines upon us waiting for us to return to the Spiritual Way of Love and Non-violence that will lead us back home to Heaven. Love only gives Life.

Jewish/Christians wrongly teach that Jesus and our Loving Creator will destroy Her children who are lost in darkness or all those who do not follow Jesus at some false Apocalypse. This is filthy slander and goes against everything

Jesus taught and demonstrated in His own life on Earth. Hell exists but it is of our own making not theirs.

She Gives us True Spiritual Life

John 6:63 Jesus said, "It is the Spirit who gives us True Life. The body of flesh profits nothing in the end."

Author: Only a Spiritual Loving Creator can create a Spiritual body for us to have True Spiritual Life in. Our Earthly mothers can only be involved in creating a body of flesh that one day has to die just like our mother's body of flesh must. But our Loving Spiritual Creator is Eternal, so our Spiritual bodies and Soul minds of Love will also be Eternal if we just accept them and live in the Way of Love and Non-violence that Jesus taught. Jesus taught we all have these two very different bodies in one with us right now but only one leaves at death. Our Spiritual body.

She is Omniscient

Luke 8:17 Jesus said, "For there is nothing concealed that will not be revealed or hidden from view that will not be known and come into the Light."

Luke 16:15 Jesus said, "You are those who justify yourselves before men, but the Loving Spiritual Creator knows the truth in your hearts. For what may be highly esteemed among earthly men may be an abomination in the sight of our Loving Creator."

Matthew 6:3-4 Jesus said, "When you perform a charitable deed do not let your left hand know what your right hand is doing or sound a trumpet before you so your charitable deed may be in secret. And your Loving Creator who sees all that you do will pour forth more of Her Loving Spiritual Life force into your Spiritual body and Soul to give you Life."

Author: Heaven and our Loving Spiritual Creator can always see us night and day and know everything we do, say and think. This is because we all have a Spiritual body and Soul within us that comes forth from Her and is connected with Her through Her Loving Spiritual Life-force that empowers our Spiritual body and Soul mind of Love. They are always with us but are we always with them?

She is with us in Life and Death

Matthew 10:29-31, Luke 12:6-7 Jesus said, "Two sparrows are sold for a copper coin. But not one of them falls to the ground and dies without our Loving Spiritual Creator being with them. And our Loving Creator even knows the number of hairs on your head. Therefore, do not fear to die to your flesh, you are of more value than many sparrows and our Loving Creator will be there with you even when your Spirit passes through the death experience of your body of flesh."

Author: Our Spiritual Eternal Life filled with Love comes forth from our Loving Spiritual Creator who's entire being is only Love. She sees us always, is with us always and always only guides us to Heaven and can never hurt us as we are Her children. We only have to accept our Spiritual Life of Love and Live out of it now. And even as our Spirits are passing through the death experience of our bodies of flesh, She is right there with us because She is Spirit.

Our Loving Spiritual Creator Is Only Love

Chapter 2
His Words Save Us
Not His Blood

Throughout the five Gospels Jesus clearly indicates what it is that will save you from sin and suffering, awakening your Spiritual Body and Soul that brings you into the Eternal Heavenly Spiritual World after the death of your body of flesh. He states repeatedly that it is His words that will save you not His blood as some Jewish/Christians wrongly teach. By listening to His words, understanding them and implementing them in your life you will become an awakened Spiritual child of our Loving Spiritual Creator in the Heavenly Spiritual World just as He did. This is the enlightenment that He and Buddha experienced and taught to help us awaken also. Without Jesus explaining His Spiritual Teachings and Spiritual Way of Love and Non-violence that He demonstrated to us, how would we know what being Spiritual means?

My Words Will Save You 1

John 8:51 Jesus said, "Truly, I say to you if anyone keeps and practices My words, he shall never see death."

Luke 6:46 "Why do you call Me Teacher, Teacher but do not do the things I tell you?"

John 14:23-24 "If anyone loves Me, they will keep My words and live by them, and our Loving Spiritual Creator will love them and will go to them and make a Spiritual home with them."

John 5:24 "He who listens to My words and understands their meaning and lives out of them and believes in our Loving Spiritual Creator who sent Me to teach them to you, cannot be judged for they will do no wrong and will pass through the death experience into Spiritual Life. The hour has now arrived when those dead to the Spirit will hear the voice of the child of our Loving Spiritual Creator and come to True Spiritual Life"

My Words Will Save You 2

John 6:63 Jesus said, "It is the Spirit who gives True Life, the flesh profits nothing. The words I have given you they are Spirit and they are Life."

John 8:31-32 "If you live out of My words, you will truly be my disciples and you will know the Truth and the Truth will set you free."

John 3:11-12 "Truly, I say to you we speak of what we know and testify of what we have seen, and you do not accept our testimony. If I told you of earthly things and you do not believe, how will you believe Me if I tell you of Heavenly things?"

Thomas 1 "Whoever understands the meaning of these sayings and Teachings will not taste death."

My Words Will Save You 3

Thomas 19 Jesus said, "Blessed is the one who came to Life before coming to Life. If you listen to my sayings and understand them, these stones will serve you."

John 4:13-14 Jesus said to the Samaritan woman, "Everyone who drinks of this Earthly water shall thirst again, but whoever drinks from the Living Spiritual Water that I shall give them shall never thirst again. And that Water that I shall give them shall cause a flow of Spiritual Water to well up inside them, lifting them up into everlasting Life."

Thomas 108 "Whoever drinks from My mouth will become like me, and I shall be like that person and what is hidden will be revealed to that one."

John 7:37-38 "If anyone is thirsty let them come to Me and drink. He who believes in Me, from his innermost Spiritual being will flow rivers of Living Spiritual Water."

My Words Will Save You 4

Mark 10:45 Jesus said, "For the child of our Loving Spiritual Creator did not come to be served but to serve others by teaching everyone how to be set free from sin and Spiritual ignorance and to dedicate His life to bring this about like a ransom paid to release someone from captivity."

John 15: 3 "You are already clean and free of sin because of the words which I have spoken to you."

John 15:7 "If you live in Spirit with Me and My Teachings and My words live in you ask whatever you desire, and it will be done for you."

Sower of the Seeds

Matthew 13:18-23 Jesus said, "My words are like Spiritual seeds, and I am the sower of those seeds. When anyone hears the words of Spiritual Life but does not understand them the evil one can come and easily snatch them away from within their hearts and Souls. Preventing them from believing and being made whole in Spirit. These are the ones where the seeds fell by the pathway.

Those who receive the seeds on stony ground, initially receive the words with great joy. But they have no deep belief within themselves, so endure only for a while. For when the challenges of suffering and persecution arise in their Spiritual Life because of the Spiritual Way, they are not strong enough in Spirit and abandon the Way.

Those who receive the seeds among the thorns are those who listen to the words but the cares of this world and delight in material riches smothers the words and their Spirit does not grow to maturity and are unfruitful.

Those seeds sown on good soil are those who hear the words, believe them, hold fast to them, understand them and patiently bring forth Spiritual fruits. Some a hundredfold, some sixty and some thirty. He who has ears to hear, listen correctly and understand My words."

My Words are the Rock of Your Life

Matthew 7:24-27, Luke 6:46-49 Jesus taught, "Everyone who comes to Me and hears My words, understands them and puts them into practice will be like a wise man who while building his home dug down deep and laid the foundation on a rock. And the rain fell, and the floods came, and the winds blew and beat violently against that home but could not shift it and it did not fall because it had been founded on the rock.

But everyone who hears these words of mine and does not understand and practice them will be like a foolish man who built his home upon sand. And the rains came, the winds blew, and the floods came and beat upon that home, and it fell down. And great was its fall."

Author: The home that cannot fall is our awakened Eternal Spiritual body and Soul mind of Love empowered only by the Loving Spiritual Life-force of our Loving Spiritual

Creator in the Heavenly Spiritual World that comes alive through understanding the words of Jesus.

We have just read seventeen independent sayings of Jesus that clearly state it is His words and Teachings that save your Spiritual Life if you just listen to them, understand their meanings, live out of them and are transformed by them. It is His words and Teachings that awaken you to who you really are. A Spiritual child of our Loving Spiritual Creator in the Heavenly Spiritual World of Love on Earth just like Him. Without them you would not know how to behave as a Spiritual child of our Loving Spiritual Creator so could not become Her Spiritual child.

His words and Teachings describe all the characteristics such as forgiveness, non-violence, compassion, generosity, equanimity and Love that must be present in us to bring our Spirit alive as our primary Eternal Spiritual identity that we need to become at one with to be able to enter the Heavenly Spiritual World. If Jesus just died on the cross and shed His blood but said nothing, we would have no way of knowing how to get to the Heavenly Spiritual World or who we really are as Her Spiritual children of Love and Non-violence.

Our Loving Spiritual Creator is Only Love

Spiritual Words are the breath of Life.

We become Spiritually alive when we drink them in.

Chapter 3
Jesus Taught We All Have Two Bodies

The following is one of the most important, overlooked and misunderstood Teachings of Jesus where He literally states we all have two very different bodies with us right now that will separate at the time of death.

One is a temporary Earthly body empowered by earthly foods, water, chemicals, minerals and gases that dies disintegrates and returns to the earth from which it was formed. The other is an Eternal Spiritual body and Soul empowered only by our Loving Creator's Spiritual Life-force which leaves our body of flesh at the time of death and returns to be in the presence of our Loving Spiritual Creator to reap as we have sown.

Two In a Single
Bed

Luke 17:33-37 Jesus taught, "He who lives an Earthly life of only the flesh will lose it. But he who separates himself out from his life of flesh, by following My Spiritual Way and Teachings, will find his Eternal Spiritual Life.

There will be two bodies in a single bed. One is Spiritual and one is flesh. The one of Spirit will be taken to be near to our Loving Spiritual Creator. The one of flesh will no longer be of any use and being redundant will be sent forth.

There will be two women grinding at a millstone in the same position. One is Spiritual. One is flesh. The one of Spirit will be taken to be near to our Loving Spiritual Creator. The one of flesh will no longer be of any use and being redundant will be sent forth.

There will be two standing in a field. One is Spiritual. One is flesh. The one of Spirit will be taken to be near to our Loving Spiritual Creator. The one of flesh will no longer be of any use and being redundant will be sent forth." The disciples asked Jesus, "Where will they be Lord?" Jesus replied, "The dead body of flesh will be where the vultures gather." This next saying was deliberately cut out by corrupt early Jewish/Christian leaders. "The body of the Spirit will be where the eagles fly." or "The body of the Spirit will be with our Loving Creator in Heaven." If our Spirit of Love is alive.

Thomas 61 Jesus said, "Two will relax on a couch. One will die; one will live. If the flesh has come into being because of the Spirit, it is a wonder. However, if Spirit came into being because of the flesh, this is a wonder of wonders. But I am amazed at this, how such great richness of Spirit could be placed in such poverty of the flesh.

When you know your True selves, then you will be known and understand that you are Spiritual children of the Loving Creator. But if you do not know your Spiritual self, then you live in poverty, and your flesh will embody that poverty."

Author: This very important Teaching of Jesus is also seen in His simple and profound sayings, "It is the Spirit who gives True life, the flesh profits nothing. Marvel not that I tell you. You must be born again from Heaven above." He is saying we all have two bodies in one that separate at death. Jesus wants us to awaken into our True Eternal Spiritual body of Light and Love as He did and become at one with it while still in our temporary body of flesh. If we do not awaken to live out of our Spiritual body of Love, He says we will only live in the poverty of our body of flesh that dies.

Only our Spiritual body lives on to reap as we have sown. We must be filled with and live out of the Loving Spiritual Life-force from our Loving Creator right now that empowers our Spiritual Life. Our dead flesh is just food for the vultures and does not come back to life as most Jewish/Christians wrongly teach children.

They also distort this very important Truth that Jesus gave us by saying there are two completely different people in the single bed, at the millstone, in the field and on the couch. They are perverting this wonderful Truth of Jesus and must stop teaching that to children. The Greek interlinear translation is very specific about the bed only being fit for a single person. And women ground flour on their own small millstone in their home, and two different women could not use it at the same time. Jesus said this deliberately.

The Gospels have been tampered with and the saying of Jesus about our body of Spirit leaving at death to be with our Loving Spiritual Creator in Heaven has been deliberately removed. This was to accommodate the Nicene agenda falsely teaching that the dead body of Jesus came back to life when in fact He left His dead body of flesh in His perfect Spiritual body of Light, which we all have within us just as Jesus did. Two bodies in one that Jesus said we must find right now.

Make the Inner Like the Outer

Thomas 22 Jesus saw some babies being nursed and said to His disciples, "These nursing babies are like those who enter the Heavenly Spiritual World." The disciples said to Him, "Then shall we enter the Heavenly World as babies?"

Jesus said to them, "When you make the two into one, when you make the inner like the outer and the outer like the inner, and the upper like the lower, when you make male and female into a single one, so that the male will not be male and the female will not be female, when you make eyes replacing an eye, a hand replacing a hand, a foot replacing a foot, and an image replacing an image, then you will enter the Heavenly Spiritual World."

Author: Jesus is explaining that once their inner Spiritual body and Soul mind of Love come fully alive and they manifest it through their temporary body of flesh, then both bodies will be as one. Just as the nursing babies are newborns so also will the disciples be, once they are born again into their Spiritual bodies. Children who awaken Spiritually all have bodies like Angels in Heaven and no longer have biological genders. Our Spiritual identity and image eventually replace our physical identity and image.

Jesus Gives Us What We Have Yet to Realise

Thomas 17 Jesus said, "I shall give you what no eye has seen, what no ear has heard, what no hand has touched and what has never arisen in a mortal mind"

Author: Jesus is referring to our Spiritual body and Soul mind of Love which He guides us to find within ourselves once we awaken our Spirit to Life. And by doing this He connects us to our Loving Spiritual Creator's Life-force and the Heavenly Spiritual World of Love.

But we cannot see our Spiritual body or touch it with our material bodies of flesh, and it has a Spiritual mind that is at One with only Love, not a dualistic mortal mind like the body of flesh. We are used to only engaging with the material body of temporary flesh with its physical senses and mortal mind through our biological brain.

Now we must open up our Heavenly Spiritual mind of Love and awaken our Spirits to True Eternal Life. Then our whole Spiritual body and Spiritual mind will be filled with the Light and Love of our Eternal Loving Spiritual Creator. Meditate on Love and Heaven every day.

Flesh gives Birth to Flesh.
Spirit gives Birth to Spirit

John 3:38 Jesus said, "Truly, truly, I say to you, unless one is born again from above, he cannot see the Kingdom of the Loving Spiritual Creator." Nicodemus said to Him, "How can a man be born again when he is old? Can he enter a second time into his mother's womb and be born?"

Jesus answered, "Truly I say to you, unless one is born of water and the Spirit, he cannot enter the Kingdom of the Loving Spiritual Creator in the Heavenly Spiritual World. That which is born of the flesh is flesh; and that which is born of the Spirit is Spirit. Do not be amazed that I say, you must be born again from above. The wind blows where it wishes and although you hear the sound of it, you do not know from where it comes and where it is going. So, it is with all children who are born of the Spirit."

Nicodemus replied, "How can these things happen?" Jesus answered him, "Are you a teacher of Israel but do not know these things? Most assuredly I say to you, we speak of what we know and testify about what we have seen, but you do not accept or believe our witness. If I have told you about Earthly things and you do not believe they are true, how will you believe Me if I speak about Heavenly Spiritual things that you cannot see?"

Thomas 112 Jesus said, "Woe to the flesh that depends on the Soul! Woe to the Soul that depends on the flesh!"

Author: The Spiritual body and Soul mind of Love of Jesus had fully awakened while He was still in His body of flesh. That is why He knew He would not die after they killed His body of flesh because He realised His Spiritual body was empowered by a Loving Spiritual Life-force from the

Heavenly Spiritual World, another dimension and Universe of Love. Jesus is trying to tell Nicodemus we all have these two very different bodies. One is Earthly flesh which we can see with our earthly eyes. One is Spiritual but we cannot see it with our earthly eyes. As Jesus said to Nicodemus, "You do not see Spiritual children come or go just as you cannot see the wind for, they are born into Spirit from the Heavenly Spiritual World above."

Jesus clearly states, "Flesh only gives birth to flesh. Spirt only gives birth to Spirit." We must all be born again into our Eternal Spiritual body through receiving the Loving Spiritual Life-force from our Loving Creator above in Heaven. This is the Living Water that gives our Spirits True Life to awaken our Spirits to live out of now while here on Earth.

The Jews had no idea about this Truth of our two bodies of Spirit and flesh in one and could not comprehend what Jesus was explaining. We see this clearly when Nicodemus who was a Jewish teacher asks if we have to climb back into our mother's physical body and womb to be reborn.

Our earthly bodies are formed from the earthly substances of our earthly mother's bodies of flesh and are temporary and eventually all die and disintegrate. Our Spiritual bodies are formed from the Heavenly substances of our Spiritual Creator's Loving Spiritual Life-force and they are Eternal. They are both very different types of bodies, and they need different types of nourishment to be alive. Jesus said, "My words they are Spirit and they are Life. Man does not live by bread alone." Spiritual food and earthly food.

Thomas 82 Jesus said, "When you see a likeness of yourself, you are happy. But when you see your images that came into being before you and that neither die nor become visible, how much disturbance will that cause in you?"

Author: This is the only known reference we have where Jesus seems to be stating that we have had many lives before this one. Many different bodies and identities but we think we have only had this present one. To realise we may have had many previous lives could be disturbing for some. But it does match the Hindu and Buddhist Spiritual Teachings that we travel from life to life until we perfect our Spiritual awakening. Then we can enter Heaven or Nirvana no longer having to be born again in this material world where everyone will suffer at some time in their life and all must pass through death to leave to be born again.

Spiritual Nourishment

John 4:31-34 While still at the well the disciples returned and were urging Him to eat something, but He said to them, "I have nourishment to consume that you are still unaware of." The disciples wondered if someone had already brought Him something to eat. Jesus said, "My nourishment comes from performing the Spiritual works of My Loving Spiritual Creator sustained by Her Loving Spiritual Life-force within My Spiritual body."

John 6-27 "Do not labor only for earthly foods which perish with your earthly body but labor for the Spiritual nourishment from Heaven, the Loving Spiritual Life-force, which endures within your Spiritual body to Eternal Life. I will give this to you for I am an awakened Spiritual child of our Loving Spiritual Creator in the Heavenly World, and this is My joy to do so."

Author: All Spiritual bodies are sustained only by our Spiritual Creator's Loving Life-force which wells up inside us like a fountain of Living Spiritual Water as Jesus taught. All our Spiritual bodies are born from above in the Heavenly Spiritual World and placed in our bodies of flesh at conception. Once born again into our True Spiritual identity of Love we become Spiritual children of our Loving Creator in Heaven on Earth and can never harm anyone.

Our body of flesh is sustained by earthly foods, water, chemicals, minerals and gases to have temporary life and is dualistic in its mind's view. Our Spiritual body and mind are singular in their view. As Jesus said, "If your eye or mind is single in Love, your whole body will be filled with Light. But if your eye or mind is dualistic you will be filled with darkness." Yahweh is a dualistic God of Love and murder.

Jesus clearly states that we need our Spiritual body and Soul mind of Love to come alive in order to enter the Heavenly Spiritual World of our Loving Spiritual Creator and this is the most important body we have. The dead body of flesh is just food for the vultures.

Just as we need blood to be circulating through our body of flesh for it to have Earthly life, likewise we need our Spiritual Creator's Loving Spiritual Life-force circulating through our Spiritual body and mind to have Spiritual Life. This is the Living Water Jesus speaks about that we need to receive from Heaven in order to awaken, activate, empower and bring our Spiritual body and Soul mind of Love alive. It then connects us to Heaven and will guide us home.

Without it our Spirit and Soul may be present but dormant like a seed waiting to be watered to sprout and come alive and grow into the fullness of Spirit. We must be 'Born again from Heaven above,' and move into our Spirit now while we have the chance. Our Spiritual mind of Love must become our primary mind expressed through our mortal body of flesh.

Gain the Material World but Lose your Soul

Matthew 16:26 Jesus said, "For what does it profit a man of flesh if he gains the whole material world but injures or destroys his True Spiritual body and Soul mind of Love. Or what earthly material thing can a man exchange for his Heavenly Spiritual body and Soul?"

Matthew 10-28 "Do not fear those who can kill your body of flesh but can do no more to you but only fear sin that can destroy your body of flesh and also lead your Spiritual body and Soul into outer darkness tormented by being separated from our Loving Creator and Heaven by your own wrongdoing."

Matthew 19:24 "Assuredly I say to you that it is hard for those who have material riches to enter the Heavenly Spiritual World. It is easier for a camel to go through the eye of a needle than for a man rich in material wealth to enter Our Loving Creator's Spiritual World."

Mark 12:17 "Give to Caesar the things that are Caesars and to our Loving Creator the things that are Hers."

Thomas 27 Jesus said, "If you do not fast from the material world, you will not find the Heavenly Spiritual World. If you do not keep the Spiritual day as a Spiritual day, you will not see our Loving Spiritual Creator."

Thomas 67 Jesus said, "Those who know everything but lack within, lack everything."

Thomas 70 Jesus said, "If you bring forth what is within you, what you have will save you. If you do not have that within you, what you do not have will be unable to save you."

Thomas 108 Jesus said, "Let the one who finds the world and becomes wealthy, renounce the world and become Spiritual."

Thomas 109 Jesus said, "The heavens and the earth will roll up in front of you at death, but he who is living on the Loving Spiritual Life-force of the Living One will not see death nor fear."

Thomas 110 Jesus said, "Whoever finds their True Spiritual self is worth more than the world."

Author: Jesus was always teaching not to place your hope in the material world, money or wealth or your temporary body of flesh as they all perish. He gave Spiritual instructions to help us all become at one with our primary Spiritual body which He knew was Eternal and vital to be alive and filled only with Love. If we have it within us, alive and well and are living out of it here on Earth we can enter the Heavenly Spiritual World of Love after passing through our death experience and not fall into the trap of thinking we only have a body of flesh that dies. We may be very successful and full of knowledge about the material world and worldly life but if we lack Spiritual Love within our Souls and Spirits, we lack the most important thing of all and are actually empty of True Life. So, we must treat every day of our life here on Earth as another day to practice being Spiritual in all we do.

Bodies Like Angels

Mark 12:24-27, Luke 20:34-38 Jesus said, "The children of this Earthly material world marry and are given in marriage in bodies of flesh. But those who are ready to arise from their dead body of flesh and live in Spirit will enter the Heavenly Spiritual World where marriage is no longer necessary. For they will have Spiritual bodies like Angels having become Spiritual children of our Loving Spiritual Creator and cannot experience death anymore. For our Loving Spiritual Creator is not a Creator of dead bodies of flesh but of Spiritual bodies that are Eternal."

Author: Although we may not be able to see our Spiritual bodies with our eyes of flesh right now Jesus tells us they will be like the perfect, beautiful bodies of Angels in Heaven. Not bodies of flesh as many Jewish/Christians wrongly teach.

Our Loving Spiritual Creator is only Love.
Our body of flesh and body of Spirit
must become at one with Love.
The inner like the outer.

Chapter 4
Children of Light

All of the following Teachings of Jesus will contain similar contents or sayings from the five Gospels, Matthew. Mark, Luke, John and Thomas. By combining these into a more consolidated presentation, the focus on what Jesus was teaching can be amplified to understand the meaning of His Words more fully. Rather than being scattered throughout the Gospels. These following sayings of Jesus all refer to our Spiritual bodies of Light and Love that leave our body of flesh at the time of our death experience.

I am the Light

John 8:12 Jesus said, "I am the Light of the world. He who follows Me shall not walk in darkness but have the Light of True Spiritual Life."

Thomas 75 "I am in the Light that is over all things. I am in all, and all came forth from the Light in Me, and all is accomplished in Me. Split a piece of wood and the Light in Me is there. Pick up a stone and you will find the Light in Me there."

John 9:4-5 "I must work the works of our Loving Creator who sent Me while it is still daylight; the Spiritual darkness of night is coming when no one can work. As long as I am in the world, I am the Light of the world."

John 11:9-10 "Are there not twelve hours in the day? If anyone walks in the day he will not stumble because he sees the light of this world. But if anyone walks in the night he stumbles because the Light is not in him."

John 12:46 "I have come as a Spiritual Light into the world so that everyone who believes in Me and My Way will not remain in darkness."

John 12:35-36 "The Spiritual Light is with you a little longer, make progress now while you have the Spiritual Light otherwise the darkness may overtake you. He who walks in darkness does not know where he is going. While you have the Spiritual Light believe in the Light so you may become Spiritual children of the Light."

Mark 9:3 Jesus took Peter, James and John up to a high mountain and He was transfigured before them. His clothes and radiance became shining, exceedingly white like snow.

You are the Light

Matthew 5:14 Jesus said, "You are the Spiritual Light of this world. A city that is set on a high hill cannot be hidden or fall. No one after lighting a lamp places it under a basket or a bed but places it on a lamp stand and it gives Spiritual Light to all who come near it. Let your Spiritual Light so shine before others, that they may see your good deeds and glorify our Loving Spiritual Creator in the Heavenly Spiritual World through being a living Spiritual child of Her's on Earth."

Luke 11:34 "The lamp of your body is the eye of your mind. Therefore, when your vision is only of Love your whole Spiritual being is full of Light and Love. But when the vision you have is evil, your whole being is full of darkness. Be warned then that the life-force in you is not darkness. If your whole Spiritual being is full of Light having no part dark, you will be completely filled with the Loving Spiritual

Life-force of Heaven as when the bright shining of a lamp gives you Light."

Matthew 10:27 "What I explain to you that has been obscured in darkness speak in the Spiritual Light. And what you hear with your ear proclaim from the rooftops."

Thomas 24 They asked Jesus, "Show us the Spiritual Way to the place where you are, for we must seek and find it." Jesus said, "Whoever has ears let him hear. Light exists within a Spiritual child of Light and he becomes a Light to the whole world. If he does not become at one with the Spiritual Light, he is in darkness."

Thomas 50 Jesus said, "If they ask you, 'where have you come from?' say, 'We have come out of the Spiritual Light from the place where the Light came into being from Her own self, establishing Herself appearing in an image of Light.' If they ask you, 'Are you the Light?' say 'We are Her children of Light and are the chosen ones of the Loving Creator.' If they ask you, 'What is the evidence of the Loving Creator in you?' say, 'It is motion and rest.'"

Thomas 61 "If one is whole, he will be filled with Spiritual Light but if he is divided within himself, he will be filled with darkness."

Author: These important Teachings of Jesus direct us to become Spiritual children of Light and Love in this dualistic material world of Good and Evil while we still have the opportunity to do so. If our mind is divided between Loving some children and hating some children, we will be filled with darkness and not be children of Light. For our Loving Creator's Love and Light shines on the good and the evil and the just and the unjust. Jesus said if our Spiritual Love is not as perfect as Her Love, we will not enter the Heavenly Spiritual World. Only Spiritual children living out of Light and Love can enter.

Jesus was a fully awakened Spiritual child of Light and Love and at one with the Spiritual Loving Life-force of our

Loving Spiritual Creator that was empowering His Spiritual body, mind and Soul. We must all be born again into our Eternal Spiritual bodies and True ultimate identity as Spiritual children of our Loving Creator in the Heavenly world.

Our Loving Spiritual Creator is only Love.

To be Her Spiritual children on Earth

we must only be Love.

Then we become

the Spiritual children of Light.

Chapter 5
Faith

We cannot see the Heavenly Spiritual World or our Loving Spiritual Creator with our eyeballs of flesh. Or any Angelic beings who live in the Heavenly Spiritual World, although some report that they can. We cannot even see our own Spiritual bodies that we have within our bodies of flesh right now. We will only see them when we leave our body of flesh behind. We cannot give physical proof to other children that this Heavenly Spiritual World exists simply because they are formed from two different life forces.

But the more we contemplate the words of great Spiritual Teachers like Jesus and Buddha and begin to implement them in our daily lives; we can open up a Spiritual connection with that Heavenly World or Nirvana from within our Spirit and Soul mind of Love that come to Life.

Then the subtle presence of our Loving Spiritual Creator and the Heavenly Spiritual World can be felt and experienced as we grow stronger in our True Spiritual identity of Love and Non-violence. And events in our life can be guided from above through what appear to be timely coincidences but are really helping hands from the Heavenly Spiritual World. This can lead us into a real deepening faith in the existence of Life after death of the body of temporary flesh and empowers us here on Earth to become Spiritual children, selfless and filled only with Love. For this is how the Heavenly Spiritual World is. Only Love.

Jesus said Have Faith 1

Mark 11:22-24 Jesus said, "Have faith in our Loving Spiritual Creator's existence. For truly I say to you if any awakened Spiritual child of our Loving Creator says to this mountain, 'Be lifted up and cast into the sea,' and has no doubt in his heart and Soul but believes that those things he says will be done for him, then whatever he has asked for will be done. Therefore, I say to you whatever things you need and ask for, believe that you receive them and you shall have them."

Matthew 17:19-21 The disciples asked Jesus why they could not heal the sick child like He did. Jesus said, "Because of your unbelief; for assuredly I say to you if you have faith the size of a mustard seed you will say to this mountain, 'Move from here to there,' and it will move and nothing will be impossible for you. However, this long-term kind of illness does not go out except by prayer and fasting."

Jesus said Have Faith 2

Matthew 18:19-20 "If two of you agree on Earth concerning anything you ask, it will be done for you by our Loving Spiritual Creator in the Heavenly Spiritual World. For where two or three are gathered together in My name and Spiritual Way, I am also there with the Spiritual Life-force in them."

Luke 17:6 The apostles asked Jesus to increase their faith. Jesus replied, "If you have faith the size of a mustard seed you can say to this sycamine tree, 'Be uprooted and be planted in the sea,' and it will happen as you say."

Author: Jesus tells us we must believe in a Heavenly Spiritual World formed by our Loving Spiritual Creator empowered and sustained by Her Loving Spiritual Life-force which can alter any material thing on Earth. Jesus said it is Her Pure Spiritual Life-force of Love in His Spiritually awakened body and mind that performs all the miracles. We must awaken our own Spiritual body and Soul mind of Love, connect with our Loving Creator's Life-force within us as Her children on Earth and She will help us perform all good works. Jesus tells the disciples to increase their Spiritual belief in Her to connect with Her in Spirit to receive more of Her Loving Spiritual Life-force as they were still Spiritually inadequate within themselves to heal the sick child.

Jesus said Have Faith 3

Thomas 106 Jesus said, "When you make the two into one, you will become children of humanity, and when you say, 'Mountain move,' it will move."

 Thomas 48 "If two make peace with each other in a single house, they will say to the mountain, 'Move!' and it will move."

 Author: Jesus is telling us we must not be divided between our body of flesh identity and our Spiritual body housed in the one bodily form. If our Spiritual intention is motivated by the Loving Spiritual Life-force in our Spiritual body, we must also bring into perfect alignment our body of flesh with its dualistic mind potential and reign it in to be in accord with our Spiritual intention of only Love. Then the two become at one in purpose to bring Heaven's Love to Earth. Then miracles can be performed by the Loving Spiritual Life-force in our Spiritual body flowing out to others through our body of flesh.

Jesus said Have Faith 4

Matthew 7:7 Jesus said, "Ask and it will be given to you, seek and you will find, knock and it will be opened to you.

For everyone who asks receives and he who seeks finds and to him who knocks it will be opened to him."

Thomas 2 Jesus said, "Let the one who seeks not stop seeking until one finds. When one finds, one will be unsettled from the old way. When one is unsettled like this, one will become amazed and will overcome all."

Mark 5:35-36 So, Jesus went with Him, but while on the way a man from the ruler's house came and said, "Your daughter is dead; do not trouble the Teacher anymore." But Jesus heard what the man was saying, and He said to the ruler, "Do not be afraid, but only trust and believe."

John 4:49-51 The nobleman said to Him, "Sir, please come down, before my child dies!" Jesus said to him, "Go your way, your son has life." So, the man believed the words that Jesus spoke to him and went his way. And as he was returning home his servants met him and told him saying, "Your son is alive and well."

Jesus said Have Faith 5

Mark 5:28-29, 33-34 A woman with a bleeding hemorrhage believed that if she could just touch the cloak of Jesus as He passed by, she would be healed and she did and her bleeding was immediately healed. She came and fell down before Jesus and told Him of her healing. Jesus said, "Daughter your faith has made you well. Go now in peace and be healed of your affliction."

Matthew 14:29-31 Jesus replied, "Come." So, Peter got out of the boat and walked on the water and came towards Jesus. But when he was distracted by the strong winds, he became frightened and began sinking, crying out, "Master, save me." Jesus immediately reached out His hand to him and held on to him saying, "O man of little faith, why did you doubt?"

Jesus said Have Faith 6

Luke 8:24-25 And they went and woke Jesus saying, "Master, Master, save us for we are perishing." Then He arose and rebuked the wind and said to the sea, "Peace, be still!" And the wind ceased and there was a great calm. And He said to them, "Why are you so afraid? Have you no faith?"

Mark 1:40-42 A leper implored Jesus saying, "If you are willing, you are able to cleanse me of this illness." Jesus, moved with compassion, stretched out His hand and touched him and said, "I am willing, be cleansed." As soon as He spoke these words, immediately the leprosy left him and he was cleansed.

Matthew 8:5-13 A centurion who had heard about Jesus came forward to Him saying, "Master, my servant is lying paralysed at my home in terrible distress, please heal him?" Jesus said, "I will come now and heal him for you." But the centurion answered Jesus saying, "Master, I am not worthy to have you come under my roof; but only say the word, and my servant shall be healed. When Jesus heard him, He marveled and said, "Truly I say to you, not even in all of Israel have I found such faith and trust in Me." And Jesus said to the centurion, "Go, be it done for you as you have believed." And the servant was healed from that moment.

Jesus said Have Faith 7

Mark 10:50-52 A blind man by the roadside calling out to Jesus was brought to Him. And Jesus asked him, "What do you want Me to do for you?" The blind man said to Him, "Master, that I may receive my sight." Then Jesus said to him, "Go your way, your faith and belief in Me has made you well." And immediately his sight was restored.

Mark 7:24-30 A Canaanite woman came to Jesus and cried out to Him saying, "Master, have mercy on me, for my daughter is severely possessed by a demon, please help me." And Jesus replied, "O woman, your faith and trust in Me is great. Be it done for you as you desire." And her sick daughter was healed from that hour.

Jesus said Have Faith 8

Mark 6:4-6 Jesus came to His own country, but they had no belief in His Spiritual wisdom or power and were offended by His Teachings. Jesus said, "A prophet is not without honour except in his own country and among his own relatives and in his own house." And He could do no mighty works there except to heal a few sick people. And He was amazed by their lack of belief.

Thomas 31 "A prophet is not popular in his home-town, and a doctor cannot heal family and friends."

Author: Jesus tells us it is imperative that we believe in the Spiritual power and Loving Life-force of our Loving Creator in Heaven which can alter any material thing on Earth including our bodies of flesh. It is clear that the best healings were attained when the person who was ill had faith in Jesus having Spiritual power from Heaven to heal them. Clearly the Spiritual Life-force of Pure Love from the Heavenly Spiritual Universe and World dimension is far superior to mere material matter and the forces that form it.

Through faith in Him being an enlightened Loving Spiritual child of Heaven on Earth they were open to receive the healing Spiritual Life-force from our Loving Creator as it flowed from Heaven into Him and through Him into their bodies of flesh. As Jesus said, "He who believes in Me and My Spiritual Way out of his inner Spirit will flow rivers of Living Water."

The people in His own locality where He grew up, could not believe in His Spiritual transformation and Spiritual power and wisdom He now had from Heaven. They judged Him because He was just a carpenter's son not a Jewish Rabbi. But this same inner Spiritual awakening and transformation that Jesus experienced connecting us to the Heavenly Spiritual World of only Love is within us all. Whether you are a carpenter, an office worker, rich or homeless, a King or Pope, a criminal or soldier Jesus taught this Spiritual treasure of Heavenly Life awaits for us all to find within our body of dualistic flesh. We then only have to accept it and become at one with it and that is what Jesus was really Teaching. His Teachings are a Universal Truth for us all.

But we must have intelligent faith in Jesus and His Teachings, understand them correctly and if we apply ourselves to open up this Spiritual Way and belief within our own minds it will awaken our True Spiritual identity. Then as Spiritual children of our Loving Spiritual Creator in the Heavenly Spiritual World, filled with Her Loving Life-force we can really make a difference in this dangerous material world by being bridges from Heaven to Earth to bring Heaven's Love to all. How else can we change this world for the betterment of all except through Love.

Our Loving Spiritual Creator is Only Love.

We must become Her Spiritual children of

only Love on Earth.

Chapter 6
In the Beginning

Author: The following is a combined account of the main events from the four Gospels, of the birth and early life of Jesus before He began teaching His Spiritual Way of Love and Non-violence to awaken children's Spirits and bring them back to True Eternal Life in the Heavenly Spiritual World of our Loving Spiritual Creator.

Our Loving Spiritual Creator is beyond gender. The Jewish/Christian tradition uses the male pronoun He. As Jesus described our Spiritual Creator as being only Love and our Spiritual source of Life, I use the pronoun She to refer to our Creator as it is our mothers who give birth to our physical life as our Loving Spiritual Creator gives birth to our Spiritual life. Also, in English the pronoun He is only male while the pronoun She has both genders in the one word and so is more inclusive. Just replace She with He while reading this book if that suits you better. It is the Teachings of Jesus about the Spiritual Way of Love and Non-violence that are the most important thing to understand to awaken our Spiritual body and Soul mind of only Love.

In the Beginning

In the beginning was the Word and the Word was with our Loving Creator and the Word was our Loving Creator. All things were made through Her and without Her was not anything made. In Jesus was Spiritual Life and that Life was the Light of men. The Light shines in the darkness and the darkness could not comprehend it or overcome it.

There was a man sent from Our Creator, whose name was John. He came to testify to bear witness to the Light, that all might believe through Him. He was not that Light but gave witness to it. The True Light that enlightens everyman was coming into the world. He was in the world, but the world did not know Him. He came to His own and His own received Him not. But to all who received Him, He empowered them to become children of the Loving Spiritual Creator. They were born again not of blood, nor by will of the flesh, nor by will of man but through the Loving Spiritual Life-force of our Loving Spiritual Creator.

The Word awoke in flesh and dwelt among us full of grace and Truth, and we have beheld His glory as an awakened Spiritual child of our Loving Creator on Earth. John testified saying, "This was He whom I spoke of, He is higher in Spiritual awakening than I am." For the old law was given through Moses, but Grace, Truth and Spirit came through Jesus of Nazareth. No man of flesh has seen the Loving Spiritual Creator, only a Spiritually awakened child of the Loving Creator can truly know Her.

Mary and the Angel

An Angel was sent from the Loving Creator in the Heavenly Spiritual World, to a woman named Mary in Nazareth who was married to Joseph. The Angel told her that she was highly favoured by the Loving Creator due to her good and virtuous nature and would give birth to a son whom she should name Jesus.

He would become an awakened Spiritual child on Earth, of the Loving Creator in the Heavenly Spiritual World and be a great Spiritual Teacher. He will help children everywhere to find their True Spiritual identity within themselves, which awakens them to also become Spiritual children of the Loving Creator, and He will lead them into the Heavenly Eternal Spiritual World of Love.

Mary asked the Angel how this could happen to someone as simple as her, and the Angel told her that the Spiritual Loving Life-force of our Loving Creator would be with Jesus and would teach and guide him until He experiences His full Spiritual awakening.

Elizabeth

The Angel also told Mary that her elderly cousin Elizabeth was pregnant, so Mary went to visit her. There was in the days of Herod, the king of Judea, a certain priest named Zacharias of the division of Abijah. He had a wife from the daughters of Aaron, and her name was Elizabeth. And they were both righteous before Our Creator.

While Zacharias was performing his priestly duties in the temple, an Angel appeared to him and told him his wife Elizabeth will become pregnant and bear a son whom he should call John. And he will be a great prophet and shall not drink wine or strong drink and shall be inspired by the Loving Spiritual Life-force of our Loving Creator. And he shall help many children of Israel who have lost their way to repent and turn the hearts of the fathers to their children and the disobedient to the wisdom of the just.

When Mary arrived to see Elizabeth and greeted her, the baby in Elizabeth's womb leaped for joy and Elizabeth was filled with the Loving Spiritual Life-force which inspired her to say, "Blessed are you among women Mary, and blessed is the fruit of your womb." And Mary stayed with her for three months and then returned home.

After Elizabeth gave birth, they named the baby John as the Angel instructed. Zacharias, inspired by the Spirit said,

"This child shall be a prophet of our Loving Creator, and teach salvation through the repentance of sins. He shall give Light to them that sit in the darkness and in the shadow of death, to guide our feet into the way of peace." And the child grew strong in Spirit and went into the wilderness to live.

Jesus is Born

Mary gave birth to a boy, as the Angel predicted, and they named him Jesus. Mary kept all the things the Angel predicted about Him to herself pondering what was to become of him in the years ahead.

Jesus Presented in the Temple

And at the end of eight days Jesus was circumcised and Mary and Joseph brought him to the temple in Jerusalem to perform the purification ceremony and offer a sacrifice of two turtledoves to the Loving Creator.

There was a man named Simeon, devout and virtuous, who was inspired by the Loving Spiritual Life-force that he would not experience physical death until he had seen the anointed one, the Messiah of the Jews and the world. Led by the Spirit to go to the temple the same day as Mary and Joseph, he saw their baby and asked to hold Him and was moved by the Spirit to announce the following.

"Now let your servant depart from this Earth in peace, according to your promise; for my eyes have beheld your salvation in this child who will be a Spiritual Light to the Gentiles and a saviour to the people of Israel. He is set for the fall and rising of many in Israel. And will be a sign from the Loving Spiritual Creator that is spoken against. And all the thoughts of people will be revealed through the Spiritual

Truth that He will bring." Mary and Joseph were amazed by what he predicted about their son Jesus.

Jesus as a Child

When Jesus was twelve years old, Mary and Joseph and their family went to Jerusalem for the Passover Feast. After the Feast they left to return home, but after one day they realised Jesus was not with them so returned to Jerusalem to find him. They searched for three days and finally found Him in the temple, talking with the Teachers listening to them and asking them questions.

And all that heard Him were astonished at His understanding of the Spiritual Teachings. And his mother asked Him why He had caused them such distress by not leaving with them from Jerusalem, and He replied, "Why were you seeking Me? Don't you know I must be doing My Loving Creator's Spiritual work?" And He then went with them, and his mother kept His response in her heart. And Jesus increased in wisdom, stature and favour with our Loving Spiritual Creator in the Heavenly Spiritual World.

John the Baptist

In those days came John the Baptist, son of Zacharias and Elizabeth the cousin of Mary, preaching in the wilderness of Judea and all the region about the Jordan. He was preaching a baptism of repentance for the forgiveness of sins, saying the Kingdom of Heaven is very close to you. Jesus later explained that the Spiritual connection to the Kingdom of Heaven is actually inside of you.

John wore a garment of camel's hair and a leather girdle around his waist, and his food was locusts and wild honey. And many went out to see him from around Jerusalem, Judea and all the region about the Jordan river. And they were baptised by him in the river Jordan, confessing their sins, cleansing their Souls and Spirits.

The Jewish leaders sent priests and Levites from Jerusalem to John to ask him who he was. He told them he was not the Messiah or a prophet, but a voice in the wilderness crying out to make straight the way of the Loving Spiritual Creator.

But when he saw many of the Pharisees and Sadducees coming to be baptised he said to them, "You brood of snakes! Who warned you to flee from the wrath to come? Bear good fruit that benefits repentance, and do not presume that just because you say you have Abraham as your father you are saved. For our Loving Creator can raise up children of Abraham from these stones. Even now the axe is laid to the root of the trees, and every tree that does not bear good fruit is cut down and thrown into the consuming fire of Truth."

And the multitudes asked John, "What then shall we do?" And he answered saying, "He who has two coats, let him share with him who has none, and he who has food let him do likewise." Tax collectors also came to be baptised and said to him, "Teacher, what shall we do?" And he said to them, "Collect no more than is legally required of you." Soldiers also asked him, "And what shall we do?" And he said to them, "Rob no one by violence or by false accusation, and be content with your wages."

John then said, "I baptise you with water for repentance, but He who is coming after me, whom you know not, is mightier in Spirit than I whose sandals I am not worthy to untie. He will baptise you with the Loving Spiritual Life-force and with the fire of Light. His winnowing fork is in his hand, and He will clear His threshing floor and gather the True wheat into the granary, but the useless chaff will pass through the unquenchable fire of Spiritual Truth, Light and Divine Love to be cleansed."

Baptism of Jesus

Jesus came from Galilee to the Jordan river to John to be baptised by him. John saw him approaching and said to his disciples, "Behold, the child of the Loving Spiritual Creator who takes away the sin of the world. This is He of whom I said, 'After me comes a man who is preferred before me, for He was enlightened before me. I did not know Him but so He would be revealed to Israel, I came baptising with water.'" John tried to dissuade Jesus from being baptised by him saying, "I am the one who needs to be baptised by You. Why do You come to me to be baptised?"

Jesus answered him saying, "Let it be so for now, for it is fitting to fulfill all righteousness." So, John baptised him. And after Jesus was baptised, He came up out of the water and while praying, the Heavens were opened and the Loving Spiritual Life-force descended upon Him like a dove. And John bore witness to this event saying, "I saw the Spirit descend as a dove from Heaven and it remained on Him. And the Holy One who inspired me to baptise with water, said to me, 'He on whom you see the Spirit descend and remain with Him, this is He who baptises with the Loving Spiritual Life-force.' And I have seen this and have borne witness that He is a Spiritual child of the Loving Spiritual Creator in the Heavenly Spiritual World."

Temptations of satan

And Jesus, filled with the Loving Spiritual Life-force, was led by the Spirit into the wilderness and fasted for forty days and nights and He became hungry. Then He was tempted by the satanic identity. And the satan tempted Him saying, "If you are a Spiritual child of the Loving Spiritual Creator in Heaven, then command these stones to become loaves of bread." But Jesus answered, "Man shall not live by bread alone, but by every word that comes out of the mouth of our Loving Spiritual Creator."

Then the satan took Him to Jerusalem, and set Him on the pinnacle of the temple and tempted Him saying, "If you are a Spiritual child of the Loving Spiritual Creator in Heaven, then throw yourself down; for it is written that She will protect you from any harm by sending you Angels from Heaven to protect you." But Jesus answered, "You shall not tempt or test our Loving Spiritual Creator."

Then the satan took Him up to a very high mountain, and showed Him all the Kingdoms of this Earth world in a moment of time and the human glory of them and said, "I will give you all this Earthly power, authority and glory for it has been given to me, and I can give it to whomever I wish. If you just fall down and worship me, it shall all be yours." And Jesus answered, "You shall only worship and serve our Loving Spiritual Creator the Holy One." And the satan was defeated and had to leave Jesus and hope for another opportunity to be able to tempt Him.

And from this time on Jesus began to teach saying, "Repent and change your beliefs and ways so I may bring you to be near to the Kingdom of the Heavenly Spiritual World."

Author: Jesus had to confront and overcome the same material, Earthly temptations to be just a body of flesh to awaken into becoming a Spiritual child of Love that we must all face and overcome. In the case of Jesus, the tempter is called satan. In the case of Buddha, the same tempter is called mara. Jesus and Buddha both chose to become Spiritually awakened enlightened children of Love and we must also follow the Way of Spiritual awakening to enter the Heavenly Spiritual World or Nirvana. We clearly see the dualistic battle that Jesus and all of us face of worshipping the material world or the Heavenly Spiritual World.

Jesus Calls the First Disciples

And as Jesus walked along the sea of Galilee the people pressed upon Him to hear Him teach, and Jesus asked one of the fishermen called Simon, to allow Him to sit in his boat a little way out from the shore to speak and teach the people more easily. Simon agreed to do it for Him.

After teaching the people He said to Simon, "Put out into the deep water and let your nets down for a catch." And Simon answered, "Master we have toiled all night and caught nothing! But at your word we will let down the nets." And when they did this, they caught a great number of fish, nearly breaking their nets. They had to call their partners in the other boat to come and help them gather in all the fish. And they came and the boats were filled with fish to the point of nearly sinking.

When Simon saw this, he fell down at the feet of Jesus on the boat saying, "Depart from me for I am a sinful man, O Lord." For they were all in awe of Jesus, including John and James the sons of Zebedee who were partners with him when they saw the great catch they had taken following the instruction Jesus gave them, to let down their nets. Jesus said to Simon, "Be not afraid, follow Me and I will make you fishers of men."

The next day two disciples of John the Baptist saw Jesus walk by and followed Him to ask if they could stay with Him. Jesus said, "Come with Me." One of the disciples of John was called Andrew. The following day, Jesus decided to go to Galilee where He found Phillip and said to him, "Follow Me." Philip then went and found Nathaniel, and said to him, "We have found Him of whom Moses in the law and the prophets spoke about, it is Jesus of Nazareth, the son of Joseph."

Nathaniel said to him, "Can anything good come out of Nazareth?" Philip replied, "Come and see." Jesus saw

Nathaniel coming and said, "Behold an Israelite, in whom there is no deceit." Nathaniel asked Him, "How do you know me?" Jesus said, "Before Philip called you, I saw you sitting under a fig tree." Nathaniel was amazed and said, "Teacher, you are a Spiritual child of the Loving Creator." Jesus said, "Just because I told you I saw you under the fig tree you believed in Me. You shall see greater things than this."

Our Loving Spiritual Creator is Only Love.

We must become Her Spiritual children of

only Love on Earth.

Chapter 7
The Miracles

The Marriage at Cana. Turning Water into Wine

John 2:1-12 There was a marriage at Cana in Galilee, and the mother of Jesus was there, along with Jesus and His disciples. During the celebration they ran out of wine and the mother of Jesus said to Him, "They have no more wine." Jesus said to her, "What does your concern have to do with Me? My time has not yet come." His mother told the servants, "Do whatever He directs you to do."

There were six stone water pots standing there for the Jewish rites of purification, each able to contain twenty or thirty gallons. Jesus said to them, "Fill the water pots with water." And they filled them to the brim. He said to them, "Now draw some out and take it to the master of the feast." So, they did as He said.

When the master of the feast tasted the water that was made into wine and did not know where it came from, but the servants knew, the master of the feast called the bridegroom and said this to him. "Every man usually places the good wine out at the beginning, and when guests are becoming intoxicated, he then serves the inferior wine, but you have kept the best wine until last."

This was the first sign and wonder that Jesus performed, manifesting His Spiritual attainment as a child of the Loving

Spiritual Creator in Heaven, on Earth. And His disciples believed He truly was a Spiritual child of the Loving Creator. After the wedding, Jesus went down to Capernaum with His mother, brethren and disciples but did not stay there for many days.

Healing a Man with an Unclean Spirit

Mark 1:21-28 While in Capernaum Jesus entered into the synagogue and taught them. And they were astonished at His Teachings, for He taught them as one who had authority and certainty, unlike the scribes. Now there was a man in their synagogue with an unclean spirit and he cried out saying, "Let us alone. What have we to do with you Jesus of Nazareth? Did you come to destroy us? I know who you are, Holy One of the Loving Creator."

Jesus rebuked him saying, "Be quite and come out of him." And after the unclean spirit caused the man to have convulsions, he cried out in a loud voice, and the unclean spirit came out of him. All in the synagogue were amazed and questioned among themselves saying, "What is this wonder we witnessed? What new Spiritual Teaching is this? For with complete authority, He commands even unclean spirits and they must obey Him." The fame of Jesus immediately spread throughout all the region around Galilee.

Healing the Man with Palsy

Mark 2:1-12 Again, He entered Capernaum and after some days everyone heard that He was staying in a certain house. Immediately people came to the house to see and hear Him, and a great crowd gathered filling the house and blocking the doorway. And Jesus taught them the word and Way of our Loving Spiritual Creator.

Four men brought a paralytic man carrying him to Jesus but could not get near Him in the crowded house. So, they uncovered part of the roof and lowered down the bed on which the paralytic was lying, so he could be seen by Jesus.

When Jesus saw their great faith, He said to the paralytic, "Son, be of good cheer, your sins are forgiven you." But some of the scribes sitting there questioned what Jesus said, thinking to themselves, "This man blasphemes God with His words, for who can forgive sins but God only."

But Jesus in His Spirit, immediately knew what they were thinking and said to them, "Why do you think such things about Me? Which is easier to say to the paralytic man, your sins are forgiven or to say arise, take up your bed and walk?

So that you may know that the Spiritual Child of Humanity has the power and authority to forgive sins on Earth, I now say to this child; take up your bed and go on your way to your home."

The paralytic immediately arose, took up his bed and walked out in the presence of them all. And they were all amazed and praised God saying, "We have never seen anyone do this before."

Author: Here we see Jesus healing the crippled man's Spiritual body and Soul first as Jesus knew that is our primary and most important Eternal identity that must be free of sin to enter the Heavenly Spiritual World after our body of flesh dies.

Only after criticism from the Jews did Jesus then heal the man's body of temporary flesh which would die later anyway and return to the earth. Our Spirit is our most important identity and is only empowered by our Loving Creator's Loving Spiritual Life-force. We must be filled only with Love and no darkness of any kind when we pass through our death experience to be able to enter the Heavenly Spiritual World. We prepare for that event that will come to us all by Loving others now while here in this material world.

Healing Simon Peter's Mother-in -law and Others

Mark 1:29-39 Now they left the synagogue and entered into the house of Simon and Andrew, with James and John. Simon Peter's mother-in-law lay sick with a fever, and they told Jesus about her being ill. So, He came and took her by the hand, rebuked the fever and lifted her up and the fever immediately left her and she served them. And in the evening when the sun was setting, they brought Him all who were sick and possessed by demons, and He cast them out with His word and healed all. The whole town gathered around the house.

As He healed those who were sick with diseases and cast out many demons, He would not allow the demons to speak because they knew He was a Spiritual child of the Loving Spiritual Creator.

And in the morning, long before daylight, Jesus went out and departed to a solitary place and there He prayed to the Loving Spiritual Creator. And Simon Peter, and others that were with Him went and searched for Him, and when they found Him they said to Him, "Stay with us and do not leave."

But He said to them, "I cannot stay, for I must teach about the One True Loving Spiritual Creator in Heaven, to other children in other towns, for this is My purpose."

And He taught in their synagogues throughout all of Galilee, teaching about the One Loving Spiritual Creator and the Kingdom of Heaven, healing every disease and sickness, and casting out demons from the possessed.

Healing the Leper

Mark 1:40-45 While He was in one of the towns a leper came to Him and kneeling before Him implored Jesus saying, "If you are willing, you are able to cleanse me of this illness."

Jesus, moved with compassion, stretched out His hand and touched him and said to him, "I am willing, be cleansed." As soon as He spoke these words, immediately the leprosy left him and he was cleansed.

Jesus then sent him away giving him strict instructions to follow. He said to him, "See that you say nothing about this to anyone. Go on your way and show yourself to the priest, and offer those things commanded by Moses for ritual purification as a witness to them of your healing by the Loving Creator."

But he went out and proclaimed his healing by Jesus to everyone, so that Jesus could no longer openly enter a town or city easily and had to stay in the countryside where people still came to Him from every direction.

Healing of the Nobleman's Sick Son

John 4:46-54 After two days He departed from there and went to Galilee. And the Galileans welcomed Him having seen all the wondrous things He did in Jerusalem at the Holy Day Feast, for they were also at the Feast. When Jesus came again into Cana of Galilee, a nobleman whose son was very sick, heard Jesus had come from Judea into Galilee. So, he went to Jesus and implored Him to come down and heal his son, for he was at the point of death.

And Jesus said to him, "Unless you see miracles and wonders you will not believe." The nobleman said to Him, "Sir, please come down, before my child dies!" Jesus said to him, "Go your way, your son has life."

So, the man believed the words that Jesus spoke to him and went his way. And as he was returning home his servants met him and told him saying, "Master, your son is alive and well." Then he inquired of them at what hour he recovered. And they said to him, "Yesterday at the seventh hour the fever left him."

So, the father knew it was at the same hour in which Jesus said to him, "Your son has life." And he himself and his whole household believed in Jesus.

Author: We can see Jesus had perfect Equanimity and had Love for all and healed anyone regardless of their profession, religion or position in society. We also must give our Love to all with the same degree of Equanimity that Jesus had to be Spiritual children of our Loving Spiritual Creator who Loves all Her children equally.

Healing Man's Withered Hand

Mark 3:1-6 Jesus again entered the synagogue and saw a man there, who had a withered hand. And the Pharisees and scribes watched Him to see if He would heal him on the Sabbath, so they could charge Him with an offense against their God. But Jesus knew their thoughts. So, Jesus said to the man with the withered hand, "Come here." Then Jesus asked them, "Is it lawful on the Sabbath to do good or do evil, to save and heal life or to destroy it? And what man among you, if he has a sheep and it falls into a pit on the Sabbath, will not lay hold of it and lift it out?" But they all remained silent.

And He looked around at them and was deeply saddened and upset by the hardness of their hearts. So, He said to the man, "Stretch out your hand." And he stretched it out, and his hand was restored as healthy as the other. And the Pharisees were filled with anger and went out and plotted with the Herodians how they could destroy Him.

Author: Jesus is saddened by their lack of Love for the child of our Loving Creator who was suffering an infirmity. He risked danger by breaking their distorted corrupt laws to perform an act of Love, and we must all do the same and break any man-made laws that go against our Loving

Creator's Spiritual Way of Love, but our actions must always be guided by Love and Non-violence when doing so.

Loaves and Fishes Feeding the Five Thousand

Matthew 14:13-21 When the crowds saw Jesus had left in a boat they followed Him on foot, and when He went ashore, He saw a great multitude coming to Him. And He had compassion for them because they were like sheep without a shepherd, and He began to teach them many things and heal all those afflicted with illness.

As it was growing late, the disciples came to Him and said, "This is an isolated place and the hour is late, send them away to go into the villages and country nearby to lodge and get something to eat." But Jesus said to them, "You give them something to eat." And they said to Him, "Shall we go and buy two hundred denarii worth of bread and give it to them?"

And He said to them, "How many loaves have you?" And when they found out they said, "We have five loaves and two fish. But what are they among so many in need?" And Jesus said, "Bring them to Me." And He ordered the crowds of people to sit down on the grass in groups of about fifty each.

Taking the five loaves and two fishes, He looked up to Heaven, gave thanks to our Loving Spiritual Creator and blessed and broke them, then gave them to the disciples to distribute among the people. And they all ate and were satisfied. And they took up what was left over and it filled twelve baskets. And about five thousand were fed.

When the crowds saw this miracle, He had performed, they said, "Truly, this must be the prophet spoken of who is to come into this world." Jesus saw they were ready to seize Him and make Him their king, so He withdrew into the countryside by Himself.

Author: In the slanderous book of Revelation that should be ripped out and burnt it states that Jesus is coming back on the clouds and will cause famine to starve children to death. A filthy slander taken from the book of Daniel in the Jewish religion to poison who Jesus and our Loving Spiritual Creator really are. Every Christian follower of Jesus must defend Jesus and our Loving Creator and call for it to be destroyed by all the Jewish/Christian churches right now. Have meetings about it and discuss this in your own church and see the Truth. Stand up for Jesus and stop them slandering Him and our Loving Creator. Don't hide your Light under a basket. Don't be intimidated see the simple Truth, speak up and destroy these lies about Him.

Walking on the Water

Matthew 14:22-33 After this, Jesus told the disciples to go before Him in the boat to the other side to Bethsaida, while He sent the crowds away. And after dismissing them He went up on the mountain to pray by Himself. And when the evening came, the boat was many furlongs out to sea, and the strong wind and waves were beating against them.

And about the fourth watch of the night, He came to them, walking on the sea and would have passed by them. But when the disciples saw Him walking on the sea, they were terrified, crying out in fear, "It is a ghost, a Spirit!" But immediately Jesus spoke to them saying, "Take heart, it is I; do not be afraid."

Peter answered, "Master if it is you, bid me to come to you on the water?" Jesus replied, "Come." So, Peter got out of the boat and walked on the water and came towards Jesus. But when he was distracted by the strong winds, he became frightened and began sinking, crying out, "Master, save me."

Jesus immediately reached out His hand to him and held on to him saying, "O man of little faith, why did you doubt?" And when they got into the boat the wind ceased. And the disciples were utterly astounded saying, "Truly you are a

Spiritual child of the Loving Spiritual Creator in the Heavenly Spiritual World."

Author: Here we see a stunning display by Jesus of what He taught about us all having two different bodies in one. His Spiritual body had awakened fully filled with the Loving Spiritual Life-force of our Loving Spiritual Creator and He just carried His body of flesh across the water with His Spiritual body. Peter was able to also briefly awaken his Spiritual body to walk on the water due to his deep faith in Jesus. But the danger of the material world's laws of gravity arose in his mind and shifted him out of his Spiritual mind and body back into his mortal mind and he began sinking.

Healing Blind Man at Bethsaida

Mark 8:22-26 And they came to Bethsaida, and some people brought to Him a blind man and begged Him to touch and heal him. And Jesus took the blind man by the hand and led him out of the village, and when He had placed spit upon his eyes and laid His hands upon him, He asked him, "Do you see anything?"

And the man looked up and said, "I see men, but they look like trees walking." Then again Jesus laid His hands upon his eyes, and the man looked intently and was healed and saw everything clearly. And Jesus sent him away to his home, saying, "Do not enter the village or tell anyone what I have done for you."

Author: When we are seeking a healing for ourselves or others through the power of the Loving Spiritual Life-force of our Loving Creator, we must not give up trying. Even Jesus had difficulty at times in healing other children. And if we never receive a healing but remain stuck in illness and suffering or are called out of our body of flesh for it is our time to leave, the practice of being connected to Heaven and our Loving Spiritual Creator while praying for Her help only deepens your personal connection with Her. Not all illnesses are healed but every one of us comes into the presence of our beautiful Spiritual Creator in our Spiritual body and Soul after we pass through the death experience of our body of flesh. And we only have to live a life of Love to be ready to be with Her forever whenever we may be called home.

Healings at Gennesaret

Mark 6:53-56 And when they had crossed over, they came into the land of Gennesaret. And as soon as they got out of the boat, the people recognised Him and spread the word of His arrival throughout the surrounding region. And they brought Him all that were sick to wherever He was. Whenever He entered into villages, cities or country areas, they laid the sick in the marketplaces and asked that they be allowed to just touch the hem of His garment, and as many who touched it, they were healed.

Healing Lame Man at the Pool

John 5:1-18 Now there is in Jerusalem by the Sheep Gate a pool, which in Hebrew is called Bethesda, having five porches. In these porches lay many sick people, some lame, blind and paralysed, waiting for the waters to move. For at certain times an Angel descended into the pool stirring up the water, then whoever entered into the water first, after the stirring of the water by the Angel, were made well from whatever disease they had.

Now a certain man was there who had a sickness for thirty-eight years. When Jesus saw him lying there and knew he had been coming there for many years, He said to him, "Do you want to become well?" The sick man answered Him, "Sir, I have no man to help me into the pool when the water is stirred up, and before I reach the water, another steps down into the water before me."

Jesus said to him, "Arise, take up your bed and walk." Immediately he was made well and took up his bed and walked. It was on the Sabbath day that Jesus healed him.

And the Jews said to the man, "It is the Sabbath. It is not lawful for you to carry your bed." He answered them saying, "He who healed me and made me whole, told me to take up my bed and walk." Then they asked him, "Who is the man who said to you, 'Take up your bed and walk?'"

But the man who was healed did not know who it was, for Jesus had quietly withdrawn from the crowd there. But afterwards Jesus found the man in the temple and said to him, "Behold, you have been made well, sin no more or something worse will happen to you." And the man departed and told the Jews it was Jesus who healed him.

Author: Jesus tells the healed man that now he is physically well but to be careful and not to sin as this will damage his Spiritual body and Soul mind of Love which is much worse than having temporary lame legs in a body of flesh that dies anyway. Jesus was always drawing our attention to the condition of our Eternal Spiritual bodies and Soul minds of Love saying not to worry too much about our body of flesh that eventually dies and is then just food for the vultures anyway. Earth returns to earth. Spirit returns to Spirit.

Healings around the Region of Judea

Luke 6:17-19 And when Jesus and the disciples came down from the mountain a crowd of His followers and a great multitude of people from all Judea and Jerusalem, and from the seacoast of Tyre and Sidon were waiting for Him. They came to listen to Him teach and be healed of their diseases, as well as those who were tormented with unclean spirits. The whole crowd sought to touch Him, for the Heavenly power of the Loving Spiritual Life-force in His Spiritual body went out from Him to heal them all.

Stilling the Storm

Luke 8:22-25 One day, at evening time, Jesus said to the disciples, "Let us cross over to the other side of the lake." And leaving the crowd they took Him with them in the boat, and as they sailed Jesus fell asleep in the stern of the boat. And a great windstorm arose on the sea, driving waves to beat against the boat and they began swamping it and filling it with water.

And they went and woke Jesus saying, "Master, Master, save us for we are perishing." Then He arose and rebuked the wind and said to the sea, "Peace, be still!" And the wind ceased and there was a great calm. And He said to them, "Why are you so afraid? Have you no faith?" They were filled with a great wonderment and said to one another, "What sort of man is this, that even the wind and the sea obey Him?"

Author: The disciples still had no understanding that they had another body that is Spiritual that does not die as they had yet to experience it like Jesus. They were still only believing they had a body of flesh that drowns. Jesus remarks their Spiritual belief is still not fully opened connecting them to our Loving Creator in Heaven and Her Loving Spiritual Life-force in their Spiritual bodies of Light.

Healing Gerasene Demonic Possessed Man

Mark 5:1-20 They came to the other side of the sea, to the country of the Gerasene's. And when He stepped out of the boat a man possessed by demons, who lived among the tombs came to meet Him. For a long time, he had worn no clothes, was very fierce and no one could bind him anymore, not even with chains and fetters which he broke to pieces. And night and day he was always crying out and often cutting himself with stones.

When he saw Jesus, he ran and fell down before Him and spoke with a loud voice, "What have you to do with me Jesus, child of the Loving Spiritual Creator? I beseech you, do not torment me." For Jesus had commanded the demonic, unclean spirit to come out of him. Jesus then asked the demon, "What is your name?" And he replied, "Legion," because many demons had entered into him.

There was a great herd of swine feeding on the hillside nearby, and the demon begged Jesus saying, "Do not cast us into the Abyss but let us enter into the herd of swine." And immediately Jesus permitted them to do so. And all the demonic spirits came out of the man and entered the herd of swine. And the herd of swine, rushed down the steep hillside into the sea and were drowned.

When the herdsmen saw all that happened, they fled into the city telling everyone what had occurred to the demon possessed man and the swine. And the people came out to see what had happened themselves. And they came to Jesus and saw the man previously possessed by demons, now clothed and sitting at the feet of Jesus completely sane. And they were amazed and frightened.

And those who witnessed what had happened, told everyone there again about the way the possessed man had been healed by Jesus. Then all the people asked Jesus to leave their neighbourhood, for they were seized with great fear by what had happened.

As Jesus was getting into the boat to depart, the man Jesus healed who had been possessed by demons, begged Him to be allowed to go with Him. But Jesus sent him away saying, "Go home and tell all your friends what a great thing the Loving Spiritual Creator has done for you, and how She had compassion on you."

And he went his way and proclaimed throughout the region all that Jesus had done for him, and everyone marveled.

Jairus' Daughter Brought to Life

Mark 5:21-24, 35-42 Now when Jesus had crossed back in the boat to the other side, a great crowd welcomed Him. And while He was speaking to them, a man named Jairus, a ruler of the synagogue, fell at the feet of Jesus and begged Him saying, "My young daughter lies at the point of death. Please come and lay your hands upon her, that she may be healed and will live." So, Jesus went with Him, but while on the way a man from the ruler's house came and said, "Your daughter is dead; do not trouble the Teacher anymore."

But Jesus heard what the man was saying, and He said to the ruler, "Do not be afraid, but only trust and believe." And when He came to the house He permitted no one to enter in with Him, except Peter, John and James and the father and the mother of the child.

At the house there was a great commotion, with many people wailing loudly and weeping over the young girl's death. Jesus said to them, "Do not weep, for the girl is not dead but is only sleeping." And they all ridiculed Him.

Jesus then put them all outside and went in to where the child was laying. Taking her by the hand, He called her saying, "Talitha cumi," meaning, "Little girl, I say to you awaken." And her Spirit returned and immediately the girl arose and walked about, for she was twelve years old. And they were completely astounded. But Jesus strictly commanded them that no one should be told what happened and then said to give her something to eat.

Author: Jesus taught we all have two different bodies in one. The girl's Spiritual body and Soul had left her body of flesh now dead. Our Loving Spiritual Creator sent the girl's Spiritual body back into her healed body of flesh because

Her Spiritual child Jesus knew She would do it for Him through the power of Her Loving Spiritual Life-force.

Jesus often told those He healed not to publicise what He had miraculously done for them. His main purpose was to awaken everyone to their inner Spiritual body and Soul that is Eternal empowered only by the Loving Spiritual Life-force of our Loving Creator. Everyone's body of flesh that He healed all died later anyway only our Spiritual body lives on and that was His main concern that it must be healthy and whole at One with Love before our body of flesh dies.

Healing Boy Possessed by a Spirit

Mark 9:14-29 And when they came down from the mountain, a man from the crowd ran up to Jesus and said, "Teacher, I beg you to have mercy on my son for he is my only child, and behold, a spirit often seizes him throwing him down, convulsing him until he foams at the mouth and becomes rigid. And I asked your disciples to heal him, but they were not able to do so."

Jesus said, "O faithless and corrupt generation, how long am I to endure you? Bring him to Me." Then they brought him to Jesus. As he was coming, the spirit convulsed him and he fell on the ground rolling about, foaming at the mouth.

Jesus asked his father, "How long has this been happening to him?" And he replied, "Since childhood. And he is often thrown into the fire or water, which nearly kills him. Please, if you can do anything to help, have compassion on me." Jesus said to him, "If you are able to believe, all things are possible to him who believes." Immediately the father of the child cried out in tears and said, "Teacher, I believe; strengthen my weak faith." And when Jesus saw the crowd come running together, He rebuked the unclean spirit saying to it, "Deaf and dumb spirit, I command you come out of him and enter no more."

Then the spirit cried out and greatly convulsed him and then came out of him. And he appeared as one who is dead, causing many to say, "He is dead." But Jesus took him by the hand and lifted him up, and he arose.

And after, when they were in the house, the disciples asked Him privately, "Why could we not cast it out?" He said to them, "Your faith was too weak. But this kind can only come out by connecting more deeply with our Loving Spiritual Creator, and Her Loving Life-force within your Soul and Spirit, and by fasting."

Author: Jesus is guiding the disciples into becoming more at one with their Spiritual bodies and Soul minds of Love by connecting more deeply to our Loving Spiritual Creator in the Heavenly Spiritual World. Then they will receive an abundance of the Loving Spiritual Life-force He has Himself to enable them to heal all children just as He does. Thinking less about or fasting from material life and its concerns will help them achieve this.

Healing Woman Crippled on Sabbath

Luke 13:10-17 Jesus was teaching in one of the synagogues. And there was a woman who had a spirit of infirmity for eighteen years and she was bent over and could not fully straighten herself. And when Jesus saw her, He called out to her, "Woman, you are freed from your infirmity." And He laid His hands on her and immediately she was made straight and glorified the Loving Spiritual Creator.

The ruler of the synagogue was very upset because Jesus had healed her on the Sabbath day. And he said to the crowd in the synagogue, "There are six days on which men ought to work; therefore, come and be healed on those days and not on the Sabbath day."

Jesus said to him, "You Hypocrite! Does not each of you loosen his ox or his donkey from their stall on the Sabbath day and lead it away to water to drink? So, ought not this daughter of Abraham, whom satan has bound for eighteen years, be loosened from this bondage and suffering on the Sabbath day?"

After He said these things, all of His adversaries were put to shame, and the crowd then rejoiced for all the glorious things that He was accomplishing.

Widow's Son Brought to Life in Nain

Luke 7:11-17 Jesus went into a city called Nain and many of His disciples and a crowd went with Him. And when He came near the gate of the city a dead man was being carried out, the only son of his mother, a widow. And a large crowd from the city was with her.

When Jesus saw her, He had compassion on her and said, "Do not weep." Then He came and touched the stretcher the body was on, and those who were carrying it stood still. And He said, "Young man I say to you, awaken and arise!"

So, he that was dead sat up, and began to speak. And Jesus gave him back to his mother. Then everyone was filled with awe, and they glorified the Loving Creator saying, "A great prophet has awakened among us, and the Loving Spiritual Creator has visited our people." And this report about the miracle Jesus performed went throughout Judea and all the surrounding regions.

Author: Jesus knew we all have two different bodies with us right now. One is our Eternal Spiritual body and a temporary body of flesh. The son's Spiritual body was sent back into his healed body of flesh by our Loving Spiritual Creator to help Jesus demonstrate and teach children this Truth.

Jesus is growing stronger in His Spiritual practice and is now bringing children back to life more publicly. Unlike the private occasion concerning the daughter of Jairus. He knows His miracles will act as a magnet for children to seek Him out and then He can also administer the healing Spiritual Teachings to them to bring their Spirits back to Life as well as healing their temporary bodies of flesh.

Healing Centurion's Servant

Matthew 8:5-13 As Jesus entered Capernaum, a centurion who had heard about Jesus came forward to Him saying, "Master, my servant is lying paralysed at my home in terrible distress, please heal him?"

Jesus said, "I will come now and heal him for you." But the centurion answered Jesus saying, "Master, I am not worthy to have you come under my roof; but only say the word, and my servant shall be healed. For I am a man under authority, with soldiers under me; and I say to one, 'Go,' and he goes, and to another, 'Come,' and he comes, and to my slave, 'Do this,' and he does it."

When Jesus heard him, He marveled and said to those who followed Him, "Truly I say to you, not even in all of Israel have I found such faith and trust in Me." And Jesus said to the centurion, "Go, be it done for you as you have believed." And the servant was healed from that moment.

Author: Jesus had perfect Equanimity of Love for all. Here a Roman centurion belonging to the occupational force asks Jesus for help and Jesus does not withhold His Heavenly Love from him. We must also follow this example of Jesus and give our Heavenly Love to all who ask us for it.

Healing Blind Man Bartimaeus

Mark 10:46-52 And as Jesus came near Jericho with His disciples and a great crowd following Him, a blind man sitting by the roadside begging, named Bartimaeus, asked what was happening. They told him Jesus of Nazareth was passing by. And he cried out, "Jesus, have mercy on me!" And many rebuked him and told him to be quiet, but he just cried out more loudly, "Jesus, have mercy on me!"

So, Jesus stood still and said, "Call him to Me." And they called the blind man saying to him, "Take heart and get up, for Jesus is calling you." And throwing aside his garment, he arose and was brought to Jesus. And Jesus asked him, "What do you want Me to do for you?" The blind man said to Him, "Master, that I may receive my sight." Then Jesus said to him, "Go your way, your faith and belief in Me has made you well." And immediately he received his sight and followed Jesus glorifying our Loving Spiritual Creator. And all who saw it, also gave great praise.

Loaves and Fishes Feeding the Four Thousand

Matthew 15:29-39 And a great crowd had been with Jesus for three days, to listen to His Teachings and they brought many who needed to be healed to Him: the lame, the blind, the dumb, the maimed and many others.

And He called His disciples and said, "I have compassion on the crowd, because they have been with Me now for three days, and have nothing left to eat. And if I send them away hungry to their homes, they may faint along the way, as some of them have travelled from far away."

And the disciples said to Him, "How can one feed these people with bread, here in the countryside?" Jesus asked them, "How many loaves of bread do you have?" And they said, "Seven." So, Jesus ordered the crowd to sit down on the ground. He took the seven loaves, gave thanks and broke them, and gave them to His disciples to place next to the crowds sitting down, for them to eat.

They also had a few small fish, and after blessing them, He told them to distribute them also among the crowd. So, they all ate and were filled, and they collected seven baskets of leftover fragments. And those that had been fed numbered about four thousand. Then He sent them on their way.

Healing Canaanite Woman's Child

Mark 7:24-30 Jesus went into the region of Tyre and Sidon. And a Canaanite woman came towards Jesus and cried out to Him saying, "Master, have mercy on me, for my daughter is severely possessed by a demon, please help me." The disciples were annoyed by her crying out for help and wanted her to go away. But she then ran and fell at the feet of Jesus pleading with Him to help her. And Jesus replied, "O woman, your faith and trust in Me is great. Be it done for you as you desire." And her sick daughter was healed from that hour.

Author: We can see the trouble Jesus had in getting the disciples to become at one with the Loving Spiritual Creator in their Spiritual bodies and minds with perfect Equanimity of Love for all. They rejected her while Jesus accepted her.

Healing Deaf Mute Man

Mark 7:31-37 When they returned from Tyre, they passed through the region of the Decapolis. And they brought to Him a man who was deaf and had difficulty speaking, and they begged Him to lay His hands on him and heal him. So, Jesus took him apart from the crowd and placed His finger in his ears, and with His spit, Jesus touched his tongue. Then looking up to Heaven, He let out a long deep breath, and said to him, "Ephphatha," meaning, "Be opened."

Immediately, his hearing was restored, and his tongue was loosened from the impediment, and he was able to speak in a correct way. Then Jesus told them they should tell no one about this, but the more He told them not to tell others, they proclaimed it even more. All were amazed, saying, "All things He does are good and commendable. He makes the deaf hear and the mute to speak."

Healing Man Born Blind

Luke 9:1-41 As Jesus passed by, He saw a man blind from birth. His disciples asked Him, "Teacher, who sinned, this man or his parents that he was born blind?" Jesus answered, "Neither this man nor his parents sinned, but rather that the works and Spiritual power of the Loving Spiritual Creator may be revealed through him. I must do the Spiritual works of Her who sent Me while it is still day; the night and dark times are coming when no one can perform Spiritual works. As long as I am in the world, I am the Light of the world."

When He had said these things, He spat on the ground and made clay with His saliva, and He anointed the eyes of the blind man with the clay. Then said to him, "Go, wash in the pool of Siloam." So, he went and washed and came back seeing. The neighbours, and those who had previously seen that he was blind said, "Is not this the man who used to sit and beg?" Some said, "It is he." Others said, "No, but he is like him." He said to them, "I am he."

They asked him, "How were your eyes opened?" He answered and said, "A man called Jesus made clay and anointed my eyes and said to me, 'Go to the pool of Siloam and wash.' So, I went and washed and I received my sight." They asked him, "Where is He?" He said, "I do not know."

They brought the man, who had been blind and healed, to the Pharisees. Now it was the Sabbath when Jesus made clay and healed his blindness. The Pharisees asked him how he received his sight. He said to them, "Jesus put clay on my eyes, told me to wash them, and now I see." Therefore, some of the Pharisees said, "This man cannot be from our God, because He does not keep the Sabbath." While others said,

"How can a man who is a sinner perform such miracles?" And there was a division among them.

They said to the blind man again, "What do you say about Him because He healed your blindness." He said, "He is a prophet." But the Jews did not believe that he had been blind and received his sight, until they called his parents to question them. Then they asked them, "Is this your son, was he born blind? If so, then how does he now see?" His parents answered them saying, "We know that this is our son and that he was born blind; but how he can now see, we do not know, or who restored his sight, we know not. He is of age; ask him. He will speak for himself."

His parents said this because they feared the Jews, for the Jews had already agreed that if anyone declared that Jesus was the Messiah or anointed one, they would be expelled from the synagogue. This is why they said to ask their son and not them.

So, they again called the man who had been blind, and said to him, "Give God the glory! We know this man is a sinner." He answered and said, "I do not know if He is a sinner or not. But one thing I do know, is that I was blind and now I see." Then they said to him, "What did He do to you? How did He heal your blindness?" He said, "I already told you, but you did not listen. Why do you want to hear it again? Do you also want to become His disciples?"

Then they abused him and said, "You are His disciple, but we are Moses' disciples. We know that God spoke to Moses; as for this fellow, we do not know where He comes from." The man answered and said to them, "Why do you not know where He is from when this is a wonderful thing He has done in healing my blindness. Now we know that the Loving Creator does not hear sinners, but if anyone is a worshipper of the Loving Creator, and does Her will, She hears him. Since the world began, it has never been heard that anyone healed someone and restored their sight who was born blind. If this man were not from the Loving Spiritual Creator, He could do nothing."

They answered him, "You were born in utter sin, and are you teaching us?" And they cast him out of the synagogue. Jesus heard they had expelled him from the synagogue, and when He had found him, He said to him, "Do you believe in the Spiritual child of the Loving Spiritual Creator?" He answered and said, "Who is He Master, that I may believe in Him?" And Jesus said, "You have now seen Him, and it is He who is talking to you." Then he said, "Master, I believe!" And he knelt before Him in reverence and thanks.

Jesus said, "I have come into this world to determine who are those who do not see correctly, but can be helped to see correctly, and those who think they can see correctly, to help them realise they are really blind." Some Pharisees nearby heard Him say this and said to Him, "Are we blind also?" Jesus replied, "If you were blind and did not see correctly, you would have no sin, but because you say, 'We can see correctly,' but you are really blind, then you live in sin."

Healing Ten Lepers

Luke 17:11-19 As Jesus was passing between Samaria and Galilee, He entered a village and was met by ten lepers who stood off at a distance. And they raised their voices crying out, "Jesus, Master, have mercy on us!" When He saw them, He said to them, "Go, show yourselves to the priests." And as they went, they were cleansed of their disease.

One of them, when he saw that he was healed returned, and in a loud voice glorified our Loving Spiritual Creator and fell down at the feet of Jesus giving Him thanks. And he was a Samaritan.

And Jesus said, "Were there not ten cleansed? Where are the other nine? Has only this foreigner returned to give glory to our Loving Spiritual Creator?" And He said to him,

"Arise, go on your way, your faith and belief in Me have healed you."

Healing Man with Swollen Hand

Luke 14:1-6 Jesus went into the house of one of the rulers of the Pharisees on the Sabbath to eat, and they watched Him very carefully. For there was a certain man there who suffered from swelling under his skin. Jesus knew why they were watching Him so He asked the Pharisees and the lawyers, "Is it lawful to heal on the Sabbath?"

But they all kept silent. And Jesus took hold of the sick man, healed him and let him go. Then He said to them, "Which of you, having a son or an ox that has fallen into a pit on the Sabbath day, will not immediately pull him out?" And they could not contradict Him regarding these things of Spiritual Truth that He taught.

Lazarus Brought Back to Life

John 11:1-44 Now a certain man was ill, named Lazarus of Bethany, from the village of Mary and her sister Martha. It was Mary who anointed the Master with ointment and wiped His feet with her hair, whose brother Lazarus was ill. Therefore, the sisters sent a message to Him saying, "Master, he whom You love is ill."

When Jesus received the message, He said, "This illness will not end in death, but for the glory of the Loving Spiritual Creator, so that the Spiritual child of the Loving Creator, may also be glorified through it. Now Jesus loved Martha and her sister and Lazarus, but when He heard that he was ill, He remained two more days in the place where He was.

Then after this He said to the disciples, "Let us go to Judea again." The disciples said, "Teacher, now the Jews seek to stone you, and are you going there again?" Jesus answered, "Are there not twelve hours in the day? If anyone walks in the day he does not stumble, for he sees the light of this world. But if one walks in the night he stumbles, because the light is not with him."

He said to them, "Our friend Lazarus sleeps, but I go so that I may awaken him." Then the disciples said, "Master, if he sleeps he will get well." However, Jesus spoke of his physical death, but they thought He was speaking about restful sleep. Then Jesus said to them plainly, "Lazarus is physically dead. And I am glad for your sakes that I was not there, that you may believe. But let us go to him." Then Thomas, called the Twin, said to his fellow disciples, "Let us also go, that we may die with him and be awakened also."

Now Bethany was near Jerusalem, about two miles away. And many of the Jews had come to be with those comforting Mary and Martha, concerning their brother. Now Martha, as soon as she heard Jesus was coming, went and met Him but Mary stayed in the house. Martha said to Jesus, "Master, if You had been here my brother would not have died. But even now, I know whatever You ask of our Loving Creator, She will give it to You."

Jesus said, "Your brother will rise again." Martha said to Him, "I know that he will rise again in the resurrection at the last day." Jesus said to her, "I am the resurrection and the life. He who believes in Me, though he may physically die, he shall live in Spirit. And whoever believes in Me, and lives in the Spirit, shall never die. Do you believe this?" She said to Him "Yes Master, I believe that You are the Messiah, a Spiritual child of the Loving Spiritual Creator, who has come into this world."

And then she went and called her sister Mary, privately saying to her, "The Teacher has come and is calling for you." As soon as she heard that, she rose quickly and came to Him. Now Jesus had not yet entered the town but was still in the place where Martha met Him. Then the Jews who were with Mary in the house comforting her, saw Mary get up and quickly go out and followed her saying, "She is going to the tomb to weep there."

Then when Mary came where Jesus was and saw Him, she fell down at His feet saying, "Master, if You had been here my brother would not have died." When Jesus saw her weeping, and the Jews who came with her weeping, He was deeply moved in Spirit and distressed. And He said, "Where have you laid him?" They said to Him, "Master, come and see." And Jesus wept. Then the Jews said, "See how He loved him." And some said, "Could not this man, who opened the eyes of the blind, also have kept this man from dying?"

Then Jesus, deeply moved again in Himself, came to the tomb. It was a cave and a stone lay against it. Jesus said, "Take away the stone." But Martha, the sister of her dead brother said to Him, "Master, by now there will be a stench, for he has been dead four days." Jesus said to her, "Did I not say to you that if you believed, you would see the glory of the Loving Spiritual Creator?"

Then they took away the stone from the entrance to where the dead man had been laid. And Jesus lifted up His eyes and said, "My Loving Spiritual Creator, I thank You that You have heard Me. And I know that You always hear Me, but for the sake of the people standing by I said this, that they may believe that You sent Me."

Now, when He had said this, He cried out in a loud voice, "Lazarus, come out!" And the dead man came out; his hands and feet bound with bandages and his face wrapped in a cloth. Jesus said, "Unbind him and let him go."

Author: Jesus is now reaching higher levels of performing Spiritual miracles. He deliberately does this spectacular one publicly while calling out loud to our Loving Creator in the Heavenly Spiritual World in front of them all to help them realise where His Spiritual power is coming from.

Only our Loving Spiritual Creator could empower Him to do these wonders as She is Pure Love and True Spiritual Life. And He is also showing them the relationship He now has with Her as an awakened Spiritual child of Hers, at one with Her Loving Spiritual Life-force as we all can be.

Jesus reveals here that we all have two different bodies with us right now. A Spiritual body that lives on to reap as we have sown and a temporary body of flesh that dies.

Healing Man's Ear

Luke 22:47-51 While He was still speaking there came a crowd with Judas, one of the twelve, leading them. He drew near to Jesus to kiss Him, so they would know which one He was to arrest Him. But as he went to kiss Him, Jesus said to him, "Judas, would you deliver the Child of Humanity with a kiss?" And then they seized Him.

And then one of the followers of Jesus suddenly drew his sword and cut off the ear of the servant of the High Priest. Then Jesus rebuked him saying, "Put your sword back into its place; for all who take the sword will perish by the sword." He then touched the servant's ear and healed him.

Author: Jesus heals the injured person who has come to help arrest Him to be trialed and crucified. Jesus has told us all that the Heavenly Spiritual World and our Loving Spiritual Creator are at one only with Love. And if we do not reach this Spiritual awakening in our own Spiritual life to Love all other children now while here on Earth, we cannot enter easily into the Heavenly Spiritual World of Love after the death of our body of temporary flesh.

He also clearly establishes that all True followers of His must be pacifists and not injure any other child of our Loving Creator or we will destroy our Spiritual Life in Heaven. This important Teaching was destroyed in the fourth century by the corrupt Christian leaders under Emperor Constantine.

Healing Woman with Bleeding Haemorrhage

Mark 5:25-34 As Jesus walked along, the crowd pressed upon Him. And there was a woman who had suffered from a haemorrhage for twelve years, and who had suffered much under many physicians, spending all that she had and was no better but rather grew worse. When she heard about Jesus, she came behind Him in the crowd and touched His garment. For she believed that if she was able to just touch His clothes she would be healed.

And as soon as she touched His garments, immediately her flow of blood dried up and she knew her body was healed of the affliction. And instantly Jesus, knowing in Himself that miraculous power had gone out of Him, turned around to the crowd and asked, "Who touched My clothes?"

The disciples said to Him, "You can see the crowds all thronging around you, and you ask, 'who has touched Me?'" And He looked around to see who had done this thing. And the woman, knowing what had happened to her after touching the clothes of Jesus, came and fell down before Him trembling, and told Him the whole truth. He said to her, "Daughter, your faith has made you well. Go in peace and be healed of your affliction."

Author: Jesus said it was the Loving Spiritual Life-force of the Loving Creator in Him that performed all the works He did. Here we see this in total clarity. Jesus has no idea who touched Him or that the woman is ill or what the illness may be, but He feels the Loving Spiritual Life-force of our Loving Creator in His Spiritual body flow out into someone in need who believes in Him.

But our Loving Spiritual Creator does know everything about the woman's condition and also her faith in believing Jesus is an unusually special child of our Loving Creator filled with Love for everyone. So, our Loving Creator Herself flows the Loving Spiritual Life-force out of the Spiritual body of Jesus into the woman to heal her as she hoped she would be through just touching His cloak.

This is how Jesus could heal all children's bodies of flesh. He had no need of biological knowledge as our Loving Creator is omniscient. He only had to let the Loving Spiritual Life-force in Himself that empowers our Spiritual bodies, flow out of His Spiritual body to any child in need and our Loving Creator healed them.

He taught the disciples how to do this, and we must also try to understand this miraculous process and become healers like Him. But it can only flow from our Loving Spiritual Creator who is only Love into us if we are truly her Spiritual children of Love. And we must be Spiritually clean to receive such a beautiful, pristine and powerful gift to use to heal other children who are suffering. This is why Christians should only acknowledge and give thanks to the Loving Spiritual Creator of Jesus for giving us True Spiritual Life if we wish to accept it. Not a two headed dualistic God like Yahweh of the Jews who murders and steals then loves and protects.

This healing that Jesus said we can all perform may have declined in power because of the corrupt Christian leaders in the fourth century taking Christians back to worship the Jewish two headed God Yahweh. This converted them into being Jewish/Christian hybrids instead of pure Christians of only Love. Yahweh is a dualistic two headed God of War and Peace and is clearly not monotheistic. All such entities divided within themselves are full of darkness as Jesus said. Our Loving Spiritual Creator is only Love, Light and True Spiritual Eternal Life. There is no evil in Her.

Jesus taught we all have two different bodies. A body of flesh that dies and returns to the earth and does not rise again. And a Spiritual body and Soul that lives on reaping as we have sown. Jesus could heal both of our bodies but only one can enter the Heavenly Spiritual World and is Eternal. His main concern was to bring those dead to their Spirit back to True Spiritual Life before their body of flesh dies. As He said, "My words they are Spirit and they are Life. He who listens to them, understands them, is awakened and transformed by them and lives out of them will pass through death to True Eternal Spiritual Life."

We have seen many examples of Jesus only healing the sick, the injured and those possessed of all of their various illnesses. In the slanderous book of Revelation, it says Jesus will knowingly be involved in instigating an Apocalypse that causes terrible painful sores to come on the bodies of people who do not follow Jesus and His Way and the God in Revelation. Along with other monstrous evils.

Stop slandering my wonderful friend of Love and Non-violence Jesus and our Loving Spiritual Creator. That is not Jesus but a satanic figure of hate, death and destruction coming on the clouds. And the God is the Godhead of War and death of the Jews Yahweh 1. Jesus actually stated, "Whoever hears My words but does not do them, I do not judge them. For I did not come to judge the world but to save the world." Rip out the book of Revelation and burn it.

Our Loving Spiritual Creator is Only Love.

We must become Her Spiritual children of

only Love on Earth.

Chapter 8
John the Baptist

John the Baptist Witness of Jesus

John 3:22-36 Jesus and His disciples then came into the land of Judea, and He remained there with them and baptised everyone there. And John the Baptist was also baptising many people in Aenon near Salim, because there was much water there. And some of John's disciples had a dispute with the Jews about ritual purification so they went to John and said, "Teacher, Jesus who was with you beyond Jordan, about whom you have testified as being a child of the Loving Spiritual Creator on Earth, is also baptising and everyone is going to Him."

And John answered saying, "A human can receive nothing unless it has been given to them from Heaven. You have heard me tell you that I am not the Messiah but have been sent before Him. He who joins as one with the bride is the bridegroom, while the friend of the bridegroom standing beside Him hearing His words, greatly rejoices because of the words of the bridegroom. Therefore, my joy is full through hearing His words and being blessed by them. He must become greater, while I become less."

He who is at one with the Spiritual Heavenly world above, is above all on Earth. He who is of the Earth is Earthly and only speaks of Earthly things. He who is at one with

Heaven is above all. And what He has come to know and understand He reports and shares freely with everyone, but no one receives His testimony. But anyone who does receive His testimony, is sealed with our Creator's Love and Truth. For He who is at One with the Loving Creator speaks the words of Her and our Loving Creator gives the Spirit fully to all who wish to receive it.

The Loving Spiritual Creator Loves all of Her children, giving all things into their hands. He who follows the Spiritual Way of the child of the Loving Creator, and becomes at one with it, will have Life everlasting. But he who does not believe in the Spiritual Way of our Loving Creator, and become at one with it, will not experience full Spiritual Life, but shall remain captured by physical desires and the restraints of the material world.

John the Baptist in Prison

Matthew 11:1-19 Herod seized John and put him in prison because John had said it was not lawful for Herod to take his brother's wife, Herodias, and for criticising the evil things he had done. When John heard of the works Jesus was doing, he sent two of his disciples to ask Him, "Are you the coming one or do we look for another?"

Jesus answered them saying, "Go and tell John the things which you hear and see. The blind receive sight, the crippled walk, the lepers are made clean, the deaf hear, those who are dead to their Spirit are awoken and raised up, and the materially poor have the good Spiritual news given to them. And blessed is he who is not enticed into sin, because of following Me and My Spiritual Way."

Jesus then said to the crowd about John, "What did you go out into the wilderness to see? A reed shaken by the wind. But what did you go out to see? A man clothed in soft garments. Behold, those who wear soft garments and live in luxury are in King's houses. But what did you go out to see? A prophet? Yes, I tell you, and one much more than a prophet. Truly I say to you, there has not risen amongst those born of women one who is greater than John the Baptist. Yet the least in the Spiritual Kingdom of Heaven is greater than he."

Thomas 46 Jesus said, "No one is much greater than John the Baptist. Yet I say to you that whoever becomes like a little child will know the Heavenly Spiritual World and will become greater than John."

"And from the days of John the Baptist and henceforth, the Kingdom of Heaven suffers violence, and the violent take it away from you by force. But what shall I liken this generation to? It is like children sitting in the town square calling to their companions saying, 'We played the flute for you, and you did not dance, we were deeply grieved about what you were doing, but you saw no reason to lament.'

For John came neither eating nor drinking and they said he has a demon in him. While the Child of Humanity came eating and drinking and they say He is a glutton and a drunkard, a friend of tax collectors and sinners. But wisdom is exhibited and declared by her children."

John the Baptist is Beheaded by Herod

Mark 6:14-29 The Governor Herod heard reports about Jesus and thought it was John the Baptist, whom he had beheaded, and who must have risen from the dead to have such wondrous powers.

Herod had imprisoned John for publicly criticising him about marrying Herodias, his brother's wife. And Herodias wanted him executed but Herod feared the people because they thought he was a prophet from God. Herod himself thought John was a just and Holy man and listened to him. But after the daughter of Herodias performed a beautiful dance before Herod during his birthday celebration, He promised her anything she desired. So, her mother told her to ask for John's head on a platter.

Although Herod was remorseful, he kept his word and had John beheaded as she requested. Then his disciples came and took away the body and buried it and went and told Jesus. When Jesus heard this news, He and the disciples departed from where He was by boat to a place in the countryside, to be by themselves.

Author: Mary the mother of Jesus was the cousin of the mother of John the Baptist and did visit her. By looking at the Teachings of John the Baptist and how similar they are to those of Jesus we have to conclude that they grew up often meeting each other on visits. It is probable that as they matured they both had a deep sense of Spiritual awakening to find the One True Loving Spiritual Creator and discussed this with each other.

John may have been the one who understood the new Spiritual Way that Jesus taught more than anyone else. This would account for Jesus being so despondent at the news of John's death. The one who He originally confided in and shared His New Way of Spiritual awakening and understanding with before teaching it to others.

**Our Loving Creator is only Love.
We must become Her Spiritual children of
only Love on Earth.**

Chapter 9
The Beatitudes

Matthew 5:3-12, Luke 6:20-23

Blessed are the materially poor, for in Spirit, yours is the Kingdom of the Heavenly Spiritual World. But woe to you who are rich in material possessions for you have received your temporary consolation.

Blessed are you that mourn, for you shall be comforted.

Blessed are you that weep now, for you shall laugh. But woe to you who laugh now, for you shall mourn and weep.

Blessed are you meek, for you shall inherit the Earth.

Blessed are you who do hunger and thirst after righteousness, for you shall be filled. But woe to you who are satisfied with inferior things for you will be in need.

Blessed are you the merciful, for you shall receive mercy.

Blessed are you the pure in heart, for you shall see the Loving Spiritual Creator.

Blessed are you the peacemakers, for you shall be called the Spiritual children of our Loving Spiritual Creator in the Heavenly Spiritual World.

Blessed are you who are persecuted for righteousness's sake, yours is the Kingdom of the Heavenly Spiritual World.

Blessed are you when men shall persecute you, expel you and revile you, and shall falsely slander all manner of evil against you because you are following My Spiritual Way. Rejoice and be exceedingly glad, for great is your reward in the Heavenly Spiritual World, for the good prophets were also persecuted in this way. But woe to you, when all men who worship material things highly praise you, for so did other such men praise the false, lying prophets of old.

Thomas 77- Blessed are those who have heard the word of our Loving Spiritual Creator and kept it.

Thomas 69- Blessed are those who have been persecuted in their hearts and minds; they truly have come to know the Love that the Loving Spiritual Creator has for them. Blessed are those who are hungry and searching so the belly of he who desires may be satisfied.

Thomas 68- Blessed are you when they hate and persecute you here in this world, but they will never come anywhere near the place within themselves where you are living in and out of the Loving Spiritual Life-force of our Loving Spiritual Creator in the Heavenly Spiritual World.

Thomas 58- Blessed is the one who is troubled in this world, he will find True Life.

Thomas 49- Blessed are those who are at one and chosen; you will find the Heavenly Spiritual World.

Thomas 19- Blessed is the one who came to Life before coming to Life.

Thomas 18- Blessed is the one who stands at the beginning; that one will know the end and will not taste death.

Author: Jesus gives us a short list of Spiritual blessings we will receive by following His Spiritual Way in this dangerous material world. They are powerful reminders of a Heavenly Spiritual World that awaits all those who awaken to become at one with the Loving Spiritual Life-force in our Spiritual bodies created for us by our Loving Spiritual Creator. All sufferings we undergo in this material world will end at the time of our death experience when our Spiritual body leaves to come into the presence of our Loving Creator to reap as we have sown.

We see in the words of Jesus how our Loving Spiritual Creator cares for us all and Her presence in our life can be a great comfort during our trials on Earth. She only wants us to follow the Spiritual Way of Love, Peace, Forgiveness, Mercy and purity of Heart and Soul so we may stay connected to the Heavenly World and enter the Heavenly Spiritual world after passing through our death experience of the body of flesh.

Of course, those who are filled with Love will receive only Love and an end to all their sufferings. While those who are filled with evil will receive the evil they created and continue to suffer until it is all consumed in the fire of their own burning realisations through the Light of Her Love and Truth shining upon them. As Jesus said, "Nothing will remain hidden that will not be disclosed."

The last two sayings of Thomas refer to our Spiritual body and Soul mind of Love awakening before our body of flesh dies. We come to Heaven in our Living Spiritual body if it is filled with the Loving Life-force of our Loving Creator. And once we awaken into our Spiritual mind of Love on Earth, we have come to the end of our dualistic mortal mind and life and entered the beginning of our Spiritual Life and mind of only Love. Jesus says if we achieve this, we have come to Life before coming to Heavenly Life.

Our Loving Spiritual Creator is only Love

We must become Her Spiritual children of

only Love on Earth.

Chapter 10
Matthew

The following Gospel of Matthew will combine any Teachings of Jesus that are repeated in the other Gospels into one account containing all the important points. The other Gospel accounts of the same Teaching are listed alongside each of Matthew's account.

Salt of the Earth

Matthew 5:13, Luke 14:34-35, Mark 9:49-50 Jesus said, "Salt is good and you are the Spiritual salt of the Earth, and everyone needs to be salted with the Light of Spiritual Life, and every material sacrifice will be seasoned with this salt. But if your salt has lost its saltness and Spiritual quality, how shall it be restored? It is no longer of any use and men just throw it away. So, always have the salt of Spirituality in you and be in peace with one another."

Author: Jesus tells us we must always hold on to and live out of our Spiritual Life while here on Earth. Then all our material life will be empowered by our Loving Creator's Spiritual Life-force in our Spiritual body but if we lose that Loving Life-force, we will be of no Spiritual use to anyone. Our physical bodies of material flesh need to be seasoned with this Spiritual Life-force to enable us to come alive to our Spirit and bring Heaven's Love to all in need on Earth. Then our body of flesh and our Spiritual body will be as one.

Jesus Fulfills the Law of Love

Matthew 5:17,20 Jesus said, "Do not think I came to abolish the Law of Love or the good prophets but to fulfill the Law of Love and make it complete and whole. I say to you, that unless you justify yourselves in greater Love than the scribes and Pharisees you will by no means enter the Heavenly Spiritual World."

Author: Jesus tried to lead the Jews out of their dualistic belief in their two headed God Yahweh of Love and Peace and War and murder and come into the fullness of only Love.

Do not be in Anger

Matthew 5:21-26, Luke 12:57-59 Jesus said, "You have heard that it was said to those of olden times, 'You shall not kill, and whoever kills will be in danger of damnation.' But I say to you, that whoever is angry with his brother for no reason, shall be in danger of damnation. And whoever says to his brother, 'Raca!' that is 'Worthless one!' shall be in danger of the judgment of the council. But whoever says, 'You fool!' shall be in danger of hell fire.

Therefore, if you are bringing your Spiritual gift to our Loving Creator and remember that another was wronged by you, go first to the one who you wronged. Then reconcile with them and make good and return to offer your Spiritual gift to our Loving Creator with a clean Spirit.

Agree with your accuser and accept responsibility quickly while you are still alive with him. Otherwise, he may deliver you to the judge, the judge hand you over to the officer and you will be cast into prison. Assuredly I say to you, you will not be released from prison until you have paid in full for your wrongdoing."

Author: Jesus reminds us that Spiritual Love goes beyond actions and includes our words. To hurt someone physically or verbally hurt their Spirits is equally wrong. And to avoid reaping the suffering we have caused to another after we die, we must go and apologise while they are still alive and offer any compensation we may need to give them. Then our own Spirits are cleansed and once again we can come into the presence of our Loving Spiritual Creator.

Lust is not Love

Matthew 5:27-28 Jesu said, "You have heard it said in the old Way, 'You shall not commit adultery.' But I say to you that whoever looks upon another with lust for them, has already committed adultery in his heart and mind."

Author: Jesus guides us to control not only our actions and words but even our thoughts that may hinder our True Spiritual Love from arising. This is moving us towards a complete Spiritual awakening of body and mind.

Cut Away Your Sin

Matthew 18:7-9, Mark 9:43-47 Jesus said, "Woe to this world because of temptations to sin. For circumstances in this world can cause them to come into existence but woe to that one who brings the temptation into this world.

If you commit a wrongdoing by using your hand or foot in an evil way and cannot stop doing so, it would be better to cut them off to prevent yourself sinning further. Then by maiming your temporary body of flesh to prevent your Spirit being taken into darkness, you can rise after death into the fullness of a perfect Spiritual body in Heaven.

But if you continue using your hands or feet in performing wrongdoings until you die you will propel your

Spirit and Soul to enter the Hell of burning realisations from which there is no escape. Until your Spirit and Soul have experienced all the wrongs you have committed to others or yourself. Those who enter into there will wail and cry aloud and be alone.

And if your eyes cause you to perform wrongdoings or evil and you cannot stop doing so, it would be better to pluck them out to prevent yourself sinning further. Then by maiming your temporary body of flesh to prevent your Spirit being taken into darkness, you can rise after death into the fullness of your perfect Spiritual body in Heaven.

But if you continue using your eyes to commit wrongdoings or evil until you die you will propel your Spirit and Soul to enter the Hell of burning realisations from which there is no escape. Until your Spirit and Soul have experienced all the wrongs you have committed to others or yourself. Those who enter there will wail and cry aloud and be alone.

Author: Jesus is giving us a dramatic example of the consequences of performing wrongdoings while here on Earth. He does not mean this to be taken literally but to be a very serious warning so we can guard ourselves from committing evil that will damage our Spiritual Life and propel our Spirit and Soul into a Hellish experience.

Think of all the soldiers and others who are murdering children of our Loving Spiritual Creator in the world today 2025-2026. They use their eyes to get the child in the sights of their bomb or gun to blow their bodies to pieces. They use their hand and finger to pull the deadly trigger that kills a child of our Loving Creator. They use their foot to drive a tank to blow a building up so the structure collapses crushing the children in it to death. Better they were all born lame and blind. The ever-flowing 'Spiritual River of Reaping as We Sow' separates Heaven from the Earth world. Be careful you have no millstones of evil tied around your neck before you try to cross over.

Speak Truthfully

Matthew 5:33-37, Thomas 6 Jesus said, "You have heard it said in old times, 'You shall not swear falsely, but shall perform your oaths to the Lord.' But I say to you, do not swear an oath at all; neither by Heaven, for it is the abode of the Loving Creator, nor by the Earth, for Her presence is also here, nor by Jerusalem, for it is the city of a great King. Nor shall you swear by your head, because you cannot make one hair white or black. But let your 'Yes' be 'Yes' and let your 'No' be 'No'. Anything else is superfluous and is from the evil one."

Thomas 6: Jesus said, "Do not lie or do what you hate since all things are clear before the Heavenly World."

Author: We can only deliberately lie to protect other children or ourselves from harm from those who wish to hurt us. And in doing so we also protect them from sin.

Charitable Works

Matthew 6:1-4 Jesus said, "Take heed not to do your charitable works before men, so as to be deliberately noticed by them. Otherwise, you are living out of a false ego identity and not living out of your True Spiritual identity of Love and have no connection to the Loving Spiritual Life-force from Heaven to empower your act.

Therefore, when you perform a charitable deed, do not sound a trumpet before you as the hypocrites do in the synagogues and streets so they may have praise from men. Assuredly I say to you they have their worldly reward. But when you perform a charitable deed do not let your left hand know what your right hand is doing that your good deed may be done privately and your Loving Creator who sees all things will give Her Love to you for doing so."

Pray from Within

Matthew 6:5-15, Luke 11:1-4 Jesus said, "And when you pray and talk to our Loving Creator do not be like the hypocrites. They love to pray in the synagogues and standing on the corners of the streets so they may be deliberately noticed by others. They have their worldly reward. But you when you pray and talk to our Loving Creator go within, into your Spirit and Soul and when you have shut out the external material world, pray and talk to your Loving Spiritual Creator in this private way hidden from the view of others. And your Loving Creator who sees and hears you in private will give Her Love to you. Like a Mother gives it to Her child.

When you pray and talk to our Loving Creator do not use vain repetitions as others do. For they think they will be heard if they speak many words. Therefore, do not be like them. For your Loving Spiritual Creator knows all the things you have need of before you even ask Her." One of His disciples asked, "Master, teach us to pray as John also taught his disciples."

Jesus said, "In this manner pray. Our Loving Spiritual Creator in the Heavenly Spiritual World hallowed be your name. Your Heavenly world come, your will be done on Earth as it is in the Heavenly World. Give us this day our daily breads, nourishment for our earthly bodies and nourishment for our Spirits and Souls. And forgive us our sins as we forgive those who have sinned against us. And lead us away from all temptation and deliver us from every evil. Amen.

Remember this, if you forgive those who sin against you, your Loving Spiritual Creator will be able to forgive you the sins you have committed. But if you do not forgive others then She cannot forgive your sins."

Author: Jesus teaches we must live an honest and caring life for others. And we connect with our Loving Spiritual Creator from within our body of flesh by being at one with our Spiritual body and Soul mind of Love when talking to Her. She is a Spiritual Being, and we must be in our Spiritual identity as a child of Hers to talk with Her.

This simple prayer of Jesus provides a short reminder and guidance for us of the basic Spiritual understandings we need to be Her Spiritual children. Jesus draws special attention to having to forgive others who sin against us so our sins may also be forgiven and cleansed to prepare us to enter the Heavenly Spiritual World of Love.

Fasting in Private

Matthew 6:16-18 Jesus said, "When you fast for Spiritual purposes do not be like the hypocrites who like having a sad appearance while doing so. For they deliberately disfigure their faces so they may be noticed by others to be fasting. They will have their little worldly reward. But when you fast for Spiritual purposes, anoint your head and wash your face so that no one notices that you are fasting. Instead, turn to face our Loving Creator in Heaven who sees you fasting for Spiritual strengthening and She will give Her Love to you."

Store Your Treasures in Heaven

Matthew 6:19-21, Thomas 74 Jesus said, "Do not lay up for yourselves temporary, material treasures on Earth where moth and rust destroy and where thieves break in and steal. But lay up for yourselves Spiritual treasures that are unfailing and abiding in the Heavenly Spiritual World that is Eternal where neither moth nor worm nor rust destroys and where thieves do not break in and steal. For where your treasure is, there your existence and heart will also be."

You Cannot Serve Two Masters

Matthew 6:24 Jesus said, "No one can serve two masters, for either he will hate the one and love the other or else he will be loyal to the one and despise the other. You cannot serve our Loving Spiritual Creator and material riches and money at the same time."

Thomas 47 Jesus said, "A person cannot mount two horses or bend two bows, and a servant cannot serve two Lords. That servant would respect one and offend the other."

Author: Jesus knew the Jews were worshipping a two headed God called Yahweh, with a Godhead of War and Death and a Godhead of Love and Peace. He warned them.

Do not Worry

Matthew 6:25-34 Jesus said, "Therefore I say to you, do not worry about your life regarding what you shall eat; nor about your body, what you shall wear. For the Spiritual Life is greater than food rations, and the body more than clothing. Observe the ravens, for they cannot sow nor reap and have no storehouse or barn, yet the Loving Creator feeds them. How much more will the Loving Creator take care of you than these birds.? And which of you by worrying could increase his stature by four centimeters? If you are unable to do the least important of things, why are you worried about the rest?

Observe the lilies how they grow yet they neither work nor spin, yet I say to you not even Solomon in all his glory was clothed like one of these. If such vegetation in the field today is then thrown tomorrow into the oven, how much more will the Loving Creator clothe you, o you of little Spiritual faith?

Do not seek after what you should eat or what you should drink, nor have a doubtful mind. For all these things the nations of the world seek after and our Loving Creator in the Heavenly Spiritual World, knows you have need of these Earthly things. But seek the Spiritual Kingdom of the Loving Creator first and Her virtuous Way, and all these things will be just additional to you.

Do not fear little flock, for our Loving Creator is pleased to give us the Heavenly Spiritual Kingdom. Sell what you have and give to those in need, make yourselves pouches which do not wear out to contain a Spiritual treasure that does not fail in the Heavenly World. So, do not worry about tomorrow today, for tomorrow will have its own trouble to care about. Today's troubles are enough to contend with."

Author: While Jesus was well aware of our daily earthly needs to keep our body of flesh alive, He constantly directed us to first keep our Eternal Spiritual body and Soul alive and well. As this is the Spiritual body, we need to be in good health and filled with the Loving Spiritual Life-force from Heaven to be able to enter Heaven after passing through our death experience of the body of earthly flesh.

Judge Not

Matthew 7:1-6, Luke 6:37-42 Jesus said, "Judge not, and you will not be judged. For with what judgment you judge, you shall be judged. Condemn not and you will not be condemned, forgive and you will be forgiven, give and it will be given to you, and whatever you give out to others will be the same you will receive back."

Author: Jesus gives these extremely important and vital characteristics of our Spiritual identity we must become at one with to enter the Heavenly Spiritual World. And He warns us of the Spiritual Law of the ever-flowing river called 'Reaping as We Sow' that we must all cross over to reach Heaven's shore. Also called Karma as taught by Buddha.

Speck in Your Eye

Matthew 7:3-5, Luke 6:41-42 Jesus said, "Why do you look at the speck in your brother's eye but do not notice the plank in your own eye? Or how can you say to your brother, 'Let me remove the speck from your eye,' while a plank is in your own eye? You hypocrite! First remove the plank from your own eye and then you will see more clearly to remove the speck from your brother's eye. If the blind lead the blind they will both fall into a ditch?"

Author: We must not forget we all have imperfections.

Pearls Before Swine

Matthew 7:6, Thomas 93 Jesus said, "Do not give what is holy to the dogs for they may drop it in a pile of manure, and do not cast your pearls before swine lest they trample them under their feet making them worthless and turn and tear you to pieces."

Author: When we share the Spiritual Teachings with other children, we must first gauge their readiness to receive them. Then we must adjust our delivery of the Spiritual Way accordingly to fit each child's personal situation, beliefs and character. This may mean a gradual unfolding of the Spiritual Way beginning with basic logical elements that could lead to an awakening of the deeper Spiritual beliefs. But to share deep Spiritual beliefs with someone who is not at all familiar with them or is against them could cause them to ridicule you and the Spiritual Teachings causing them to move further away from Spiritual belief.

The Narrow Way

Matthew 7:12-14, Luke 13:23-24 Jesus said, "Therefore, whatever you want others to do to you, do also to them for this is the Spiritual Way of the Law of Love and the good prophets. Enter by the narrow gate for wide is the gate and broad is the way that leads to destruction and there are many who go in that way. Because narrow is the gate and difficult is the Way that leads to True Spiritual Life and there are few that find it."

Author: We must find the elusive Spiritual path and Way of only Love and Non-violence that leads us through this dangerous material world to Heaven. By awakening to our True Spiritual body and Soul mind of Love guided and inspired by the words of Jesus we will be able to navigate through the dangerous waters of this Earth world and reach the haven of Heaven. And the golden rule to guide our Spiritual practice is to treat others as you would like to be treated by them. Remembering, we all reap as we have sown.

Known by Their Fruits

Matthew 7:15-20, Matthew 12:33-37, Luke 6:43-45 Jesus said, "Beware of false prophets who come to you in sheep's clothing but inwardly are ravenous wolves. You will know them by their fruits. Are grapes gathered from thorny bushes or figs from thistles? For no good tree can bear evil fruit, nor does a bad tree bear good fruit. A good person out of the good treasure of their heart brings forth good, and an evil person out of the evil treasure in their heart brings forth evil. For out of the abundance of the heart their mouth speaks. I say to you that for every idle word men may speak they will give account of it on their judgement day at death. For by your words, you will be justified and by your words you will be condemned.

Either make the tree good and its fruit good, or make the tree evil and its fruit evil, for the person is known by their fruit. Therefore, every tree that does not bear good fruit, is removed and must enter into the cleansing fire of Truth and burning realisations."

Author: Jesus warns us of children who can lead us astray from the Spiritual path of Love and Non-violence that leads us to Heaven. We only have to observe their behaviour and speech to see if they match the Spiritual Way of True Love as Jesus taught. Jewish/ Christians say Yahweh, the two headed God of War and Love of the Jews, is the One God of Jesus. Christians like me say only the One Loving Spiritual Creator is the source of the Spiritual Life and Way of Love that Jesus became at one with and taught us to be also at one with.

We must dedicate our life to bringing Loving actions into this world from within our Spirit and Soul and never manifest anything evil. Jesus also reminds us to guard our words as they echo the state of our heart and Spirit. And at the time of our death experience every word we have ever spoken is known by our Loving Creator just as the state of our Spirit is known by Her. Jesus warns us we will all reap as we have sown.

And any child on Earth who lives out of the Loving Spiritual Way that Jesus taught will enter the Heavenly Spiritual World whether they know Him or not. It is His Spiritual Way of Life that leads any child to the Heavenly Spiritual World so a Muslim, Christian, Buddhist, Hindu, Jew, Zoroastrian, Bahai, Atheist, Humanitarian, Native spiritual child or any other child can become a Spiritual child of our Loving Spiritual Creator by following the same Way of Love from within their own life or religion. But it must be Love only. Many Jewish/Christians falsely teach only Christians will be allowed to enter Heaven. They should not say that. Jesus is inclusive, not exclusive like the Jews or others.

I Never Knew You

Matthew 7:21-23, Luke 6:46 Jesus said, "Why do you call Me Lord, Lord but do not follow what I tell you to do? Not everyone who calls Me Lord shall enter the Heavenly Spiritual World but only he who lives out of the Spiritual Way of Love of our Loving Spiritual Creator will enter.

Many will say to Me in that day, 'Lord, have we not prophesied coming events in Your name, cast out demons in Your name and performed many miracles in Your name?' And I will say to them, 'I never knew you. Depart from Me you who practice violations of the law.'"

Luke 13:25-27 Jesus said, "When the master of the house has risen up and shut the door and you begin to stand outside and knock at the door saying, 'Lord, Lord open for us,' he will answer, 'I do not know you or where you are from.' Then you will say, 'But we ate and drank in your presence, and you taught in our streets.' But he will answer, 'I tell you I do not know you, for you are from a different place to me. Depart from me all you workers of iniquity.'"

Author: There are two groups here. Some people love Jesus and follow Him around praising Him but do not listen to or want to implement His Spiritual Words to awaken their Spiritual Lives. He says it is of little use just praising Him but not becoming Spiritually awakened to enter Heaven.

The other group seem to be people who used His name to perform questionable miracles for some self-serving purpose that He condemns as being evil. We can only conclude the ones He is referring to here were using the miracles and other wonders they performed in His name for personal gain not as True caring Spiritual children of our Loving Spiritual Creator.

However later at **Mark 9:39** and **Luke 9:49-50** He told the disciples that those who work a miracle in His name are for Him and should be allowed to do so. There may be some missing words from these original translations that could give a better understanding of what the 'violations of the law' were that Jesus was referring to, accounting for this variance in His responses.

Commit to the Spiritual Way

Matthew 8:18-22, Luke 9:57-62 A scribe came up to Jesus and said to Him, "I will follow you wherever you go." Jesus replied, "Foxes have holes, birds of the air have nests, but the Spiritual child of our Loving Creator in Heaven has nowhere here on Earth to lay His head and call His home." Then another who wanted to follow Jesus said, "Lord let me first go and bury my father." Jesus replied, "Follow Me and let those dead to their Spirit bury their own dead. But you go now and proclaim the Heavenly Spiritual Kingdom of our Loving Spiritual Creator."

Another said, "I will follow you Lord, but let me first say farewell to those of my household." Jesus replied, "No one who puts his hand to the plough and looks back is fit for the Heavenly Spiritual World of our Loving Creator."

Author: While these requests made by the followers seem reasonable, Jesus uses them to convey the urgency for all of us to first become Living Spiritual children before our body of flesh dies. Earthly, worldly affairs are secondary to our Spiritual awakening. Jesus Himself says this Earth is no longer His True home since He became Spiritually awakened and at one with the Heavenly Spiritual world. This requires an ongoing daily commitment to awaken to our True Spiritual identity and live as a Spiritual child right now.

Jesus Loves Sinners

Matthew 9:9-13, Luke 5:27-32, Mark 2:13-17 Jesus saw a tax collector named Matthew sitting at the tax office. And He said to him, "Follow Me." So, Matthew arose and followed Him. Now Matthew made a great feast in his house for Jesus and His disciples and many tax collectors and sinners came and sat down with them at the table.

When the Pharisees saw this, they asked the disciples, "Why does Jesus eat with tax collectors and sinners?" Jesus heard them and answered, "Those who are Spiritually well have no need of a doctor but those who are ill do. Go and learn what this saying means, 'I desire compassion not sacrifice.' For I do not come to call those who are already Spiritually well but sinners who need to change their ways to become Spiritual."

Author: Jesus had no need to save children who were already Spiritually minded in Love. He had to bring the Spiritual Way of Love to those in society who were outcasts, sinners, doers of evil or those condemned who needed to know the Loving Spiritual Creator cares about them as much as any other child. And there is a place in Heaven for them also if they just change their ways and awaken into their True Spiritual identity of Love, Truth and Non-violence.

Fasting Without Jesus

Matthew 9:14-15, Mark 2:18-20, Luke 5:33-35 The disciples of John came to Jesus and asked, "Why do we and the Pharisees fast often but your disciples do not fast?" Jesus replied, "Can the descendants of the bridal chamber grieve as long as the bridegroom is with them? But the days will come when the bridegroom will be taken away from them, and then they will fast."

Author: The question they asked Jesus concerned fasting from eating earthly food for physical nourishment. But Jesus turns it into an answer referring to His disciples no longer having the nourishment of His words after He leaves as if fasting. But while He is still with them, they have His words to nourish their Spirits.

New Wine Old Wine

Matthew 9:16-17, Mark 2:21-22, Luke 5:36-39 Jesus spoke a parable to them, "No one tears a piece of cloth from a new garment and sews it onto an old garment. For if he does, the patch will not match the old and it will lift away from it, the new from the old and a worse split or schism is made between the two.

And no one puts new wine into old worn-out wineskins, if he does the new wine will burst the old skins as they cannot hold it and the new wine will be lost and the old skins destroyed. But new wine must be put into new wineskins to preserve its purity, and both are preserved. And no man used to drinking old wine desires to drink the new wine for he only knows the old wine and thinks it is good enough."

Thomas 47 Jesus said, "A person cannot mount two horses or bend two bows, and a servant cannot serve two Lords. That servant can only respect one but offends the other by doing so"

Author: Jesus warned His followers not to try and mix our One Loving Spiritual Creator He was at one with, in with the Old Testament two headed God Yahweh of the Jews because they do not match. Yahweh is a dualistic God with one body called Yahweh but two heads. One Godhead is a brutal, murdering, thieving War God the same as the Roman War God Mars, Greek War God Ares and Egyptian War God Sekhmet. The other Yahweh Godhead is a God of Love and

Peace the same as the Roman God Pax, Greek God Eirene and other Gods of Peace and Love at that time.

The garment analogy Jesus uses is talking directly about the different Spiritual identities. You cannot take a piece of our Loving Spiritual Creator who is only pure Love and try to sew it onto a dualistic God who loves and saves and hates and murders. If you do you will lose the understanding of the True Loving Creator that Jesus taught us about and pervert and distort Her Spiritual identity. Unfortunately, all Jewish/ Christian churches have done this, mixing the two different Gods together in one wineskin falsely teaching they are the same God. And they call the one wineskin the Bible.

I always advise followers of Jesus to cut the Bible in two, rip out the book of Revelation, which is the Jewish book of Daniel and put the Jewish religion up on the shelf with all the other different religions. As they usually all have some Love in them. And just stay with the words of Jesus about our Loving Spiritual Creator and the Spiritual Way of Love and Non-violence that He gave us to follow to reach Heaven.

Few Spiritual Laborers

Matthew 9:36-38, Mark 6:34, Luke 10:2 When Jesus saw the multitudes, He was moved with compassion for them for they were harassed and scattered like sheep without a shepherd. Then He said to His disciples, "The harvest is truly plentiful, but the Spiritual laborers are few. Therefore, pray our Loving Spiritual Creator sends out laborers into the harvest to gather Her children home."

Author: With the rise of the cult of the materialists in this world and the satanic warmongers still prowling and murdering children, more than ever we need True Spiritual children of Love and Non-violence to awaken and stand forth against all the evil in this world.

The Twelve Disciples

Matthew 10:1-15, Luke 6:12-16, Mark 3:17-19 Jesus called His twelve disciples, and He taught them how to have mastery over unclean Spirits, to cast them out and to heal all kinds of disease and weakness. Now the names of the twelve apostles were these: Simon who is called Peter, and Andrew his brother; James the son of Zebdee, and John his brother; Philip and Bartholomew; Thomas and Matthew the tax collector; James the son of Alphaeus and Lebbaeus, whose surname was Thaddaeus; Simon the Canaanite, and Judas Iscariot, who betrayed Him.

Disciple's Instructed

Matthew 10:5-15, Mark 6:7-11, Luke 9:2-5, Luke 10:3-11, 17 And before sending them out two by two Jesus said to the disciples, "Before going on the road to the Gentiles and entering the cities of the Samaritans first go to the lost sheep of Israel. And as you go, proclaim saying, "I bring the Kingdom of the Heavenly Spiritual World for you to find and be near to." Heal the sick, raise those dead to their Spirit back to Life, cleanse the lepers and cast out demons. Freely you have received the Loving Spiritual Life-force of Heaven so freely give it to others.

Procure neither gold, silver nor copper coins for your money belts, nor a bag for your journey, nor two tunics, nor sandals, nor staffs; for a good worker is worthy of his keep. And whatever city or town you enter inquire who is suitable to hear you and stay with them until you leave that place. As you enter the house say, 'Peace be upon this house,' and if the household is suitable to hear you let your peace rest upon it and stay in that house eating and drinking whatever they offer you. However, if the household is not suitable to hear you, let your peace settle back into yourself. And if anyone will not receive you or listen to your Spiritual words then leave that house or town and let the dust falling from your feet as you walk away be a witness to them."

So, they went out and taught people that they must have a change of mind and heart and become Spiritual. And they cast out many demons and anointed with oil many who were sick and healed them. When they returned, they joyfully told Jesus, "Master, even the demons are subject to your name."

Author: The original Teachers of the Spiritual Way of Jesus were like beggars relying on the generosity of those they taught just as Jesus did. And He advised them to be frugal and only carry the essentials that they needed and avoid excess material things. This is where the vow of poverty comes from for many Christians so they may concentrate on their Spiritual Life and share it with other children. Some Jewish/Christian church leaders no longer follow this Way of simple living and amass fortunes setting a bad example for other followers of Jesus. Jesus also said to keep searching for anyone ready to hear the Spiritual Way of Love that leads to Heaven even if some others may reject it.

Be Sheep Among Wolves

Matthew 10:16-23, Luke 12:11-12, Luke 21:12-19 Jesus said, "Behold I send you forth as sheep in the midst of wolves. Therefore, be as discreet as serpents and harmless as doves. But beware of worldly men, for they can deliver you up to the councils to punish and whip you in their synagogues.

You will be brought before governors and kings on account of following Me, to be a witness of the Spiritual Teachings and Way of Love for them and for the Gentiles. But when they deliver you up to them, do not worry about what you should say or how you will say it. For you will be given the words to speak in that hour. For it is not you that speaks, but the Spiritual Life-force of the Loving Creator in you that inspires the words for you to speak.

You will be betrayed even by parents and brothers; relatives and friends and they will even put some of you to death. You will be hated by all because you follow My Spiritual Way of Love and Non-violence but endure in this Way until the end of your journey here and then your Spirit and Soul will be alive and well and safe in Heaven. And whenever they persecute you in one city, flee to the next.

Author: All followers of the Spiritual Way of Love and Non-violence in this temporary Earth world can expect to be persecuted. But we must stay strong in our Spiritual body and Soul identity of Love keeping it filled with our Loving Creator's Spiritual Life-force. And be an example to others and be ready to enter the Heavenly Spiritual World after the death of our body of flesh.

Students Become Teachers

Matthew 10:24-26, Luke 12:2-5, John 13:16, Thomas 5 Jesus said, "A disciple is not above his Teacher nor a servant above his master. It is fulfillment that a disciple becomes the same as his Teacher, for when he is fully taught and understands the Spiritual Way he will be like his Teacher of the Way just as a servant will be like his master. If they call the master of the house satan how much more will they call those of his household satanic. But do not fear them for there is nothing covered that will not be revealed and hidden that will not be known.

What I explain to you that has been obscured in darkness speak in the Spiritual Truth of Light. And what you hear with your ear proclaim from the rooftops. Do not fear those who can only kill your body of flesh but do no more harm to you. But rather fear sin that can destroy both your body of flesh and also lead your Spiritual body and Soul into outer darkness tormented by being alone and separated from our Loving Creator and Heaven by your own wrongdoing."

Thomas 5 Jesus said, "Know what is within your sight and what is hidden from you will become clear to you. For there is nothing hidden that will not be revealed."

Author: Jesus taught we can all become exactly like Him right now by understanding His Teachings and Spiritual Way to awaken our Spiritual Life. He is not the only child of our Loving Spiritual Creator as the Jewish/Christians wrongly teach but certainly a fully awakened child as we must also become. He warns the disciples not to fear those who will hate them for being His followers of Love and Non-violence even if they kill their bodies of flesh for, they have another Spiritual body to leave in.

He tells them their Spiritual body is more important and to only fear sin as it can harm both their physical and Spiritual Lives and prevent them entering Heaven. Others can damage our body of flesh but only we can damage our Spiritual Life by performing wrongdoings or evil.

He understands the darkness that existed covering the Truth of our Loving Creator who is only Love and He removed it to reveal and bring us into the Truth and Light of Her Pure Love and Eternal existence in Heaven. And He tells them to be courageous and speak out about the One True Loving Spiritual Creator and Way of Love and Non-violence to Heaven.

In Thomas Jesus tells us if we understand the nature of the material world around us, we will realise it is temporary and imperfect. Prompting us to search for the Spiritual Heavenly World instead which is Eternal connected within us through our Spiritual body and Soul mind of Love which will then awaken and become our True life.

Those Who Know Me

Matthew 10:32-33, Luke 12:8-9 Jesus said, "Whoever acknowledges Me and lives out of My Spiritual Way of Love and Non-violence before men will be acknowledged and known in Heaven by Me, our Loving Creator and the Angels in Heaven. But he who does not acknowledge or live by My Spiritual Way of Love and Non-violence cannot be in the Heavenly Spiritual World of our Loving Creator."

Author: Jesus says if we follow His Spiritual Way of Love and Non-violence, we can all become exactly the same as Himself and be awakened Spiritual children of our Loving Creator in the Heavenly Spiritual World while still here on Earth. Then enter the Heavenly Spiritual world after death.

Jesus Challenges Social Identity

Matthew 10:34-39, Luke 12:49-53,14:25-27 Thomas 82 Jesus said, "Do not think My coming will bring peace on Earth for I bring a sword of Spiritual Truth that causes division amongst children. The Spiritual Truth will cause a son to go against his father, a daughter to go against her mother, a daughter-in-law against her mother-in-law and a man's foes will be those of his own household.

He who loves father or mother more than our Loving Spiritual Creator is not comparable to Me. And he who loves son or daughter more than our Loving Spiritual Creator is not comparable to Me. And he who does not take up his cross and follow after Me in the Spiritual Way of Love is not comparable to Me.

He who finds only his Earthly life of flesh will lose it. But he who loosens himself from his life of flesh by following My Spiritual Way and Teachings will find his Spiritual Life. I came to cast the fire of Spiritual Light upon the Earth, and I wish it were already alight. I have a baptism to undergo, and

I must hold this all together until it is fully accomplished."
Thomas 82: "Whoever is close to me is close to the fire. And whoever is far from Me is far from the Heavenly World."

Author: The Spiritual Truth of the One Loving Spiritual Creator that Jesus taught about contradicted the two headed God Yahweh belief of the Jews. This caused serious division within the Jewish community between the believers of the old false dualistic God Yahweh and the new believers in the One True Loving Spiritual Creator of Jesus. Jesus warns them they will face serious opposition from within their own social structure if they believe and follow Him.

He also states we should hold our Loving Spiritual Creator above all other Loves for She gives us all True Spiritual Life. And we must find, move into and live out of our primary Spiritual identity by following His Way and not be overly attached to our physical body or social identity which all end at death anyway. If we stay close to Him and His Way, we will be close to the Heavenly Spiritual World.

You Represent Me

Matthew 10:40-42, Mark 9:41, Luke 10:16, John 13:20
Jesus said, "He who receives whom I send receives Me and he who receives Me receives our Loving Spiritual Creator who sent Me. Each shall receive a compensation according to the extent of their belief and understanding.

He who accepts Me as a prophet shall receive a prophet's compensation, and he who receives Me as a righteous man shall receive a righteous man's compensation. And even someone who gives you a cup of water because you are a follower of Me and My Way will also receive a compensation. But he who rejects you rejects Me and My Spiritual Way of Love. And he who rejects Me rejects the Way of our Loving Spiritual Creator in the Heavenly Spiritual World."

Author: Children connect with Jesus at different levels of understanding. Some have no interest in Him so gain nothing from Him. Some believe He was just a good man while others believe He was a philosopher who taught a good way to live on Earth but do not believe in the Heavenly Spiritual World He taught about.

But others who believe He was an enlightened Spiritual child of our Loving Spiritual Creator in Heaven receive His words, are transformed by them and awaken their Eternal Spiritual body and Soul ready to leave their body of flesh at death and enter Heaven to be with our Loving Spiritual Creator. As Jesus said, "To he who has, more will be given."

This Generation is Like

Matthew 11:16-17 Jesus said, "To what shall I liken this generation? It is like children sitting in the marketplaces and calling to their companions saying, 'We played the flute for you, but you did not dance. We mourned for you, but you did not lament.'"

Thomas 28 Jesus said, "I took My stand in the middle of the material world, and in flesh I appeared to people. I found them all drunk, and I did not find any of them thirsty. My Soul ached for these mortal children because they are blind of heart and do not see that they came into the world empty and they will also seek to depart from the world empty. But now they are drunk. When they become sober, they will change their minds."

Author: Jesus is sorrowful that children were being intoxicated with temporary material things and were not thirsting after the Spiritual Truth and Heavenly Life that He was bringing to them. But once the material civilisations with its material way of life collapse children turn back to search for a deeper meaning and Spiritual Life.

Children Find the Truth

Matthew 11:25-27, Luke 10:21-24 Jesus said, "I thank you Loving Creator of the Heavenly Spiritual World that you have hidden these things from the clever and cautious ones and have revealed them to simple children. For in this manner your purpose comes before you.

All things have been entrusted to Me by our Loving Creator, and no one knows the Spiritual child of our Loving Creator except the Loving Spiritual Creator. Nor does anyone know our Loving Spiritual Creator except Her Spiritual child and the one to whom that child reveals Her too.

Blessed are your eyes that see what you have seen. For I say to you that many prophets and kings desired to see what you see and did not see it and to hear what you hear, and they did not hear it."

Author: Jesus sees the wisdom of our Loving Spiritual Creator guiding Him to teach simple fishermen and ordinary people these profound Spiritual truths as they are not filled with their own self-importance. Jesus says that only awakened Spiritual children will really know our Loving Spiritual Creator and they can help others find Her.

Take My Yoke Upon You

Matthew 11:28-30 Jesus said, "Come and follow Me all you who are wearied and heavy laden and I will refresh you. Take My yoke and Spiritual Way upon you and learn from Me for I am gentle and humble in heart and you will find rest for your Souls. For My yoke is pleasant and My burden is light."

Author: The Spiritual Way of Love of Jesus taught refreshes our Spirits and Souls through receiving the Loving Spiritual Life-force from Heaven to lift our Spirits up and sustain our journey through this temporary material world and help us carry all burdens through the power of Love.

Plucking Grain

Matthew 12:1-8, Luke 6:1-5, Mark 2:23-28 One Sabbath Jesus and His disciples were going through a grainfield, and the disciples plucked some grain to eat. The Pharisees saw this and said to Jesus, "Look, your disciples are doing what is not lawful on the Sabbath." He replied, "Have you never read what David did when he and those with him were hungry and entered the sacred house of Yahweh and ate the sacred bread there meant only for priests, which is not lawful to do?

If you only knew what, 'I desire mercy not sacrifice,' means you would not have condemned the guiltless. For I tell you a greater sacred place exists right here in Me. Making the Spiritual child of Humanity master of the Sabbath. The Sabbath was made for man, not man for the Sabbath."

Author: Jesus was not that interested in man's laws but was referring to the Loving Spiritual Life-force of our Loving Creator in His Spiritual body that comes from the Heavenly Spiritual World. A far greater and sacred Spiritual presence of our Loving Creator than any found in a Temple of stone of the two headed God of the Jews Yahweh. Heaven is within you. Not in a temple of stone.

A Divided House Falls

Matthew 12:22-30, Luke 11:14-23, Mark 3:20-27 A demon possessed blind and mute man was brought to Jesus and He healed Him so he could speak and see. All the multitudes were amazed but the Pharisees said, "He casts out demons by the power of satan the ruler of demons."

Jesus said, "Every kingdom divided against itself is brought to desolation and every city or house divided against itself will not stand. If satan casts out satan, he is divided against himself. How then will his kingdom stand? And if I by satan's power cast out demons, by whom do your sons cast them out? By this let them be your judges. But if I cast out demons by the Loving Spiritual Life-force of our Loving Creator surely the Heavenly Spiritual World has arrived upon you.

Or how can anyone enter the strong man's house and carry off his property unless he first binds the strong man? Then he will be able to plunder his house. He who is not with Me is against Me and he who does not gather with Me scatters abroad."

Thomas 103 Jesus said, "Blessed is the person who knows where the robbers will enter. Then the person may arise and bring his resources together and prepare himself before they break in."

Author: Jesus often warns us not to be divided within ourselves, or we will be in darkness, and our Spiritual house will fall but always be at one only with Love. He was able to perform these miracles by only acknowledging the Loving Spiritual Creator and Her Loving Spiritual Life-force which opposes all satanic evil just as Light destroys all darkness. The Jews worshiped a satanic War God along with a God of Love and called them both Yahweh, so that was poisoning the understanding of the One True Loving Spiritual Creator.

He also warns us not to lose our Spiritual strength by being tempted and having our Spirits bound by sin. For only if we let temptation and sin into our Spiritual home and Life can we be robbed of our Spiritual merit and Life-force. If we become aware of a temptation or dark way about to encroach on our life, we must counterattack it with the Spiritual weapons of Love, Light and Truth that come forth from Heaven and are within our Spiritual body and mind. All children in this material world who follow the Spiritual Way of Love and Non-violence that Jesus taught are with Him.

No Sign Given

Matthew 12:38-39, 16:1-4, Mark 8:11-12, Luke 12:54-56 Then some scribes and Pharisees began to argue with Jesus and to test Him they asked Him to give them a sign from Heaven. He sighed deeply in His Spirit and said, "Why does this evil generation seek a wonderous sign? Truly, I say to you, no wonderous sign shall be given to this generation. When it is evening you say, 'It will be fair weather, for the sky is red,' and in the morning, 'It will be foul weather today, for the sky is red and threatening.' Hypocrites! You know how to discern the face of the sky, but you cannot discern the signs of the times."

Thomas 91 They said to Jesus, "Tell us who you are so we can believe in you." He said to them, "You study the face of the sky and the earth, but you have not come to know the one who is before you, and you do not know how to understand this moment."

Author: The Jews who opposed Jesus rejected Him and His Spiritual Teachings that could transform them. Instead, they wanted a wonderous magic trick to believe in Him but that does not produce the Spiritual awakening that His words do when they are heard and understood.

Unclean Spirit Returns

Matthew 12:43-45, Luke 11:24-26 Jesus said, "When an unclean spirit goes out of a man it passes through dry places seeking rest but does not find any. Then it says, 'I will return to the house from which I came out from.' And when it comes back it finds it unoccupied, swept and put in order.

Then it goes and takes with it seven other spirits more wicked than itself, and they enter and dwell there and the last state of that man is worse than the first. So, shall it be with this wicked generation."

Author: Once we clean ourselves of all wrongdoings or bad habits, we must never let them into our life again as they leave an imprint or memory that is easily reignited, quickly escalating making things far worse than the first time.

The Families of Jesus

Matthew 12:46-50, Mark 3:31-35, Luke 8:19-21 Jesus went home and the crowd came together again with so many that they could not even eat. And people were saying, "He is possessed by a Spirit Himself." And when His family heard of this, they went out to seize Him and stood outside because of the large crowd, calling to Him. And they told Jesus His mother and brothers were outside calling Him. But He replied, "Who are My mother and brothers?" And stretching out His hand to those gathered around Him He said, "Here are my mother and brothers. For whoever follows the Spiritual Way of our Loving Spiritual Creator in Heaven of Love and Non-violence is My mother, brother and sister."

Author: We all have two different families. Our biological Earthly family and all those children in this world who have awakened to become Living Spiritual children of Love and Non-violence of our Loving Creator in the Heavenly World.

Sower of Seed Parable

Matthew 13:1-9, Mark 4:1-9, Luke 8:4-8 Jesus began to teach by the sea and as the crowd was large on the shoreline He sat in a boat in the water to speak to them. And He taught many things using parables. He said, "A Sower went out to sow seeds and as he sowed some of them fell along the path, were trodden underfoot and birds came and devoured them.

Other seed fell on rocky ground without much soil, and it sprang up. But because they had no depth of soil, when the sun rose, they were scorched as they were not deep rooted and lacking moisture they withered away. Other seed fell among thorns, and the thorns grew up and choked the seed and it yielded no grain. And other seed fell into good soil and grew strong and brought forth grain, some thirty-fold some sixty-fold and some a hundred. He who has ears to listen and understand let him hear and understand."

Author: We must always remember that not everyone has come into good contact with the beautiful Spiritual Teachings of great Teachers like Jesus and Buddha. Life's circumstances can have a serious impact on whether we find the Spiritual Teachings or not. Never judge those who have no Spiritual belief for you do not know their background. Rather, cherish your own good fortune and share your Spiritual beliefs with those who may be interested.

Why Parables

Matthew 13:10-13,16-17, Mark 4:10-12, Luke 8:9-10 The disciples came to Jesus asking Him, "Why do You speak to them in parables?" He answered, "Because it has been given to you to know the mysteries of the Heavenly Spiritual World but to them it cannot be given yet. For whoever has more will be given and he will have an abundance of understanding. But whoever has no understanding, what he already has must first be taken away. Therefore, I speak to them in parables for they will not see or understand what they hear if I give the same to them as I do to you.

Blessed are your eyes for they see and your ears for they hear and understand, for truly I say to you that many good prophets and righteous men desired to see what you see and did not see it and to hear what you hear, and they did not hear it."

Thomas 38 Jesus said, "Often these sayings that I am telling you have been desired to be herd. But you have no one else from whom to hear them. There will be days when you seek me but will not find Me."

Author: The disciples were with Jesus every day and He taught them daily. He slowly led them away from their old two headed Yahweh God beliefs to bring them into a Spiritual awakening that would transform them into becoming Living Spiritual children of our Loving Spiritual Creator in the Heavenly Spiritual World. Other children hearing Him for the first time teach this new Spiritual understanding needed a gentler approach with simple parables and analogies that held a deeper Spiritual meaning within them.

This avoided a serious backlash from occurring between the believers in the two headed God Yahweh of the Jews and the One True Loving Spiritual Creator and Way of Love and Non-violence that Jesus taught about. Then over time they could slowly receive higher Teachings and be led out of the dualistic religion of the Jews into the monotheistic Spiritual Way of Love of Jesus and our Loving Spiritual Creator.

Sower of Seed Explained

Matthew 13:18-23, Mark 4:10-20, Luke 8:11-15 Jesus sent the crowds away and His disciples came to ask Him to explain the parable's meaning to them. Jesus said, "Do you not understand this parable? How then will you understand all the other parables? To you it has been given to know the mystery of the Heavenly Spiritual World but those who are not with you must receive it in parables for they are not yet ready to receive it directly.

My words are like Spiritual seeds describing the Spiritual Way of Love and Non-violence that leads children to our

Loving Creator in Heaven. The seed that falls along the path are those who hear the words of Spiritual Life but do not understand them. This allows satan to come and distract them, taking their attention away from becoming Spiritual towards other worldly things and they lose the words and the Way to awaken into Spirit.

The seed sown on rocky ground are those who hear the Spiritual words and immediately receive them with joy, but they do not have a deep enough belief. So, they endure only for a while until the Spiritual Way is challenged by temptation, suffering or persecution and because they are not strong enough in belief, they depart from the Spiritual Way.

The seed sown among thorns are those who hear the Spiritual words but the cares of this material world and delight in riches and physical pleasures overtake them and choke the words and their Spirit does not ripen.

The seed that is sown on good soil are the ones who hear the Spiritual words, understand them and hold onto them with an honest and good heart, and they bring forth Spiritual fruit some thirty-fold, some sixty-fold, some a hundred-fold."

Author: To hear the Spiritual Teachings and understand them and live out of them in a dangerous, dualistic material world full of distractions, sufferings and evils is indeed a real achievement. Jesus lists a few of the reasons why some children fail to understand and receive the Spiritual Words and Way that Jesus taught that awakens our Spiritual bodies and minds bringing us to True Eternal Life in Heaven.

We must not be attached to this material world and once we receive the Spiritual words or seeds of awakening, we need to cultivate them, water them, nourish them and strengthen them by turning to our Loving Spiritual Creator in the Heavenly Spiritual Universe and World, to be filled with Her Loving Spiritual Life-force to bring our Spirits alive. Then we can manifest Loving Spiritual fruits on Earth.

Tares and Wheat

Matthew 13:24-30, Thomas saying 57 Jesus said, "The Kingdom of the Heavenly World is like a person who sowed good seed in his field, but while men slept his enemy came and sowed false grains among the true wheat and went on his way. When the wheat grain had sprouted and produced a crop the false grains appeared also amongst them.

So, the servants came to the owner and said to him, 'Sir, did you not sow good seed in your field? How then does it contain false grains?' He said to them, 'An enemy has done this.' The servants asked, 'Do you want us to go and gather them all up?' But he said, 'No, for while you gather up the false grain you may uproot the good grain with them. Let both grow until they are harvested and then gather the false grains into bundles and burn them with fire and gather the good grain into my barns.'"

Author: Here Jesus is talking about the Spiritual Law of Reaping as we Sow. All children who live a True Spiritual life will enter the Heavenly Spiritual World of Love. All those children who have created a false shadow identity to live out of to commit evil will have to undergo burning realisations of suffering to be cleansed because of the suffering they caused to others.

The harvest time is the day when each one of us passes through our death experience to reap as we have sown. Not an end of world Apocalypse as some Jewish/Christians wrongly teach children misleading them. Jesus never said any of the things concerning the Apocalypse or Himself coming on the clouds. These have all been placed in by an Apocalyptic Jew to damage the image of Jesus and our Loving Spiritual Creator. Jesus taught we must always be ready to die every day by living out of a Spiritual Life now.

Mustard Seed Parable

Matthew 13:31-32, Mark 4:30-32, Luke 13:18-19 Jesus said, "The kingdom of the Heavenly Spiritual World is like a mustard seed which a man receives and sows in his field, which indeed is the least of all seeds in that field but when it has grown to fullness it is greater than all the herbs and becomes a tree so that the birds of the air come and nest in its branches."

Author: The mustard seed represents the Spiritual words that we receive from Spiritual Teachers of Love like Jesus that are planted in our minds and hearts. A Spiritual seed in a material world that seems to dominate our lives on Earth. Compared to the material world around us the Spiritual words seem to have little real substance in comparison. But they can grow and become the dominant Spiritual identity and Life-force we live out of in this material world that will lead us to the Heavenly World.

Our connection to the Heavenly Spiritual World is within us in the form of our Spiritual body and Soul mind of Love. And eventually if these Spiritual words grow in us to fully open, we will have our Spiritual homes in Heaven. In a material world dominated by physical things including our temporary body of flesh and the sensations it can produce, it is easy to only believe in these temporary material things and not search for Spiritual Truths and our Spiritual Life.

Leaven in Bread

Matthew 13:33, Luke 13:20-21 Jesus said, "The kingdom of the Heavenly Spiritual World is like leaven which a woman took and hid in three measures of flour until it was all leavened."

Author: Bread made from flour does not rise and remains flat without leaven or yeast being mixed in with it. The yeast multiplies with moisture and warmth and produces pockets of air that make the dough rise and become soft. Likewise, the words of Jesus awaken our True Spiritual body and Soul mind of Love that is within our body of flesh. They bring us the Living water, and the warmth of our Loving Creator's Love that we need to arise in Spirit like the bread rises with yeast. His words transform us and we awaken into our Spiritual Life of Love and Non-violence which we need to become at one with to enter the Heavenly Spiritual World.

Hidden Treasure in the Field

Matthew 13:44 Jesus said, "The kingdom of the Heavenly Spiritual World is like a treasure hidden in a field which a man found and hid; and in joy over finding it he goes and sells all his material possessions and buys that field."

Thomas 109: "The Kingdom of Heaven is like a person who had a treasure hidden in a field but did not know it. At death the owner left the field to his child. The child did not know about the treasure either but took over the field and sold it. The new owner went plowing and discovered the treasure and began to lend the treasure at interest to whomever he pleased."

Author: Jesus is saying that the Spiritual treasure of our life is buried within the field of our body of flesh, but we must plow or dig beneath our Earthly identity of flesh or ego to uncover it. Many do not know about it so cannot tell their children how to find it either. Jesus again directs us to not let material things dominate our life and it is more important to gain this Spiritual treasure and Eternal Life than holding onto material things that all perish. Once we do find our Spiritual Life, we can share or lend the Loving Spiritual Life-force that sustains us with everyone we meet.

And the more Love we give to others, the more interest or Love we receive from our Loving Spiritual Creator.

One Pearl

Matthew 13:45-46, Thomas 74 Jesus said, "The kingdom of the Heavenly Spiritual World is like a merchant who had a supply of merchandise seeking beautiful pearls. The merchant was wise for when he found one pearl of great value he went and sold all that he had and bought it and made it his own."

Author: Jesus repeats the same message to be wise and find our True Spiritual Eternal Life within us all of great value. But we must seek it to find it and not be attached to all our material belongings. Once we have awakened into our Spiritual body and Soul mind of Love it becomes our primary identity to live out of here on Earth and in Heaven. We need no material possessions in Heaven.

Jar of Flour Empty

Thomas 97 Jesus said, "The Kingdom of the Heavenly Spiritual World is like a woman who was carrying a jar full of flour. While she was walking on a road far from home, the handle of the jar broke, and the flour spilled behind her on the road. She did not know this was happening, she had not noticed the problem. When she reached her house, she put the jar down and discovered that it was empty."

Author: Jesus is saying that the material substances and Earthly life-force that support our physical journey as we walk along the road of life in our body of flesh are always slowly running out. When we are born, we start our journey from Earth to Heaven and are at the farthest point from our

Spiritual Home but as time goes by through following the Spiritual Way, we can come closer to Heaven.

Just like the woman carrying the jar of flour, our Spirits must carry our body of flesh with us until we get home to the Heavenly Spiritual World. Then one day our body of flesh will run out of its material energy and lay down upon the earth empty of all life like the woman's jar was empty of flour when she finally reached her Heavenly home.

Then, if we have used our temporary physical life and its material energy to become Spiritually alive with the Loving Spiritual Life-force and are ready, we will enter the Spiritual Heavenly World in a Spiritual body fully alive and leave behind our body of flesh now empty of life.

The woman in this Teaching of Jesus only discovered she now had another Spiritual body to live out of when she left her dead body of flesh at the time of its death. Which is now just food for the vultures as Jesus said in His Teaching about two bodies in one woman's body grinding at the millstone. One dies and is food for vultures. And one is taken to be near to our Loving Spiritual Creator in the Heavenly Spiritual World of Love.

If we are well and our life is rich in daily activities, we do not think much about dying or how we are getting closer to our death experience every day. But we should, as it helps us to prepare by really valuing and making the most of what time we have to Love others and grow stronger in Spirit.

Sword Through Wall

Thomas 98 Jesus said to them, "The Heavenly Spiritual World is like someone who wanted to put a powerful one to death. He drew his sword at home and thrust it into the wall to find out if his hand would go through. Then he killed the powerful one."

Author: A Spiritual child may find themselves surrounded and imprisoned by a wall of sinful behaviour which has powerful control over their life. From within our Spirits, we must draw the Spiritual sword of Light and Truth wielded by the hand of Love and thrust it into the wall of false sin to break through it and kill the powerful temptation that took control of us and regain our Spiritual Life.

Net Cast in the Sea

Thomas 8 Jesus said, "A person is like a wise fisherman who cast a net into the sea and drew it up from the sea full of little fish. Among them the wise fisherman discovered a good, great fish. So, the fisherman threw all the little fish back into the sea and with no hesitation kept the good, great fish. Whoever has ears to listen and understand then hear."

Thomas 56 Jesus said, "Whoever has come to know the material world has discovered a carcass of flesh, and whoever has discovered a carcass of flesh is worth more than this material world."

Author: This is the original and correct saying of Jesus regarding the net parable. Again, He directs us to find the One great and good fish or our Spiritual Life amongst all the other little identities we may have here on Earth. Then we can let go of them and live out of our One True Spiritual Life and identity of Love and Non-violence and express it through our unique Earthly identity of the temporary flesh. By doing this we help to consolidate our Spiritual identity and bring it alive, getting ourselves ready to leave in our Spiritual body at death and enter the Heavenly Spiritual World. This is what Jesus meant when talking about realising our body of flesh is eventually just a carcass, which ignites the search for our Spiritual body and Soul mind of Love that lives on in Heaven.

The Matthew Gospel version has been deliberately manipulated and distorted to portray the fish as good and bad who will face judgement at an Apocalypse at the end of the age. This was done throughout the Gospels especially Matthew, to lay a false trail that will lead Christians to the slanderous book of Revelation portraying Jesus as a bringer of death, starvation, war and sickness. A complete assassination of who He and our Loving Spiritual Creator really are. I personally advise all True followers of Jesus to rip out the book of Revelation and burn it.

Jesus Rejected at Nazareth

Matthew13:53-58, Mark 6:1-6, Luke 4:16-24 Jesus came to His own country and His disciples followed Him. And on the Sabbath, He began to teach in the synagogue and many that heard Him were astonished saying, "Where did this man get all of this wisdom? And how does He perform mighty works by His hands? Is not this the carpenter, the son of Mary and brother of James and Joses and Judas and Simon, and are not His sisters here with us?"

And they took offense at Him teaching like this. But Jesus said to them, "A prophet is not without honour except in his own country and among his own kin and in his own house." And He could do no mighty works there except laying His hands on a few sick people to heal them because they had no respect or belief in Him.

Thomas 31 Jesus said, "A prophet is not popular in his hometown, a doctor does not heal family and friends."

Inner Defilement

Matthew 15:1-20, Mark 7:1-23, Luke 11:37-41 The scribes and Pharisees came to Jesus asking, "Why do your disciples transgress the tradition of the elders? For they do not wash their hands when they eat bread." He answered, "Why do you transgress the commandment of your God for the sake of your tradition? For your God commanded, 'Honour your father and mother,' and 'He who speaks evil of father or mother let him surely die.' But you say if anyone tells his father or mother that what they should have received from them is given to God, then they no longer have to honour their father or mother. So, for the sake of your tradition you have made void the word of your God.

You hypocrites! Well did Isaiah predict saying, 'This people honours me with their lips, but their heart is far from me; in vain do they worship me teaching as doctrines the laws of men.' You prefer the laws of men such as washing of pitchers and cups and many other such unimportant things instead of the laws of your God."

Jesus said to the crowd, "Hear and understand. It is not what goes into the mouth that defiles a man, but what comes out of it, this defiles a man." Then the disciples came to Jesus and said, "The Pharisees were offended by what you just said." Jesus answered, "Every plant which our Loving Spiritual Creator has not planted will be unable to survive without Her Loving Spiritual Life-force. Leave them to themselves. They are blind leaders of the blind. And if the blind leads the blind both will fall into a ditch."

Peter then asked Jesus to explain the parable to them. Jesus said, "Are you still without understanding? Do you not yet understand that whatever enters the mouth goes into the stomach and then is eliminated? But those things that proceed out of the mouth come from the heart and they defile a man. For out of the heart proceed evil thoughts, murders, adulteries, fornications, thefts, covetousness, wickedness, deceit, lewdness, pride, foolishness, false witness and blasphemies. These are the things which defile a man but to eat with unwashed hands does not defile a man."

Author: Jesus reminds us again that our inner Spiritual body and Soul mind of Love are the most important part of our life to keep clean. Our physical bodies are literally made of the earth and dirt anyway and return to it at death.

Leaven of the Pharisees

Matthew 16:5-12, Mark 8:14-21, Luke 12:1 The disciples had forgotten to bring bread when they set off in the boat with Jesus. Then Jesus said to them, "Be careful about the leaven of the Pharisees, Sadducees and Herod." They thought Jesus was talking about not bringing bread. But Jesus was aware of what they were saying and said, "O you of little faith, why do you think what I just said was about you not bringing bread? Do you not understand or remember the five loaves of the five thousand and how many baskets you took up? Nor the seven loaves of the four thousand and how many large baskets you took up? How is it then that you do not understand I was not talking about bread? I was talking about the leaven of the Pharisees, Sadducees and Herod." Then they understood He was talking about the Teachings of them, not about bread.

Author: The Jews were teaching that their two headed God Yahweh was the only True God. Jesus warns the disciples not to listen to or believe them as He was teaching them about the One True Loving Spiritual Creator and the correct Way of Love that leads us all to the Heavenly Spiritual World.

Peter Calls Jesus the Anointed One

Matthew 16:13-20, Mark 8:27-30, Luke 9:18-21 When Jesus came into the region of Caesarea Philippi, He asked His disciples saying, "Who do men say that I am?" And they told Him, "Some say John the Baptist and others say Elijah and others Jerimiah or one of the old prophets." Jesus asked, "But who do you say that I am?"

Peter answered saying, "You are the anointed one, a child of the Loving Creator." Jesus said, "Blessed are you Simon Bar-Jonah, for flesh and blood has not revealed this to you but My Loving Spiritual Creator who is in the Heavenly Spiritual World has. And I also say to you that you are Peter and upon this rock I will build My church and the gates of Hell shall not prevail against it.

And I will give you the keys of the Heavenly Kingdom and whoever is bound against the earth will be bound from entering Heaven and whoever is loosed from the earth will be loosed into Heaven." And He told them not to tell anyone that He was the anointed child of Our Loving Creator.

Thomas 12 The disciples said to Jesus, "We know you will leave us. Who is going to be our leader then?" Jesus said to them, "No matter where you reside, you are to go to James the Just. For the care of Heaven and Earth he came into being."

Thomas 43 His disciples asked Him, "Who are you to teach us all these things?" Jesus replied, "Don't you know who I am from what I have been saying to you? You have become like the Jews; either they love the tree but hate its fruit or they love the fruit but hate the tree."

Thomas 13 Jesus said to His disciples, "Compare Me with someone and tell Me whom I am like." Simon Peter said, "You are like a just Angel." Matthew said, "You are like a wise philosopher." Thomas said, "Teacher, my mouth is utterly unable to say whom you are like."

Jesus then said to Thomas, "I am no longer your Teacher for you have become intoxicated after drinking from the bubbling Spiritual spring that I have tended." And He took Thomas and withdrew and told him three things. When Thomas joined the others again, they asked him, "What did Jesus tell you?" Thomas said to them, "If I tell you even one of the things He told me you will pick up rocks and stone me. Then fire will come forth from the rocks and devour you."

Author: The keys to the Kingdom of the Heavenly Spiritual World that Jesus gave to Peter and the other disciples are His words and His Teachings of the Spiritual Way of Love and Non-violence that opens the Way for all children to follow to Heaven.

In Thomas Jesus picks James to be their leader not Peter and Thomas receives special Spiritual Truths that the other disciples are not yet ready to hear or understand. For example, Jesus may have openly told Thomas that Yahweh was not the real God but a hybrid between satan and a Loving God. This sort of Truth would be seen as blasphemy by Jews, and they would stone you to death for speaking it. The other disciples may have found this too confronting to be told.

Also, in Thomas we see different answers about who the disciples believe He might be and the disciples questioning Him about who He was. This may have been at an early time when the disciples were just beginning to follow Jesus.

Jesus Predicts His Death

Matthew 16:21-23, Mark 8:31-33, Luke 9:22 Jesus began explaining to the disciples that He must go to Jerusalem and suffer many things and be rejected by the elders and chief priests and scribes and be killed and rise again from the dead. Then Peter took Him aside and said, "Far be it from You Master that this should happen to You!" Jesus turned and said to Peter, "Get behind Me satan! You are an offense to Me, for you are not thinking about the Spiritual things of our Loving Spiritual Creator but of the things of man."

Author: Peter had no idea about the deeper Spiritual Teachings of Jesus and still did not realise we all have two different bodies in one as Jesus was teaching. Jesus needed to die to the flesh in order to reveal to them His Living Spiritual body after it leaves His body of flesh at the time of death. Peter could only think of His body of flesh dying.

Take up Your Cross

Matthew 16:24-28, Mark 8:34,9:1, Luke 9:23-27 Jesus said to the disciples and the crowd, "If anyone desires to come after Me let them become selfless, die to the flesh and take up their cross and follow Me in Spirit. For whoever desires to just save their physical life will lose it, but whoever gives their physical life over for their Spiritual Life by following My Way and Teachings will find their True Eternal Life. For what profit is it to a person if they gain the whole temporary, material world but lose their own Eternal Spirit and Soul? Or what material thing can anyone exchange for their Spirit and Soul? I say to you, there are some standing here who will not die before they see the Spiritual child of our Loving Spiritual Creator going into Her Heavenly Spiritual World."

Thomas 42 Jesus said, "Be wanderers."

Author: Again, we see Jesus saying it is vital that we bring our Spiritual Bodies and Souls to Life as He did by following His Way and Teachings and not be overly attached to this material, temporary world. Flesh is not Spirit. Spirit is not flesh. For a while they are at one in purpose while here to bring Heaven's Love to Earth for all children. In the short Thomas saying Jesus directs us to remember we are just wandering through this world not staying here. So, set your course for Heaven as you travel along the road filled with various experiences of your life on Earth.

Spiritual Circumcision

Thomas 55 The disciples then asked Jesus, "Is circumcision useful or not?" Jesus answered them, "If it were useful then a father would produce children already circumcised from their mother. Rather, the True Spiritual circumcision is useful in every respect."

Author: Jesus is not concerned about the body of flesh too much as it is only temporary. The Jews thought that if they circumcised an infant that would somehow make them a child of Yahweh. Jesus says it is useless. But becoming an awakened Spiritual child of our Loving Spiritual Creator filled with Her Loving Life-force is the True way to become a child of our Loving Creator.

Transfiguration Spiritual Body

Matthew 17:1-9, Mark 9:2-3, 7-10, Luke 9:28-36 Jesus took Peter, James and John his brother up onto a high mountain by themselves. And as He was praying the visible form of His appearance changed and His clothing became like radiant white Light. And when Peter and the disciples saw this happening to Jesus they were perplexed. Then a cloud overshadowed them and a voice from the cloud said, "This is My beloved Spiritual child listen to Him." When the disciples heard this voice, they fell to the ground in fear.

And when they raised their eyes to look, they saw no one but Jesus there. And as they were coming down the mountain Jesus ordered them to tell no one what they had seen until the Spiritual Child of Humanity is raised from the dead. So, they kept what they saw to themselves and wondered what the rising from the dead meant.

Author: Here we see the awakened Spiritual body of Jesus still within His body of flesh that He was teaching about on full display before the disciples. This is the body of Light and Spirit that Jesus said we all have within us like a treasure in a field of flesh to find, bring alive and live out of. He only chose a few close disciples to see His Spiritual body glowing as the others were less prepared, but even they were confused by seeing the radiance of His Spiritual body.

Later, after He rose in His Spiritual body from His dead body of flesh and appeared to them in His Spiritual body only, these three disciples would then understand He already had His Spiritual body while still in His body of flesh. Just as we all do and so they protected His Teachings about this Spiritual Truth to pass on to us all. But not everyone has found their Living Spiritual body empowered only by the Loving Spiritual Life-force of our Loving Creator. And sadly, some children even become evil shadow figures, beasts of the flesh formed out of their own imaginations and egos.

Jesus Again Predicts His Fate

Matthew 17:22-23, Mark 9:30-32, Luke 9:43-45 Jesus again tells the disciples of His coming fate saying, "The Spiritual Child of Humanity will be delivered into the hands of men, and they will kill Him and when He is killed, He will rise again." But the disciples had no idea about what He meant, and they were afraid to ask Him about this saying.

Author: The disciples still did not understand we all have two different bodies with us right now. As Jesus taught, one dies and is food for the vultures which is our body of flesh. And one is Spiritual raised up from the dead flesh to be taken to be near to our Loving Spiritual Creator in the Heavenly Spiritual World to reap as we have sown.

Jesus Pays the Tax

Matthew 17:24-27 When they came to Capernaum those who were collecting the two drachmae tax came to Peter and asked, "Doesn't your Teacher pay the two drachmae Tax? He said, "Yes, He does." And when Peter came to Jesus, He asked Peter, "What do you think Peter? From whom do the kings of the Earth take taxes, from their children or from strangers?"

Peter said, "From strangers." Jesus then said, "Then the children are exempt. Nevertheless, so we cause no scandal go to the sea, cast in a hook and take the fish that comes up first. And when you have opened its mouth, you will find a piece of money. Take it and give it to them for Me and you."

Author: Jesus is a fully awoken Spiritual child of our Loving Creator in Heaven. He is no longer of this world. He has little regard for the material earthly order to pay tax money but so He and Peter are not charged with an earthly offense He pays the tax.

Who is Greatest?

Matthew 18:1-6, 10-11, Mark 9:33-37, Luke 9:46-48, 17:2
When they came to Capernaum and were in the house Jesus asked them what they were discussing amongst themselves along the way. But they were silent, for they were discussing who was the greatest follower amongst them. Jesus called them together and said, "If anyone wants to be first, he must be last of all and servant of all."

And He took a child and put him in the middle of them saying, "Truly, I tell you, unless you turn back and become like little children you will never enter into the Heavenly Spiritual World. And whoever humbles himself like this child is greatest in the Heavenly World. Whoever receives one such child in My name receives Me and whoever receives Me receives the Loving Creator who sent Me.

But whoever causes one of these little ones to sin, it would be better for him if a heavy millstone were hung around his neck and he was drowned in the depth of the sea. Take heed that you do not despise one of these little ones for I tell you in the Heavenly Spiritual World their Angel guardians are always in the presence of our Loving Spiritual Creator who knows all things."

Thomas 81 Jesus said, "Let the one who is Spiritually rich overcome the material world and let the one who has power renounce it and serve others."

Thomas 4 Jesus said, "The older person many days old should not hesitate to ask a little child seven days old about the realm of life and this person will live. For many of the first will be last and will become a single one."

Author: Jesus came to serve those in need both Spiritually and physically. He gives us this beautiful dialogue of who we should all be like using a simple innocent child as the guiding instruction. As adults we can develop egos and arrogance that block our Spiritual Love flowing to others and from being at the surface. Jesus tells us to look back to when we were newly alive and at the innocence we all had then and return into that childlike innocence devoid of ego. It is the ego that creates a duality in our identities, but Jesus teaches we must only have One identity. A Spiritual child of Love.

Lost Sheep Parable

Matthew 18:11-14, Luke 15:3-7 Jesus said, "The Spiritual child of humanity has come to save the lost from perishing. What do you think? If a man has a hundred sheep and one of them goes astray, does he not leave the ninety-nine and go into the mountains to seek after the one that is straying until he finds it? And when he has found it, he lays it on his shoulders, and he rejoices more over that one lost sheep than the ninety-nine that never went astray.

And when he returns home, he calls together his friends and neighbours saying to them, 'Rejoice with me, for I have found my sheep that was lost.' Likewise, I tell you there will be more rejoicing in the Heavenly Spiritual World over one sinner who changes their ways than over ninety-nine who never sinned. Even so it is the will and intention of our Loving Spiritual Creator in the Heavenly World that not even one of these lost and least in Spirit should perish."

Author: Jesus clearly states that our Loving Spiritual Creator and Jesus never destroy any of Her children lost in darkness. But She continually tries to help us find our way back to who we really are or were as Spiritual children filled with Her Loving Spiritual Life-force from Heaven who can do no wrong. Then we may enter Her Heavenly Spiritual World after death.

However, we all must reap as we sow after death. So, we must listen now while still alive to the voice of Jesus calling us all, sinners and saints to become awakened Spiritual children of our Loving Spiritual Creator in the Eternal Heavenly Spiritual World.

A Sinning Brother or Sister

Matthew 18:15-18, Luke 17:3-4 Jesus said, "If your brother or sister sins against you go and confront them about their fault between you and them alone. If they listen and acknowledge their fault you have restored your friendship again. But if they refuse to listen, take with you one or two witnesses to confirm the facts of the matter. If they still refuse to admit to sinning against you tell it to the church. But if they refuse to listen to the church then accept that they have estranged themselves from you.

However, if your brother or sister sins against you confront them and if they are sorry then forgive them. And if they sin against you seven times in a day and seven times say sorry still forgive them every time. And whoever is bound against the earth will be bound from entering Heaven and whoever is loosed from the earth will be loosed into Heaven."

Author: We must always forgive those who sin against us as the first rule. Then we can try to restore that break in trust by talking it over with the one who committed the act against us. Out of Love for them we hope to guide them into seeing the wrong that has damaged their Spirit and your friendship and restore them to good Spiritual health. But if they chose not to admit their wrong, we must accept the loss of their trusted friendship but still Love them. Jesus then comments if we are bound to the material world it prevents entry to the Heavenly Spiritual World. But loosening yourself from things of the material world including sin, will allow you to enter the Heavenly Spiritual World.

Forgive and Forgive and Forgive

Matthew 18:21-35 Peter came to Jesus and asked, "Master, how often shall my brother sin against me and I forgive him? Up to seven times?" Jesus replied, "I do not say up to seven times but up to seventy times seven. For the Heavenly Spiritual World is like a king who wanted to settle accounts with his servants. And when he had begun to settle accounts, one was brought to him who owed him ten thousand talents. But as he was not able to pay his master ordered he be sold with his wife and children and all that he owned so payment could be made.

The servant fell down before his master saying, 'Have patience with me and I will pay you all.' Then the master of that servant was moved with compassion, released him and forgave him all the debt. But that servant went out and found a fellow servant who owed him a hundred denarii, and he laid hands on him and took him by the throat saying, 'Pay me what you owe me!' And his fellow servant fell down at his feet and begged him saying, 'Have patience with me and I will pay you all.' And he would not but went and through him into prison until he could pay all the debt.

When his fellow servants saw what had been done, they were very grieved and came and told their master all that had been done. Then the master called back the servant he forgave and said to him, 'You wicked servant! I forgave you all that debt because you begged me. Should you not also have had compassion on your fellow servant, just as I had pity on you?' And his master was angry and delivered him to the torturers until he should pay all that he owed. So also, shall our Loving Spiritual Creator not be able to forgive you your sins, if you fail to forgive from your heart others who sin against you."

Author: Forgiveness is a vital characteristic we must all have as a Spiritual child of our Loving Creator. Just as we ask our Loving Creator to forgive us when we stray into sin against Her perfect Way of Love, so we must do the same for others. The torturers mentioned by Jesus are the burning realisations of our sins we must undergo after death, if we have not cleansed ourselves of sin before death. This is the Spiritual Law of Reaping as we Sow.

Divorce and Marriage

Matthew 19:3-9, Mark 10:2-8 The Pharisees came to test Jesus asking, "Is it lawful for a man to divorce his wife for any reason?" Jesus replied, "Have you not read that our Loving Creator made them male and female? And for this reason, a man shall leave his father and mother and be joined to his wife and the two shall become one flesh. So, they are no longer two but one in body. A man and his wife are naturally joined together in this way and therefore they should remain so. However, if one of them gives reason for divorcing such as infidelity or abuse then they have the right to break the bond of marriage."

Children of Heaven

Matthew 19:13-15, Mark 10:13-16, Luke 18:15-17 Then little children were brought to Jesus that He might lay His hands on them and bless them. But when the disciples saw them coming, they stopped them. When Jesus saw what they were doing He was angry with them and said, "Let the little children come to Me and do not forbid them for ones such as these will be in the Heavenly Spiritual World. Truly I say to you whoever does not receive the Heavenly Spiritual World like a little child will by no means enter in." And He laid His hands upon them and blessed them.

Author: Jesus often uses the analogy that we must become as unpretentious and humble as little children to become Spiritual children in Heaven.

Rich Young Man

Matthew 19:16-26, 29-30, Mark 10:17-31, Luke 18:18-30 A man came up to Jesus and asked Him, "Good Teacher, what good thing shall I do that I may have eternal Life?" Jesus said, "Why do you call Me good? No one is wholly good but one, our Loving Spiritual Creator of Love. But if you want to enter into Life keep the commandments." He asked, "Which ones?" Jesus replied, "You shall not murder, you shall not commit adultery, you shall not steal, you shall not lie, honour your mother and father and love your neighbour as yourself."

And he said, "Teacher, all these things I have followed from my youth." And Jesus looked at him saying, "There is one thing you still lack. Sell all that you own and distribute it to the poor, and you will have treasure in the Heavenly Spiritual World and come and follow Me." But when he heard this, he became sorrowful for he had a great number of earthly possessions.

Then Jesus said to His disciples, "Assuredly I say to you, how hard it will be for those who have earthly riches to enter the Heavenly Spiritual World." And Jesus said, "I tell you again just how hard it is for those who trust in earthly riches to enter the Heavenly Spiritual World. It is easier for a camel to go through the eye of a needle than for a rich man to enter the Heavenly Spiritual World."

And the disciples were astonished and surprised at His words for rich Jews were considered especially blessed by their God Yahweh. The disciples then asked, "Who then can be saved if not those blessed with riches?" Jesus replied, "For a man who is only mortal it is impossible but for one who is with our Loving Spiritual Creator all things are possible."

Peter asked Jesus what they who have left their homes to follow Him will have. Jesus replied, "Everyone who has left houses or brothers or sisters or father or mother or wife or children to follow and share My Spiritual Way with others will receive a vast amount more than these things by inheriting Eternal Life in the Heavenly Spiritual World of our Loving Creator. For many who are first on Earth will be last and the last will be first."

Author: Jesus again draws a definite line between the Earthly, material, temporary world and the Eternal Heavenly Spiritual World. If we only spend our life accumulating earthly material things then we will have missed out on accumulating the Loving Spiritual Life-force from Heaven that we need to be Spiritually alive when our body of flesh dies and returns to the earth from which it was formed.

That is what empowers our Spirits and Souls to have True Eternal Life in Heaven after our material body of flesh dies. Once attached to material wealth it is like an addiction that goes nowhere and can destroy our opportunity to prepare to be Spiritual children in Heaven after death.

Workers in the Vineyard

Matthew 20:1-16 Jesus said, "For the Heavenly Spiritual World is like a man who is the head of the family who went out early in the morning to hire laborers for his vineyard. Now when he had agreed with the laborers to be paid a denarius a day, he sent them into his vineyard. And he went out about the third hour and saw others standing idle in the marketplace and said to them, 'You also go into the vineyard and whatever is just I will pay you.' So, they went. Again, he went out about the sixth and ninth hour and did likewise. And about the eleventh hour he went out and found others standing idle and said to them, 'Why have you been standing here idle all day?' They said to him, 'Because no one hired us.' He said to them, 'You also go into the vineyard and whatever is just you will receive.'

So, when evening had come the owner of the vineyard said to the steward, 'Call the laborers and give them their wages beginning with the last to the first.' And when those came who were hired about the eleventh hour they each received a denarius. But when the first came they supposed that they would receive more but they also received a denarius. And when they had received it, they complained against the landowner saying, 'These last ones have worked only one hour, and you made them equal to us who have borne the greater burden and heat of the day.' But he answered saying, 'Friend I am doing you no wrong. Did you not agree with me for a denarius? Take what is yours and go your way. I wish to give to this last man the same as to you. Is it not lawful for me to do what I wish with my own things? Or is your eye malicious because I am good?' So, the last will be first and the first will be last. For many are called but few are chosen."

Author: Jesus teaches we can all become Spiritual children of our Loving Spiritual Creator in Heaven at any stage of our life on Earth. And once we are committed to being

Spiritual and begin to bring the Loving Spiritual Life-force of our Spiritual Creator in Heaven to all children in need we are all equally Her children regardless of the Earthly time spent as one. The one denarius for all represents this Truth along with the saying of Jesus about the last being equal to the first and the first being equal to the last to convey this Spiritual Truth that we are all equally Loved as Her children by our Loving Spiritual Creator.

He also points out the fault of how some Spiritual children fall into the trap of feeling superior to others due to the amount of their works being greater. When it is the Love flowing through us from Heaven to others that is all that really matters as that is our True Heavenly reward while here on Earth. And Love is Love and it has no quantity attached to it as it is one and complete and flows like an unending wellspring to all who wish to receive it and share it.

Jesus Predicts His Death

Matthew 20:17-19, Luke 18:31-34, Mark 10:32-34 As Jesus was going up to Jerusalem, He took the twelve disciples aside and He began to tell them what will happen to Him. He said, "Behold, we are going up to Jerusalem, and the child of Humanity will be delivered to the chief priests and scribes, and they will condemn Him to death and deliver Him to the Gentiles who will mock Him, spit on Him, scourge Him and kill Him and then he will rise again." The disciples understood none of these things Jesus was saying and could not grasp or understand what was said.

Author: Even after listening for a few years to Jesus teach about the New Spiritual understanding that we all have two different bodies with us, one of flesh that dies and one of Spirit that rises from death and lives on, they still had no real concept of this Spiritual Truth. Or that Jesus was going to allow His body of flesh to be killed so that He could appear briefly to them only in His Spiritual body to demonstrate this ultimate Spiritual Truth before He went to Heaven.

To Serve is Greatest

Matthew 20: 25-28 Mark 10:42-45, Luke 22:25-27 Jesus called the disciples together and said, "You know that the rulers of the Gentiles have lordship over them and their greater men have authority over them. But it shall not be this way among you for whoever desires to become great among you must be your assistant and servant. And whoever would be first among you must dedicate their whole life to you.

Just as the Spiritual child of Humanity came not to be served by others but to serve. And dedicate His life like a ransom paid to free children from being captured by ignorance and sin, through giving His words to them to set them free from the bondage of sin and ignorance by awakening their Spiritual life to the Truth of who they really are."

Author: Jesus teaches selflessness which we need for the Loving Spiritual Life-force to flow easily through us to all children in need. To serve others in need is to be at one with that Love within you which links you to Heaven and sustains your Spiritual body, Soul and Life. We can dedicate our life in this way to whatever degree our circumstances permit. Jesus gave up His career as a carpenter to teach these Spiritual Truths to awaken our Spiritual Life once He found His and guide us all home to Heaven.

Jesus Enters Jerusalem

Matthew 21:8-11, Mark 11:8-10, Luke 19:36-40, John 12:12-13, 17-19 And many heard in the city that Jesus was approaching, so they went and spread their garments on the road in front of Him and others cut down branches and spread them also on the road to honour Him. And when they saw Him arriving, knowing all about the mighty works He had done in the name of our Loving Spiritual Creator they cried out, "Hosanna, blessed is he who comes in the name of our Loving Creator! Peace in Heaven Hosanna in the highest."

And the whole city was stirred up asking who He was. And they were told, "It is Jesus the prophet from Nazareth of Galilee." And the Pharisees, seeing this said to each other, "Look, we are accomplishing nothing. The world is following after Him." So, some of the Pharisees upset by this said to Jesus, "Master, rebuke your followers." He answered saying, "I tell you, if they were all silent these stones would cry out. Have you not read, 'Out of the mouths of children and nursing babies you have perfect praise.'"

Author: Things were getting more dangerous for Jesus as many Jews were beginning to follow His understanding of our Loving Spiritual Creator who is only Love and were leaving the two headed God Yahweh that that Pharisees were teaching about. He was undermining the old God of the Jews and the Pharisees wanted to get rid of Him as He was a threat to their power base and the distorted two headed God Yahweh.

Jesus Cleanses Temple

Matthew 21:12-17, Mark 11:15-17, Luke 19:45-46, John 2:13-22 Jesus entered the temple of Yahweh, the two headed God of the Jews and drove out all those who sold and bought goods in the temple and He overturned the tables of the moneychangers and the seats of those who sold pigeons, sheep and oxen. And he drove all the animals out too. And would not allow anyone to carry goods through the temple. And He said, "My house shall be a house of Spiritual prayer says the Loving Creator, but you have gone and made it a den of thieves."

And the Jews asked Him, "What sign will you show us that gives you the right to do these things?" Jesus answered, "Destroy this temple and I will raise it up again." Then the Jews said, "It has taken forty-six years to build this temple, and will you raise it up again by yourself?" But Jesus was speaking about the death of His body of flesh and being raised up again in His Spiritual body after death.

And the blind and the lame came to Him in the temple and He healed them. But when the chief priests and the scribes saw the wonderful works He did and the children crying out, "Hosanna to the Spiritual child of our Loving Creator," they were angry and said to Him, "Do you hear what these children are saying?" And Jesus said, "Out of the mouths of little children and babes you have brought perfect praise." And the scribes and the chief priests talked about how they could destroy Him for they feared Him because all the people were amazed and enthralled by His Teachings. And then leaving He went and sort lodging in Bethany.

Author: Jesus would have known about the slaughter at Jericho incited by the Yahweh 1 War God that the Jews worshiped and followed, who instructed them to commit genocide and go and kill every man, woman and innocent child in Jericho and steal all their gold, silver and brass to bring back and place in the temple of the two headed God Yahweh and steal all their land. This is exactly the sort of thing Jesus was referring to when He rightly said, "You have turned this Spiritual Temple into a den of thieves."

Jesus is Questioned

Matthew 21:23-27, Mark 11:27-33, Luke 20:1-8 One day when Jesus entered the temple the chief priests, the scribes and the elders came to Him and asked Him, "By what authority are you doing these things and who gave you this authority?" Jesus answered, "I will also ask you a question and if you give me an answer then I will tell you by what authority I do these things. Was the baptism of John from Heaven or men?"

They discussed this with each other saying, "If we say it was from Heaven He will say, 'Why then didn't you believe him?' If we say it was from men, all the people will be against us for they believe John was a prophet." So, they answered Him, "We do not know." Jesus then said, "Well neither will I let you know by what authority I do these things."

Author: Jesus had great Spiritual insight and wisdom as a Living Spiritual child of Heaven on Earth and was able to deal with such attacks and traps in a very clever way that prevented them from stoning Him to death for committing blasphemy with His answers.

Two Sons Parable

Matthew 21:28-32 Jesus said, "What do you think? A man had two sons, and he said to the first one, 'Son, go and work in the vineyard today.' And he answered, 'I will not,' but afterwards he regretted his answer and changed his mind and went. Then he went to the second son and said the same, and he answered, 'I will go sir,' but he did not go. Which of these two sons did the will of his father?" They said, "The first one."

Jesus said to them, "Truly I say to you the tax collectors and prostitutes enter the Kingdom of the Heavenly World before you. For John came to you in the way of virtue and moral decency and you would not believe him, but the tax collectors and prostitutes believed him and even when you saw this you still did not change your mind and believe him."

Author: The first son represents those who are lost in sin but then change their ways and become Spiritual. The second son represents the Jews who do not follow Jesus to become children of our Loving Creator but remain worshiping their two headed God Yahweh.

Wicked Tenants Parable

Matthew 21:33-46, Mark 12:1-12, Luke 20:9-19 Jesus said, "There was a certain householder who planted a vineyard and set a hedge around it and dug a pit for the wine press and built a tower and let it out to tenants to farm. He then went away to another country. When the season of the fruit harvest drew near, he sent a servant to the tenants to collect his portion of the fruit.

But they seized him and beat him and sent him away empty handed. Again, he sent them another servant, and they threw stones at him wounding him in the head and treated him shamefully. So, he sent another and they killed him and likewise with others he sent, some were beaten and some killed. So, the owner decided to send his son saying, 'They will respect my son.' But when the tenants saw the son, they said among themselves, 'This is the heir, come let us kill him and claim his inheritance for our own.' So, they killed the son and cast him out of the vineyard.

What do you think the owner of the vineyard will do? They replied, "He will come and cast those tenants out of the vineyard and give it to others to bring forth the fruit." Jesus said, "Have you not read this scripture, 'The very stone which the builders rejected has become the head and primary cornerstone, this is our Loving Creator's doing and it is marvelous in our eyes.' So, our Loving Creator's Heavenly Spiritual kingdom will be taken away from you and given to others to bring forth the fruit.

And anyone who comes against this stone, his false identity covering his Spirit will be broken to pieces, and on whomever this stone rests it will winnow them of their sins and reveal their True Spiritual identity." The Pharisees and the scribes knew He was talking about them and wanted to arrest Him but were afraid of the crowd following Jesus.

Author: Jesus is talking about all the good prophets who were leading the Jews towards only a Loving God being rejected and killed by them throughout time. The servant wounded in the head could be a reference to John the Baptist whom they rejected and was beheaded. Jesus was an awakened Spiritual child of our Loving Spiritual Creator in Heaven and He was bringing a new understanding about our Loving Creator who is only Love to the Jews. This would destroy the old two headed God Yahweh that they worshiped and was their power base. So, they also killed Him, a true Spiritual child of our Loving Creator to keep and protect their distorted understanding of God.

This correct translation concerning the cornerstone is perverted in nearly all the Gospels of the world which translate it this way. "Everyone who falls upon this stone will be broken to pieces, but whomever this stone falls on it will crush him." Because of this distorted translation many followers of Jesus are wrongly taught this means Jesus and our Loving Spiritual Creator are going to destroy and kill anyone who stands against them. That refers to Yahweh 1 the War God of the Jews not Jesus and our Loving Creator who only Love us even if we are lost in sin.

Banquet Invitations Refused. The Original Saying

Thomas 64 Jesus said, "A certain person was entertaining guests. When the dinner was ready the host sent a servant to invite the guests. The servant went to the first one and said, 'My Lord invites you.' The guest said, 'Some merchants owe me money, and they are coming to me tonight. I must go to give instructions to them. Please excuse me from the dinner.'

The servant went to another guest and said, 'My Lord invites you.' The guest said, 'I have bought a house and have been called away for the day. I have no time.' The servant went to another guest and said, 'My Lord invites you.' That guest said, 'My friend is to be married, and I must arrange the dinner, so I shall not be able to come. Please excuse me from the dinner.'

The servant went to another guest and said, 'My Lord invites you.' The guest said, 'I have bought a farm, and I am going to collect the rent so I shall not be able to come. Please excuse me.' The servant returned to the Lord and said, 'Those whom you have invited to the dinner have all asked to be excused.' The Lord then said to the servant, 'Go out onto the streets and bring back whomever you find to eat my dinner.' Business people and merchants shall not enter the Heavenly Spiritual World of our Loving Spiritual Creator.'"

Thomas 23 Jesus said, "I will choose you one from a thousand and two from ten thousand and these will stand to their feet, being as One."

Author: This is the original correct saying of Jesus concerning the banquet. It is another reinforcement He gives to not become attached to the material world, riches and possessions. But rather except the invitation to join Him in the feast of Spiritual awakening that He prepares for us to receive through the nourishment of His Teachings. It can also refer to the Jews whom He taught first who rejected His Spiritual Way of Love and Non-violence of the One True Loving Spiritual Creator so He must look for others who wish to receive it.

But few find this Oneness with Love for as He said, "Many are called but few are chosen." In Thomas Jesus refers to being at One or whole in Spirit. We see this also in His saying, "If your eye is single your whole body will be filled with Light." These are the awakened Spiritual children of Love and Non-violence who are the Living Children of our

Loving Spiritual Creator on Earth. The children of Light that Jesus spoke about. No one in this correct version is killed for refusing to come or thrown into outer darkness after coming in to join Him regardless of who they are.

Banquet Invitations Refused. Altered Versions

Matthew 22:1-5, 8-10, Luke 14:15-24 Jesus said, "The Kingdom of Heaven is like a King who arranged a wedding for his son, prepared a great banquet and sent his servants to call those who were invited, 'Come to the banquet, for all things are now prepared.' But they all began to make excuses. The first said to him, 'I have bought a field and must go out and see it, I ask you that I be excused.' And another said, 'I have bought a team of five oxen, and I must go to test them, I ask that I may be excused.' And still another said, 'I have married a wife and therefore I cannot come.'

(And the rest seized his servants treated them spitefully and killed them. When the King heard about this, he was furious. And he sent out his armies, destroyed those murderers and burned up their city.) The master of the house said to the servants, 'Go out quickly into the streets and lanes of the city, and bring in here, the poor, the maimed, the lame and the blind.'

They then said, 'It is done as you ordered and still there is room for more.' So, the master said to the servants, 'Go out into the highway and hedges and convince them to come in, so that my house may be filled.' And the servants went and did as they were told and brought in both the (good and the bad.) The king saw one man who had no wedding garment and asked him how he gained entry without one. And he was speechless. Then the king said, 'Bind him hand and foot and take him away and cast him into outer darkness, there will be weeping and gnashing of teeth. For many are called, but few chosen."

Author: Matthew has distorted this parable by inserting a fictitious episode where the 'certain person' in Thomas is replaced by a King, representing our Loving Creator, who murders all those who treated Her servants badly or killed them after refusing to come and join in with the wedding of Her son who represents Jesus. That is what the War God Yahweh 1 of the Jews does not Jesus or our Loving Creator who teach us to 'Love our enemies.' And as Jesus said, "Whoever hears My words but does not follow them, I do not judge them. I have come to save the world not to condemn it."

And as always Matthew tries to make it about those who believe in Jesus being good and saved and those who don't are bad and destroyed. And he shifts the original focus from the materially minded children not being Spiritual enough to enter the Heavenly Spiritual World to being about the non-believers being killed or thrown into outer darkness and the believers being saved. A very heavy Jewish overlay viewpoint.

Caesar's Tax

Matthew 22: 15-22, Mark 12:13-17, Luke 20:20-26 And the Jewish leaders sent some of the Pharisees and the Herodians to Jesus to try and trap Him in His words so they may have something against Him to report Him to the Roman Governor. They said to Him, "Master, we know that You are True, and teach the Way of our Creator in Truth, nor do you have any regard for the position of men and show no favouritism. Tell us, is it lawful to pay taxes to Caesar or not? Should we pay, or not?"

But Jesus, aware of their malicious intent to trap Him asked, "Why do you test Me like this? Bring Me a coin and let Me see it." And they brought one to Him. And holding up the coin, He asked them, "Whose likeness and inscription is this?" And they said to Him, "Caesar's." Jesus then said,

"Give therefore the things that are Caesar's to Caesar, and the things that are the Loving Spiritual Creator's to the Loving Creator." And they marveled at His answer and left Him and went their way.

Thomas 100 They showed Jesus a coin and said to Him, "Those who work for Caesar, demand we pay taxes." Jesus said, "Give to Caesar what is Caesar's, give to the Loving Creator what is the Loving Creator's and he who is Mine, give him to Me."

Author: We see the Spiritual wisdom again of Jesus as He avoids being brought to punishment by their trap. And as always, He is directing them to realise they have two different lives going on at once. One is material involving money and daily needs and the other is Spiritual involving their Loving Spiritual Creator and the Spiritual Life She has given them.

It is also worth noting that even the heavily biased Jews knew Jesus had perfect equanimity towards all. This was because He was at One with the Loving Life-force from our Loving Creator who Loves all Her children good and bad. In the Thomas version we also see Jesus actually telling them to let those Jews who are following Him and His new Spiritual Way of Love to be allowed to do so unhindered.

Resurrection Question

Matthew 22:23-33, Mark 12:18-27, Luke 20:27-40 The Sadducees who say that there is no resurrection, came to Jesus and asked Him this question. "Teacher, Moses said, 'If a man dies leaving his wife but has no children, his brother must marry the wife and raise up children for his brother.' Now there were seven brothers: the first took a wife and died without children then the second and third took her and also died the same up to the seven brothers all without children to her. Last of all the wife died. In the resurrection whose wife will she be? For they were all her husbands."

Jesus said, "You are wrong for you do not know the scriptures or the Spiritual power of our Loving Creator. For when they rise from their dead bodies of flesh they neither marry nor are given in marriage and cannot die anymore for they have Spiritual bodies like the Angels.

And as for the dead bodies of flesh being raised have you not read in scriptures that our Loving Spiritual Creator is not a Creator of dead bodies of flesh but of Living Spiritual bodies." And when the crowd heard Him, they were astonished at His Teaching.

Author: Jesus clearly states that we all have two different bodies with us right now. Our body of earthly flesh dies and returns to the earth from which it was formed, and it does not rise again. And we no longer have a biological body of flesh in Heaven.

Instead, we have a Spiritual body that rises from our dead body of flesh at the time of death which is Heavenly like the Angels. And it is formed and sustained by the Spiritual Loving Life-force given to us to have True Life in Heaven from our Loving Spiritual Creator. The Jews had no understanding of this at all and were amazed at such Teachings of Spiritual Truth by Jesus.

First Spiritual Practice

Matthew 22:34-39, Mark 12:28-34, Luke 10:25-28 A lawyer asked Jesus a question to test Him. "Teacher, what Spiritual practice is the most important? " Jesus replied, "First you must change and understand this correctly O Israel; our Loving Spiritual Creator is only Love and One and is not a dualistic God. Then the first Spiritual practice is to Love and be thankful to your Loving Spiritual Creator with all your heart, all your strength, all your Spirit and Soul and with all your mind for giving you a Spiritual Life. The second Spiritual practice is similar; you must love your neighbour as yourself. All the good prophets and other Spiritual practices depend on these two Spiritual practices."

And the lawyer said to Him, "You are correct Teacher and you have truly revealed that our Loving Creator is only One and there is no other but She. And to Love Her with all our heart, and with all the understanding, and with all the strength, and to love one's neighbour as oneself is more than all the burnt offerings and sacrifices." Jesus saw he understood and said, "You are not far from the Heavenly Spiritual World of our Loving Creator."

Author: The first thing Jesus does is to point out to the Jews that our Loving Spiritual Creator is only One and is not the two headed dualistic God Yahweh of the Jews. He had to be very careful about the words He used to convey this new Spiritual understanding to them for if He spoke too openly about the two headed God Yahweh they would have stoned Him to death for blasphemy.

He then gives the main Spiritual Way of Love as being the most important thing of all to follow. Not like the War Godhead Yahweh 1 of murder, genocide, thieving, revenge and corruption but more like the Yahweh 2 of love your neighbour as yourself.

Jesus Criticises Pharisees

Matthew 23:1-34, Mark 12:38-40, Luke 20:45-47 Jesus warned the multitude, "The Pharisees are hypocrites by teaching certain things to you to obey while they do not follow them. For they bind heavy burdens hard to bear and lay them on men's shoulders while they will not help you lift them with even a finger.

Woe to you Pharisees, you should give for alms to those in need, those Spiritual things that are within you, then everything is clean for you. But woe to you Pharisees, hypocrites, for you give mint and rue and all types of herbs, but do not give justice, mercy, faith and the Love of our Loving Creator. These must be done, along with the other smaller things.

Woe to you Pharisees! For you love the best seats in the synagogues and at feasts, and love to be greeted and saluted in the marketplace. Woe to you Scribes and Pharisees, hypocrites! For you are like graves which are hidden, and those who travel upon them are unaware they have no Spiritual life in them. For you are like whitewashed tombs which indeed appear beautiful outwardly, but inside are full of dead men's bones and all uncleanliness. You appear outwardly in the flesh to be righteous to men, but your Spirit within is full of hypocrisy and iniquity.

Woe to you scribes and Pharisees, hypocrites, for you travel the seas and land to make one convert to Judaism and when he does convert you make him even more a son of hell than you are. You are blind guides who strain out a gnat yet swallow a camel. You blind guides say, 'Whoever shall swear by the temple it means nothing, but whoever swears by the gold ornaments of the temple he is bound by it.'

Fools and blind ones! For which is greater, the ornaments of gold or the temple that makes them Holy? And you say, 'Whoever swears by the alter it means nothing, but whoever swears by the gift that is on it he is obliged to be bound by it.' Fools and blind ones! Which is greater, the gift or the altar that makes the gift Holy?

Therefore, he who swears by the altar swears by it and all things on it. He who swears by the temple swears by it and the One who dwells in it. And he who swears by the Heavenly World, swears by the throne of our Loving Creator who sits upon it. All the works you do are to impress those watching, such as when you enlarge your script holders, phylacteries, along with the borders of your garments.

But he who is greatest among you shall be your servant. And whoever exalts himself shall be humbled, and he who humbles himself will be exalted. Woe to you scribes and Pharisees, hypocrites! For you devour widow's houses and pretend to make long prayers. Therefore, you will receive a greater condemnation.

Woe to you Scribes and Pharisees, you hypocrites! You build the tombs of the prophets and adorn the tombs of the righteous your forefathers killed then say, 'If we had lived in the days of our fathers, we would not have partaken in the blood of the good prophets.' Therefore, you bear witness against yourselves, that you are the sons of those who murdered the good prophets. Therefore, you continue to complete your father's portion.

You snakes, you offspring of poisonous vipers! How can you escape hell's judgement? She sends you good prophets, wise men and scribes, some of them you kill and crucify, and some you will flog in the synagogues and persecute from city to city.

O Jerusalem, Jerusalem, you that killed and stoned the good prophets sent to you! How often the Loving Spiritual Creator wanted to gather your children, as a hen gathers her chicks under her wings, but you were not willing. So, your house is left desolate, empty and alone, apart from the Loving Spiritual Creator. And I tell you, you will not understand Me or the Loving Creator until you say, 'Blessed is He who comes in the name of the Loving Spiritual Creator.'"

Then one of the lawyers said to Him, "Teacher, by saying these things, you also insult us." And Jesus answered, "Woe to you Scribes and Pharisees, for you clean the outside of the cup and dish, but inside they are full of extortion and self-indulgence. Blind ones, first clean the inside of the cup and dish that the outside may be clean also. Woe to you lawyers! For you have taken away the key to knowledge and shut up Heaven to men. You did not enter in yourselves, and those who were entering in, you prevented."

As Jesus spoke, they began to vehemently quarrel with Him, trying to provoke Him into saying something so that they may charge Him with an offense of blasphemy.

The disciples came later to Jesus and said, "Do you know that the Pharisees were offended when they heard these sayings?" Jesus answered, "Disregard them, for they are blind guides of the blind and if the blind guide the blind, then both will fall into a ditch."

Thomas 102 Jesus said, "Woe to you Pharisees, for you are like a dog resting in the food trough of some oxen. He never eats of it but prevents the oxen from eating it."

Author: Jesus exposes the egotistical, worldly way of the Pharisees and scribes who are devoid of the Loving Spiritual Life-force of our Loving Spiritual Creator that empowers our Spiritual bodies and Souls. He draws attention to the two different bodies they have by using the analogy of a cup.

Our outer body of flesh can be covered in earthly dirt but that means nothing and is unimportant. But if our inner Spiritual body is covered with filth from our mind and bad actions we are in serious Spiritual trouble. Our Spiritual Life must be clean and full of the Loving Spiritual Life-force. As long as our Spiritual body and Soul are clean then all our actions with our bodies of flesh will also be clean and empowered by Love.

Temple Destroyed

Matthew 24:1-2, Mark 13:1-2, Luke 21:5-6 As Jesus left the temple one of the disciples said to Him, "Look Teacher, what wonderful stones and what wonderful buildings are here!" And Jesus said to him "See these great buildings? The day will come when not one stone will be left upon another."

Author: Jesus predicts that one day the temple will be completely destroyed. Following this dialogue in the Gospels a false dialogue has been placed in supposedly spoken by Jesus where He is saying He will come again on the clouds at the end of the Apocalypse and instigate great calamity and sufferings in the world. This is slander.

This is all from the Jewish book of Daniel that Matthew in particular wants people to believe is talking about Jesus and slanders Jesus and our Loving Creator as it links them to the filthy slanderous book Revelation.

The evil slanderous book of Revelation states Jesus and our Loving Creator will return causing wars, famines, sicknesses and many other horrible afflictions and calamities to kill children undeserving of Heaven. This is the exact opposite of everything that Jesus did while here on earth as a Spiritual child of our Loving Spiritual Creator who's entire being is only love. As Jesus said, "I can only do what My Loving Creator shows Me to do."

Anyone who Truly knows Jesus and His Spiritual Way of Love and Non-violence and the Loving Spiritual Creator of Love He leads us to will know Revelation is a load of rubbish. It should be ripped out of all New Testaments and burnt. Unfortunately, many devout Jewish/ Christians are fooled into keeping it in and believing this poisonous garbage and still teach this slander to children. I wish they would wake up and stop doing so.

Always Be Spiritually Ready

Matthew 24:42-43, 45-51, Mark 13:32-37, Luke 12:42-46 Jesus said, "Take heed and stay alert for you do not know the day you will go to our Loving Creator. Take note of this, that if the master of the house had known what hour the thief would come, he would have watched and not allowed his house to be broken into to be robbed.

It is like a man going to a far country who left his house and gave authority to his servants, and to each one his particular work and ordered the gatekeeper to stay alert. Always be awake and aware for you do not know when you will be called into the presence of the master of your house, in the evening, at midnight, at the crowing of the rooster or in the morning so do not fall asleep. For not even the Angels in Heaven know the hour but only your Loving Creator knows the hour and day.

Faithful is the wise servant who does the work allotted to him so that when he comes into the presence of his master he will be welcomed. But if a servant is forgetful about being called to be in the presence of his master at any moment and becomes evil abusing others and eating and drinking with drunkards, he will fail in his duty. And therefore, when coming into the presence of his master cannot be welcomed. And he will be set apart with the hypocrites and there will be wailing and crying."

Author: Jesus warns us we do not know the day we will pass through our death experience and come into the presence of our Loving Creator or Jesus in Heaven. So, we must all remain ready by living out of the Spiritual Way of Love and Non-violence that He taught us to follow and not allow sin to break into our life that robs us of our Spiritual Life-force. And we must not fall asleep or fall away from the Spiritual Way to Heaven but walk it every day of our life ready for our Spirits to be called into the presence of our Loving Spiritual Creator in the Heavenly Spiritual World at any moment. We must continue to walk in Love every day.

Be Ready Ten Maidens

Matthew 25:1-13 Jesus said, "The Kingdom of the Heavenly Spiritual World is like ten maidens who took their lamps and went out to meet the bridegroom. Now five of them were wise, and five of them were foolish. Those who were foolish took their lamps but took no oil with them, but the wise took oil in their vessels with their lamps. The bridegroom was delayed, and they all nodded off to sleep.

And at nighttime a cry went out proclaiming; 'Look, the bridegroom is coming; go to meet him!' All those maidens arose and trimmed their lamps. And the foolish said to the wise, 'Give us some of your oil, for our lamps are going out.' But the wise ones answered, 'No, in case there will not be enough for us and you; but rather go to those who sell oil and buy some for yourselves.'

And while they went to buy, the bridegroom came and those who were ready went in with him to the wedding, and the door was shut. Later, the other maidens came back saying, 'Lord, open to us.' But he answered and said, 'Truly I say to you, I do not know you.' Therefore, always be prepared, for you know neither the day nor the hour when you will come into the presence of our Loving Creator and the Child of Humanity in the Heavenly Spiritual World."

Thomas 75 Jesus said, "There are many standing at the door, but only those who are at One within themselves, will go into the place of marriage."

Author: The lamps represent our Spiritual Bodies and Souls that are enlightened or empowered by the Loving Spiritual Life-force of our Loving Spiritual Creator in the Heavenly World. The oil represents all the Loving goodness we accumulate throughout our life before we die to the flesh and rise in Spirit. Some have more than others but cannot share it with others to be their own. They must acquire it themselves through their own good works of Love.

At the time of our death experience some will be filled with an abundance of Love even if in their last years they were too physically tired or ill to manifest Love anymore. And they will pass into the Heavenly Spiritual World of Love. Those whose Spirits had little Love will be too weak to enter and will need to accumulate more to also be filled and become enlightened. As Jesus said, "You are to be children of Light and Love." Again, Jesus reminds us we do not know the exact time or day of our death experience so always be ready and filled with Light and Love.

The Thomas version reminds us not to be divided within ourselves but if we are at One with the Loving Spiritual Life-force our whole body will be filled with Light, and we can enter the Heavenly Spiritual World of our Loving Spiritual Creator to be with Her forever.

The Talents Parable

Matthew 25:14-30, Luke 19:11-27 Jesus said, "You must grow in Spirit. It is like a householder going on a journey, who called his servants and gave one five talents, which equals thirty thousand denarii; to another two talents, which equals twelve thousand denarii; and to another one talent, which equals six thousand denarii and said, 'Work with these things I give to you and increase them until I return.' Then their Master left.

He who had received five talents went at once and worked with them; and he made five talents more. Likewise, he who had two talents made two talents more. But he who had received one talent went and dug a hole and covered the gift with the earthly dirt, so it remained hidden from view and unused.

When their Master returned, he called them to him to see what increase they had made with his gifts. And he who had received the five talents came forward and said, 'Master, you have given me five talents, and I have made five talents more.' His Master said to him, 'Well done good and faithful servant, you have been faithful over a little, so I will place you in charge of more; enter into the joy of your Master.'

And he who had two talents came forward and said, 'Master, you have given me two talents, and I have made two talents more.' His master said to him, 'Good and faithful servant, you have been faithful over a little, I will place you in charge of more; enter into the joy of your Master.'

And he who received one talent came forward and said, 'Master, I know you delegate work to be done for you, but I was afraid to do it, so I hid your gift and did only earthly things. I give back to you the gift you gave to me, unused.'

And his Master said to him, 'You worthless and lazy servant, you knew I delegate work to be done, so you should have used the gift I gave you to increase your gifts and join them with mine. Take the gift of one talent from him and give it to he who has ten. For to everyone who has, more will be given, and he will have an abundance; but from him who does not have, even what he has will be taken away from him, and he will be left with only earthly things that perish away to nothing.'"

Author: We all have certain gifts or abilities through which we can manifest the Loving Spiritual Life-force that empowers our Spiritual bodies and Souls. Some have more than others and so can achieve more. But Jesus points out it is not about the quantity but about giving one hundred percent of what you have to work with. The more Love we give the more Love we receive from our Loving Spiritual Creator and She receives all the Love we give to others because they are also Her children as are we.

Jesus points out the one who buried their Spiritual life and Spiritual works under earthly worldly activities received no extra Spiritual Love and so lost what little they had. He was frightened to be Spiritual and invest in Spiritual works so remained earthly and material, wasting his opportunity to grow in Spirit. We must increase our Spiritual life, build on what we have been given to use, and shine the Light of

Spiritual Love while here on Earth as brightly as we can, unless what we are born with diminishes and goes out.

Sheep and the Goats

Matthew 25:32-46 Jesus said, "Children of all nations shall come before the Loving Spiritual Creator, and they will be separated like a shepherd divides sheep from the goats. And our Loving Creator will say to the virtuous sheep, 'Come into the Heavenly Spiritual World prepared for you; for I was hungry, and you gave Me to eat, I was thirsty and you gave Me to drink, I was a stranger and you welcomed Me, I was naked and you clothed Me, I was sick and you visited Me, I was in prison and you came to Me.'

Then the virtuous children will answer the Loving Creator, saying, 'When did we see You hungry and feed You, or thirsty and give You drink? When did we see You a stranger and take You in, or naked and clothe You? When did we see You sick or in prison, and come to You? And the Loving Creator will answer and say to them, 'Truly I say to you, whenever you did these things to one of the least of My children, you did it to Me.'

Then the Loving Creator will say to the self-serving goats, who were cold hearted and lacking in the Spirit of Love, 'Depart from Me for you are not ready to enter the Heavenly Spiritual World, travel on with your selfish ways and inner darkness. For when I was hungry you gave Me no food; I was thirsty and you gave Me no drink; I was a stranger and you did not take Me in; naked and you did not clothe Me; sick and in prison and you did not come and help Me.'

Then they will answer, 'Loving Creator when did we see You hungry or thirsty or a stranger or naked or sick or in prison and did not help You?' And the Loving Creator will answer them, 'Truly, I say to you, whenever you did not do these things to one of the least of My children, you did not do it to Me.'

These will then leave and experience a painful awakening, exposing them to their selfish ways and false identities they lived out of, which will be like a burning realisation for their Souls and Spirits so they may be cleansed. It will last as long as it takes for each Soul.

While the virtuous and kind ones who lived out of Love, will be immediately welcomed into the Eternal Heavenly Spiritual World of our Loving Spiritual Creator. Peace, Joy and Love will be all around them and within them in the Heavenly Spiritual World beyond all suffering forever."

Author: Jesus taught the Universal Spiritual Law of 'Reaping as We Sow' for with what measure we give to others we shall receive back after death. Jesus and our Loving Spiritual Creator can never harm us in any way as their entire being and consciousness is only Love. As we are all Her children whether lost or found. And She does not commit infanticide like the two headed God Yahweh of the Jews with its violent Godhead Yahweh 1 of War and murder.

If we end up in a Hellish burning realisation after passing through our death experience, we have created it for ourselves by lacking in Spiritual Love and being selfish and causing suffering and harm to others. Buddha taught this exact same Spiritual Law known as Karma.

And all Christian charities around the world have been built on this beautiful Spiritual Teaching of Jesus to help all those in need in whatever way they can. These simple six points of Love in action that Jesus gives us to follow can be the foundation stones of our whole Spiritual awakening.

This is a powerful Teaching and to practice it is to be a Living Spiritual child of our Loving Spiritual Creator in Heaven on Earth ready to enter the Heavenly Spiritual World of Love when your body of flesh dies.

Plot to Kill Jesus

Matthew 26:1-5, Mark 14:1-2, Luke 22:1-2 It was two days before the Passover and the feast of Unleavened Bread. And the chief priests and the scribes were seeking how to arrest him by stealth and kill Him. But they said, "Not during the feast incase the people become outraged."

Woman Anoints Jesus

Matthew 26:6-13, Mark 14:3-9, Luke 7:36-50, John 12:1-8 Jesus went to have supper with a Pharisee who invited Him named Simon. While at table a woman of the city, who was a known sinner, heard Jesus was there in the house and went to Him. She brought an alabaster flask of expensive ointment called nard and came and stood behind Jesus crying and her tears fell on His feet as He lay at table. She then wiped His feet with the hair of her head and kissed His feet and anointed them with the ointment, and the fragrance filled the house.

Some disciples complained it was a waste and could have been sold to raise three hundred denarii for the poor. And they were upset with the woman and criticised her. Jesus heard them and said, "Leave her alone, why do you trouble her? For she has done a beautiful thing for Me. You always have the poor with you and whenever you wish you can do good for them, but you will not always have Me."

Now the Pharisee who invited Jesus after seeing what the woman did said, "If this man were a True prophet, He would have known who and what sort of woman this is who is touching Him, for she is a sinner." But Jesus heard this and said to him, "Simon, I have something to ask you." And he replied, "What is it, Teacher?" "A certain creditor had two debtors; one owed five hundred denarii, and the other fifty. When neither could pay, he forgave them both. Now, which of them will love him more?" Simon answered, "The one I suppose to whom he forgave more." Jesus said, "You have judged rightly."

Then turning to the woman he said to Simon, "Do you see this woman? I entered your house and you gave Me no water to wash My feet, but she has wet My feet with her tears and wiped them with her hair. You gave Me no kiss of greeting, but from the time she came in she has not stopped kissing My feet. You did not anoint me with oil, but she has anointed My feet with oil.

Therefore, I tell you her sins which are many are forgiven for she has loved much; but those who are forgiven little love little." And He said to her, "Your sins are forgiven." Then those who were at table with Him began to say among themselves, "Who is this, who even forgives sins?" And Jesus said to the woman, "Your faith has saved you; go in peace."

Author: No matter how great our sins may be, they can always be cleansed while still alive by feeling remorseful, asking for forgiveness and coming into the Spiritual Way that Jesus taught. The further we have gone into darkness, the greater will be our relief and joy when we return to the Light and the Loving Way of our Loving Spiritual Creator as Jesus taught us to do. The woman in this story was remorseful and overwhelmed with Love and respect for Jesus and knew intuitively that He would Love her despite her sins. Jesus Loved everyone but we see here how the woman was being judged by others as being unworthy of Love.

Jesus at Passover

Matthew 26:17-25, Mark 14:12-17, Luke 22:7-14, John 13:21-30 Now on the first day of Unleavened Bread the disciples asked Jesus, "Where will you have us prepare for you to eat the Passover?" He said, "Go into the city and a man carrying a jar will meet you; follow him and wherever he enters say to the householder, 'The Teacher asks, where is the guest room where I may eat the Passover with My disciples?' And he will show you a large upper room furnished and ready to prepare for us." And they went and found it just as Jesus told them and prepared the Passover.

When evening came, He sat at table with the twelve disciples. Jesus said, "Truly I say to you, one of you who is eating with Me will betray Me." The disciples looked at one another and were saddened uncertain of whom He was speaking about. And one after another they asked if they were the one saying, "Is it I Teacher?" Jesus said, "It is the one who is dipping bread into the dish with Me. "

One of His disciples whom Jesus loved, was lying close to the breast of Jesus; so, Simon Peter beckoned to him and said, "Tell us who it is of whom He speaks." So, being close to Jesus, he asked Him, "Teacher, who is it?" Jesus answered, "It is he to whom I shall give this morsel after I have dipped it." So. when He had dipped the morsel, He gave it to Judas the son of Simon Iscariot. Judas asked, "Is it I Teacher?" Jesus replied, "You have said so."

Then after eating the morsel Jesus said to him, "What you are going to do, do quickly." Now, no one at the table knew why He said this to him. Some thought that because Judas had the money box, Jesus was telling him to buy more for the feast or that he should give something to the poor. So, immediately after receiving the morsel he went out, and it was night.

Author: Some believe Jesus actually wanted one of the disciples to lead the Chief Priests to Him later that night when they were alone and vulnerable so He could be arrested without causing trouble for the crowds who followed Him. And then be charged and crucified and rise in His Spiritual body from His dead body of flesh to fulfill His Spiritual

Teachings He was giving the disciples about us all having two different bodies in one.

So, His statement could have been, "One of you at this table will have to betray Me tonight." Mark records how sad they all were that Jesus asked someone to do this for Him. Then they each reluctantly asked Him, "Is it I Teacher?" Hoping it would not be them otherwise they would have replied, "I will do it for you Teacher." So, Jesus had to select one of them to do it for Him.

And maybe Judas was not a betrayer at all but in fact the only disciple willing to do as Jesus asked which is why Jesus handed him the morsel of bread he dipped, to select him for the task. Only someone who had a deep belief and trust in Jesus could voluntarily perform such an act as this at His Teacher's request. Judas may have been an evil betrayer but either way Jesus knew what He was going to do and set it in motion Himself at that specific chosen time of the Passover with the help of Judas.

The Last Supper

Matthew 26:26-30, Mark 14:22-26, Luke 22:15-20 And as they were eating, Jesus took bread, blessed it and broke it and gave it to the disciples and said, "Take this and eat for this represents My body of flesh which I will give up for you. Do this in memory of Me." Then He took the cup and giving thanks said, "Drink of it all of you; for this is the cup of My blood which is poured out for many to reveal the new character and body of your True Spiritual identity. After singing a Hymn, they went out to the mount of olives.

Author: Jesus taught we all have two different bodies with us right now. The temporary body of flesh is just food for the vultures when it dies and has no life anymore. It is our Spiritual body and Soul mind of Love that leaves our dead body of flesh, to be taken to be near our Loving Spiritual

Creator who created them for us to have in the Heavenly Spiritual World, if they are alive and filled with Love.

The new covenant, as it is called, is in fact our new Spiritual body and character that lives on as a Spiritual child of our Loving Creator in Heaven. Jesus had to let His body of flesh be killed to release His fully awoken Spiritual body and then appear to the disciples briefly in it, so they finally understood the main message of His Teachings.

Disciples Fall Away

Matthew 26:30-35, Mark 14:26-31, Luke 22: 31-34, John 13:37-38 Jesus said, "You will all fall away from me this night; for it is written, 'I will strike the shepherd, and the sheep will be scattered.' But after My Spiritual body is raised up from My dead body of flesh I will go before you into Galilee to meet you there."

Peter said, "Though all may fall away from you, I will never fall away. Master, I am ready to go with you to prison and to death." Jesus said to him, "Truly, I say to you this very night before the cock crows, you will deny Me three times. Indeed, satan has asked for you, that he may sift you as wheat. But I have prayed for you, that your faith should not fail; and when you have returned to Me, strengthen your brethren." But Peter adamantly replied, "Even if I must die with you, I will not deny you." The others all agreed.

Author: The Spiritual commitment is based on understanding we have another Spiritual body with our body of flesh that does not die. If we doubt that or are not yet Spiritually awakened enough to have full belief in this Truth, we will be reluctant to let go of our earthly life whether threatened by other children with death or threatened by illness with death. Our Spirit is not the flesh.

Jesus Waits to be Arrested

Matthew 26:36-46, Mark 14:32-42, Luke 22:39-45 Jesus and His disciples went to the mount of olives to a garden called Gethsemane. He said to His disciples, "Rest here while I pray." And He took Peter, James and John with Him saying to them, "My Spirit is very sorrowful, remain here and wait with Me."

He then went on a little further and spoke with our Loving Spiritual Creator saying, "If you want to save Me from going through this do so. However, I realise this is the real purpose of everything you have shown Me. And I will do it." And after saying this He came back to the disciples and found them sleeping and said to them, "Why do you sleep? Rise up for now the hour has come and pray that you may not fall into the way of temptation."

Jesus Arrested

Matthew 26:47-56, Mark 14:43-52, Luke 22:47-53, John 18:2-12 While Jesus was speaking, a band of soldiers with swords and clubs and some officers from the chief priests and the Pharisees led by Judas approached them for Judas knew where he would be found. Then Jesus stepped forward and said, "Whom do you seek?" They answered, "Jesus of Nazareth." Jesus said, "I am He." They stumbled backwards in surprise after hearing Him say this so openly.

Again, He asked them, "Whom do you seek?" And they said, "Jesus of Nazareth." Jesus answered, "I told you that I am He; so, if you only seek Me then let these others go." Then one of His followers drew his sword and struck the slave of the high priest and cut off his ear. But Jesus said, "No more of this! Put your sword back into its place; for all who take the sword will perish by the sword." And He touched the ear of the slave and healed him.

Jesus then said to those who came to arrest Him, "Why have you come out with your swords and clubs as if to arrest a robber? Day after day I was with you in the temple teaching and you did not seize Me. But this is your hour and the power of darkness." And all the disciples were frightened and fled from Jesus. And the band of soldiers and officers seized Jesus and bound Him.

Author: Jesus heals the injured person who has come to help arrest Him to be trialed and crucified. Jesus has told us all that the Heavenly Spiritual World and our Loving Spiritual Creator are at one only with Love. And if we do not reach this Spiritual awakening in our own Spiritual life to Love all other children now while here on Earth, we cannot enter easily into the Heavenly Spiritual World of Love after the death of our body of temporary flesh. Jesus taught, "I say to you, Love even your enemies."

He also clearly establishes that all True followers of His must be pacifists and not injure any other child of our Loving Creator with a sword, a gun, a drone or missile or we will destroy our Spiritual Life in Heaven. This important Teaching was perverted in the fourth century by the corrupt Christian leaders under Emperor Constantine so Christian Roman soldiers could still go to war and kill other children. They became Jewish/Christian hybrids not True Christians. Jewish/Christians still go to war to this day murdering other children. No True Christian and follower of Jesus or Buddha can do that.

Peter's Denial

Matthew 26:69-75, Mark 14:66-72, Luke 22:54-62, John 18:25-27 Simon Peter followed Jesus with another disciple and as he entered the courtyard of the high priest the maid who kept the door said to Peter, "Are you not also one of this man's disciples?" Peter said, "I am not." And he went out to the porch where another maid saw him and said to the bystanders, "This man was with Jesus of Nazareth." And again, he denied it saying, "I do not know the man."

Then a little while later another bystander said to him, "Certainly you are one of them; for you are a Galilean." But he began to swear by an oath that he did not know Jesus. And then the cock crowed and Peter remembered what Jesus had predicted, "Before the cock crows you will have denied Me three times." And he broke down and wept bitterly.

Jesus Interrogated

Matthew 26:57-68, Mark 14:55-65, Luke 22:67-71, John 18:19-24 Those who had seized Jesus led Him to Caiaphas the high priest, where he and the scribes had gathered to question Jesus. Now the chief priests and the whole council questioned Jesus about His Teachings and His disciples. Jesus answered, "I have always spoken openly to the world and have taught in synagogues and in the temple where all Jews come together. I have said nothing secretly. Why do you ask Me these things? Ask those who have heard Me for they know what I have spoken."

One of the officers standing by struck Jesus with his hand saying, "Is that how you answer the high priest?" Jesus said, "If I have spoken wrongly, tell Me what it was I said, but if I have spoken correctly, why do you strike Me?" And the chief priests and the whole council tried to find witnesses to testify He had spoken blasphemy.

And some bore false witness against him, but their testimony did not agree. And the high priest then stood up and said to Jesus, "Have you no answer to these accusations and testimonies against You?" But Jesus remained silent.

Then the high priest said to Him, "Tell us, are you the anointed one of our God?" Jesus said, "If I tell you, you will not believe Me, and if I ask you, you will not answer. But as you say I am." And the high priest tore his garments and said, "We need no more witnesses for He has uttered blasphemy Himself. You have all heard His blasphemy. What is your judgement?"

They all answered, "He deserves death." Then they spat on His face and put a cover over His head and struck Him saying mockingly, "Prophesy to us anointed one, who just struck you?"

Pilate Questions and Judges Jesus

Matthew 27:11-26, Mark 15:2-15, Luke 23:2-25, John 18:29-40, 19:1-16 When morning came, all the chief priests and the elders and scribes, took council with each other how to put Him to death. They decided to take Him and deliver Him to Pilate the Governor. Pilate went out to them and said, "What accusation do you bring against this man?" They said, "We found this man perverting our nation, and forbidding us to give taxes to Caesar, and saying that He Himself is the anointed one and king."

Then Pilate asked Him, "Are you the king of the Jews?" Jesus said to him, "You have said so. But I am not of this Earthly world. I came into the world to bear witness of the Spiritual Truth. Everyone who is of the Spiritual Truth, hears My voice." Pilate then asked, "What is Spiritual Truth?" After he had said this, Pilate went out to the Jews and told them, "I find no crime in this man." Then the Jews became angry saying, "He stirs up the people, teaching throughout all Judea, Galilee and even here." And they accused Him of many other things.

Pilate returned to Jesus and said, "Do you hear all of these charges they are making against you? Have you no answer to make?" But Jesus did not say anything, and this made Pilate wonder greatly about the situation. So, when Pilate heard

He was a Galilean, which belonged to Herod's jurisdiction, he sent Him to Herod who was in Jerusalem at that time.

Herod was glad to see Jesus, having heard so much about Him, and hoped He would show him a sign or miracle. He questioned Him at some length; but Jesus made no answer. The chief priests and scribes stood by vehemently accusing Him. So, Herod and his soldiers treated Him with contempt and mocked Him, placed a splendid robe on Him and sent Him back to Pilate.

Pilate Judges Jesus

When they brought Jesus back to Pilate, he said to them, "You said this man was perverting the people; but after examining Him before you, I did not find this man guilty of any of the charges you made against Him. Herod also found no guilt in Him, sending Him back to me. Therefore, I find nothing He has done is deserving of death; I will chastise Him and release Him." So, Pilate had Him scourged and the soldiers made a crown of thorns and put it on His head and draped Him in a purple robe. Then they said, "Hail the king of the Jews!" And they struck Him with their hands.

Pilate then brought Jesus before the crowd. But the crowd continued to cry out against Jesus all the more. Pilate knew the custom at Passover was that he would release one prisoner they asked to be set free. So, Pilate brought out a violent prisoner called Barabbas, who had committed murder in the insurrection, and asked the Jews if they wanted him set free or Jesus. For he knew that it was out of envy of Jesus, that the chief priests had delivered Him up to be put to death.

But the chief priests stirred up the crowd, getting them to call out to release Barabbas. Pilate asked them again who they wanted set free, hoping they would choose Jesus. But they cried out all the more loudly, to release Barabbas not Jesus. Pilate then asked them, "What do you want me to do with this man Jesus, whom you accuse?" They called out, "Let Him be crucified." Pilate said, "Why, what evil has He done?" And they said, "If you release this man, you are no friend of Caesar, for He said he was the anointed one, the king of the Jews, which means He opposes Caesar." And Pilate said to them, "Do you want me to crucify your king?" And they shouted back, "We have no king but Caesar." And they all shouted even more loudly, "Crucify Him, crucify Him and kept on shouting." So, Pilate did as they wanted and set Barabbas free.

When Pilate saw that he was gaining nothing, but rather a riot was beginning to form, he finally gave in to their demands. So, Pilate washed his hands in front of them and said, "I am innocent of this man's blood." And he gave sentence that their demand should be granted to crucify Him and he was led away to be crucified.

Jesus is Crucified

Matthew 27:32-61, Mark 15:21-47, Luke 23:26-56, John 19:18-34 And as Jesus carried His cross, a great number of people followed Him some crying, and the soldiers forced an onlooker, Simon of Cyrene, to help carry the cross. And when they came to the place called Golgotha, they offered Him vinegar mixed with myrrh; but he refused it. There they crucified Him with two others. They divided His garments among them, casting lots for them and sat down and kept watch. And over His head, they put the charge against Him, which read, "Jesus of Nazareth the King of the Jews."

Standing near to the cross were His mother, and His mother's sister, Mary the wife of Clopas, and Mary Magdalene. When Jesus saw His mother, and the disciple whom He loved standing near, He said to His mother, "Woman behold your son." Then He said to the disciple, "Behold your mother." And from that hour the disciple took her to his own home to care for her. Jesus then said, "Loving Spiritual Creator, forgive them, for they know not what they do."

And those who passed by derided Him, wagging their heads saying, "You said you would destroy the temple and build it again. If you are the anointed one of God, save yourself and come down from the cross." And the chief priests and scribes mocked Him saying, "He saved others; but He cannot save Himself. If He comes down from the cross, we will believe in Him. He trusted in God, so let God deliver Him now, for He said He was the anointed one."

One of the criminals crucified beside Jesus complained to Him saying, "Aren't you the anointed one? Save yourself and us." But the other criminal rebuked him saying, "Do you not fear God, since you are under the same sentence of judgment? For we justly deserve this result for our bad deeds, but this man has done nothing wrong." And he said, "Jesus, please remember me when you come into your Spiritual Kingdom." And Jesus said to him, "Truly I say to you, today you will be with Me in the Heavenly Spiritual World."

And about the ninth hour Jesus cried out in a loud voice, "My God, My God why have you forsaken Me." After this, Jesus knowing that His physical body was about to die, said, "I thirst." And one of them standing by, took a sponge, dipped it in vinegar; put it on a reed and held it to His mouth. After Jesus received the vinegar, He cried out, "It is finished. My Loving Creator, into your hands I commit My Spirit!" And having said this, He breathed His last breath.

The centurion standing nearby, witnessing the death of Jesus said, "Truly, this was a righteous man." And many of His followers, including the women who had followed Him stood off at a distance and saw these things take place.

As it was Preparation Day for the Sabbath, and to prevent the bodies remaining on the cross on the Sabbath, the Jews asked Pilate to break their legs to hasten their death, so they may be taken down. So, the soldiers came and broke the legs of the two criminals beside Jesus, but when they came to Jesus His body was already dead, so they did not break His legs. But one of the soldiers pierced His side with a spear and at once blood and water flowed out.

Jesus is Buried

Matthew 27:57-61, Mark 15:42-47, Luke 23:50-55, John 19:38-42 As evening came a man named Joseph of Arimathea a disciple of Jesus who was a member of the Jewish council, went to Pilate. He asked Pilate if he could take the body of Jesus for burial. So, Pilate ordered it to be given to him. Joseph, with help from Nicodemus who also listened to Jesus teach, gathered a hundred pounds of myrrh and aloes and came to get the body of Jesus from the cross.

They took it down and wrapped it in a clean linen shroud with the spices they had brought. And they quickly laid it in Joseph's own tomb that he had recently prepared, as it was nearby and the day of Preparation was ending. Then they rolled a stone against the door and left. Mary Magdalene and Mary, the mother of Joses, saw where they laid Him.

Author: The account in Matthew about Pilate placing a Roman guard on the tomb is false and never happened. It was contrived by Matthew to help cover up the Truth that Jesus actually rose and appeared to the disciples in His full Spiritual body and not His dead body of flesh bought back to life. They had to do this as the Jews were not Spiritually advanced enough to understand this Spiritual Truth that Jesus was teaching about us all having two different bodies with us right now. Flesh is only flesh. Spirit is only Spirit.

The one of flesh dies and is food for the vultures. The one of Spirit leaves to be near our Loving Creator in the Heavenly Spiritual World, to reap as we have sown. So, they had to hide His dead body of flesh so the Jews could not find it and accuse them of lying about seeing Jesus alive and well. And they had to leave the tomb empty as if Jesus came back to life in His body of dead flesh and went to Heaven. They could then honestly say they saw Jesus alive and well but pretend he was in a body of flesh brought back to life instead of saying He was only in His Spiritual body now. The Jews already had in their scripture accounts of some prophets being taken up to Heaven while still alive. So, this would aid in their deception being believed by the Jews so they would not be afraid to follow Jesus and His New Spiritual Way of Love and Non-violence that leads all children to the One Loving Spiritual Creator in the Heavenly Spiritual World. Then they could come away from the distorted two headed God Yahweh that the Jews were worshipping.

Jesus Rises in Spirit

Matthew 28:5-10, 16-20, Mark 16:1-8, Luke 24:1-12, John 20:1-18 On the day after the Sabbath, Mary Magdalene came to where they had laid Jesus in the tomb and saw the stone had been rolled away. And when she looked in, the tomb was empty. So, she ran back to Simon Peter and the other disciple whom Jesus loved and said to them, "They have taken the Master's body out of the tomb, and I do not know where they have taken Him."

Peter then went with the other disciple towards the tomb. The disciple who reached the tomb first looked in and saw the linen cloths lying there, but did not go in. Then Simon Peter came after him and went into the tomb and saw the linen cloths lying there and the towel which had been over His head, rolled up in a place by itself. Then the other disciple at the entrance also entered in and saw the same thing as Peter. And they had forgotten Jesus had said to them, that He will rise again in Spirit from the dead. And the disciples went back home.

Mary stood outside the tomb weeping, and she stooped down and looked in the tomb. She saw two Angels in white sitting there where the body of Jesus had lain, one at the head and one at the feet. And they said to her, "Woman why do you weep? Why do you seek the living among the dead? He has risen in Spirit and is not here."

She said to them, "But I do not know where He has been taken, and where He now is." After saying this, she turned round and saw Jesus but did not recognise Him. Jesus then said to her, "Woman, why are you weeping? Whom do you seek?" Mary thought He was the gardener and said to Him, "Sir, if you have carried Him away tell me where you have laid Him, and I will take Him back."

Jesus then called her by name, "Mary." She then turned and recognised Him and she said, "Teacher!" Jesus said to her, "Do not try to hold Me Mary for I am now in the Spirit, and I am at One with our Loving Spiritual Creator. But go and tell My followers you Have seen Me, and I have ascended into Spirit with My Loving Spiritual Creator and your Loving Spiritual Creator." Mary then went and told the disciples that she had seen the Master alive and all that He had said to her.

Author: The Gospels have different accounts about the resurrection sequences and the people involved. The main points that seem consistent and logical with what really happened are that Mary Magdalene found the tomb open on Sunday morning and the dead body of Jesus was missing. She went and only told Peter and John. Jesus appeared to Mary in His Spiritual body, not His dead body of flesh bought back to life. We know this fact to be True because John gives us the strongest clue and records that Jesus told Mary she could no longer hold onto Him anymore like she did when He had a body of flesh.

The other clues are that they didn't easily recognise Him when He appeared to them after death because He was now only in His Spiritual body which must appear similar but different to us here on Earth. And He can now just materialise and disappear at will like Angels who also have Spiritual bodies just as Jesus said we will all have if we enter the Heavenly Spiritual World.

The Jews had no understanding of this and would have been frightened to follow a Spirit that had left Sheol, a shadowy underworld where they believed all Souls went after death and who was now walking around amongst them. So, based on the clues particularly in John's Gospel we can rightly speculate that Peter and John with Mary showing them the way, went to the tomb after Jesus appeared to the disciples briefly in His Spiritual body probably Friday night after the crucifixion. There they rolled back the stone door, unwrapped the bandages to make certain it was Jesus and found His dead body was still there.

They then realised the deeper meaning of all the Teachings He had given them to help them understand this Spiritual Truth about our two different bodies in one that we have on Earth now. And Jesus literally manifested this at the time of His death by appearing to them briefly in only His Spiritual body, now set free from the dead body of flesh, before He went to the Heavenly Spiritual World.

This separation of our two different bodies is exactly what happens at death as Jesus Himself taught. The dead body of flesh including His, is just food for the vultures and has no life in it anymore. But the Spiritual body rises from the dead body of flesh to be taken to be near to our Loving Spiritual Creator in the Heavenly Spiritual World if we are awakened Spiritual children of Love on Earth. Jesus was an awakened Spiritual child of our Loving Spiritual Creator, and before going to Heaven He provided a brief and powerful demonstration for the disciples of being alive and well in His Spiritual body while His body of flesh was dead.

They then had a very difficult problem. If they said they saw Jesus and He was alive and well and spoke to them, the Jewish leaders would just go to His tomb and find His decaying body of flesh and then accuse the disciples of all being charlatans and liars. This could cause everyone to leave them and the beautiful Spiritual Way of Love and Non-violence that Jesus gave us to reach the Heavenly Spiritual World, and it could have died out and been lost.

So, I believe Peter and John with Mary's involvement, hid the dead body of Jesus and left the tomb open and empty so they could say He rose again in His body of flesh which was not unheard of in the Jewish scriptures. This could make Jesus more acceptable to the Jews, and they may be more willing to leave their two headed God Yahweh and follow His Spiritual Way of Love and Non-violence of our Loving Spiritual Creator who is only Love.

This meant they had to invent coverup stories as red herrings to convince everyone Jesus had a body of flesh that rose from the dead and not a True Living Spiritual body only. So, they fabricated different little scenarios such as Jesus eating some fish or still having wounds on His body or even going so far as to have Jesus Himself saying He is not a Spiritual body, but He has a body of flesh and bones. But amongst these red herrings they also left the clues to the Spiritual Truth which at those times the Jews were not ready to understand, believe and follow. But now we are ready to see Jesus more clearly as He intended and we must remove these Jewish overlays to reveal the simple Spiritual Truth Jesus taught.

"Flesh only gives birth to flesh. Spirit only gives birth to Spirit. Marvel not that I tell you, you must be born again from above." Further discussion about this topic can be found in the book, 'The Teachings of Jesus Unplugged.'

Matthew's Resurrection Ending

Matthew 28:9-10, 16-20 When Mary Magdelene and the other Mary came to the tomb, an Angel appeared to them and said, "Do not be afraid, I know you seek Jesus who was crucified. He is not here for He has risen in Spirit from the dead (body of flesh.) Go and tell His disciples He has risen from the dead (body of flesh) and will go before them to meet them in Galilee. And as Mary Magdelene and the other Mary were on the way back to tell the disciples what the Angel said, Jesus appeared to them saying, "Rejoice!"

And they came (and held Him by His feet) and praised Him. He said to them, "Do not be afraid. Go, tell My brethren to go to Galilee and they will see Me there." The disciples went to Galilee where they saw Jesus who told them, "Authority from Heaven has been given to Me. Go and make disciples of all the nations teaching them to observe all the things that I taught you and I am with you always."

Author: In this traditional account Matthew adds the red herring stating that Mary Magdelene and the other Mary fell down and held the feet of Jesus to make out He still had a body of flesh. Instead of Him actually having a fully Spiritual body that they could not hold as John states in his more correct version and very important clue.

Mark's Resurrection Ending

Mark 16:1-8 Mary Magdelene and Mary, the mother of James and Salome went to the tomb Sunday morning and found it open. They went in and an Angel was there and said, "Do not be afraid. You seek Jesus of Nazareth who was crucified. He is risen! He is not here. Go and tell His disciples he will meet them in Galilee." So, they went out quickly and fled from the tomb for they were trembling and bewildered. And they said nothing to anyone for they were afraid.

Author: This is the original ending of Mark's Gospel as all Theological scholars generally agree. The extension was added later made up from the other accounts to bring Mark's Gospel into alignment with them.

Luke's Resurrection Ending

Road to Emmaus

Luke 24:13-35 Two men who had left Jerusalem after the crucifixion of Jesus were walking on the road to Emmaus discussing what had happened concerning Jesus and the reports that His tomb was found empty, and some women had seen an Angel who told them He was alive. Jesus drew near to them and walked along with them, but they did not recognise Him. As they walked together, they told Him all about the events in Jerusalem concerning the crucifixion of Jesus and other accounts that He was alive.

Jesus said, "Ought not He have suffered these things to enter into His Heavenly glory?" And as the night was drawing in, they asked if He wanted to stay and eat with them to which Jesus said He would. Then while they were eating Jesus took bread, blessed it and broke it and gave it to them. Then they suddenly realised it was Jesus and then He just vanished.

Appearing to Disciples Including Thomas

Luke 24:36-40 They immediately rushed back to tell the disciples what had happened. They found them all, including Thomas, gathered together in a room and told them about Jesus walking with them and talking with them then just vanishing. As they were speaking Jesus suddenly appeared amongst them and said, "Peace to you." And they were frightened and terrified thinking they were seeing a Spirit, which they actually were. Jesus said, "Why are you troubled? And why do doubts arise in your hearts? Behold it is I Myself.

(Behold My hands and My feet, that it is I Myself. Handle Me and see, for a Spirit does not have flesh and bones as you see I have." And He showed them His hands and His feet. He then asked, "Have you any food here?" And they gave Him a piece of fish and honeycomb and He ate them.) And the disciples could still not believe it but were filled with joy and wonder at seeing Him. And He led them out to Bethany and lifted up His hands blessing them and then vanished from their sight.

Author: This correctly states that all eleven disciples were there including Thomas, if Judas had left their company. Luke adds all the cover up words in brackets concerning Jesus still having a body of flesh to also help hide the fact that Jesus was actually only now in His Spiritual body. John's Gospel puts in the false doubting Thomas incident as a strong red herring to also spread the belief that Jesus rose in His body of flesh and also help cover up that He actually rose in a Spiritual body.

But John also puts in the strong counter Spiritual Truth that Mary Magdelene could not hold onto Him anymore because He was actually now only in His Spiritual body. They planted these clues for those who understood the Teachings of Jesus correctly while providing a red herring buffer for those still not familiar with His deeper Spiritual Teachings and Truths in order not to frighten them away. For even in these accounts, we can see that His own disciples were frightened of His Spiritual form appearing to them.

John's Resurrection Ending

Appearing to Disciples

John 20:19-29 After Mary Magdelene saw Jesus at the tomb in His Spiritual body He later appeared to the disciples.

In the evening the disciples gathered together in a room with the doors all shut for fear of the Jews. Jesus suddenly appeared among them and said, "Peace be with you." And the disciples were glad when they saw it was Jesus. Jesus again said, "Peace be with you. As our Loving Spiritual Creator in the Heavenly Spiritual World has sent Me, I also now send you." And when He had said this, He breathed on them and said to them, "Receive the Loving Spiritual Life-force of our Loving Creator. If you forgive those who sin against you, they are forgiven by you. If you do not forgive, it still remains for you to forgive them."

(Now Thomas, called the twin, was not there when Jesus appeared to them. The other disciples told him, "We have seen our Master." Thomas said, "Unless I see His hands and the print of the nails, and put my finger into the print of the nails and put my hand into His side, I will not believe you."

And after eight days the disciples were again inside, and Thomas with them. The doors were shut but Jesus suddenly appeared in the middle of them and said, "Peace to you." He then said to Thomas, "Reach your finger here and look at My hands, and reach your hand here, and put it into My side. Do not be unbelieving but believing." And Thomas answered and said, "My Teacher!" Jesus said, "Thomas, because you have seen Me you have believed. Blessed are those who have not seen yet believe.")

Author: This Thomas account in brackets is only found in John. It is a very dramatic description of Jesus still having wounds in His body supposedly of flesh. I doubt greatly that our bodies that are Eternal and beautiful like Angel's bodies, and the risen Spiritual body of Jesus can have any wounds in them at all.

This is the equally strong red herring that John created to counter the more accurate account of Mary not being able to hold onto Jesus as He was now totally Spiritual. John was clever to put both in but only those who really listen to the words of Jesus and understand them will see which one is True and which is false. I personally only believe the Mary account based on the words of Jesus Himself.

Appearing at Tiberias

John 21:1-19 Jesus appeared one last time to the disciples at the Sea of Tiberias. Some of the disciples had gone fishing together at the Sea of Tiberias. There was Peter, Thomas called the Twin, Nathanael, the sons of Zebedee and two others. They fished all night long but caught nothing.

In the morning Jesus stood on the shore, but the disciples did not recognise Him. Jesus called out to them, "Children, have you caught anything?" They said, "No." He said, "Cast your net on the right side of the boat, and you will catch some." So, they cast the net and caught a great haul of fish. Then one of the disciples said to Peter, "It is the Master." When Peter realised it was Jesus, he dived into the water and swam to shore immediately. The others came in the boat, dragging the net filled with the many fish they had caught.

When they came ashore, Jesus said, "Bring some of the fish you caught and have some breakfast." So, they made a fire of coals and laid some of the fish on it and some bread. None of the disciples dared to ask Him who He was, knowing it was the Master. Then Jesus took the bread and fish they had cooked and gave it to them. This was the last time Jesus appeared to the disciples after His Spirit was raised from His dead body of flesh.

When the disciples had eaten breakfast, Jesus said to Peter, "Son of Jonah, do you love Me more than these?" He said, "Yes, Teacher. You know that I love you." Jesus said, "Feed My lambs." He said to him a second time, "Simon, son of Jonah, do you love Me?" He said, "Yes Teacher, You know that I love You." Jesus said to him, "Care for My sheep." Jesus asked a third time, "Simon, son of Jonah, do you love Me?"

Peter was sorrowful because He asked a third time, 'Do you love Me?' And he said, "Teacher, You know all things; You know that I love You." Jesus said to him, "Feed My sheep."

Jesus then said, "When you were younger, you tied your own belt around yourself and walked wherever you wished, but when you are older, you will stretch out your hands, and another will tie a belt around you and take you where you do not wish to go." Jesus spoke this predicting Peter's death.

He then said to him, "Follow Me."

Author: Again, the disciples do not easily recognise Jesus now that He is in His Spiritual body only. This beautiful dialogue between Peter and Jesus is so full of Love and forgiveness that it sets a wonderful example for us all to forgive others who let us down and always welcome them back into our Love. It is worth noting that the last words of Jesus spoken to Peter were "Follow Me."

We must all follow Jesus to the Heavenly Spiritual World by being Spiritually awakened and transformed by the words He gave us and then live out of the Spiritual Way of Love and Non-violence now while here on Earth. This will bring our True Spiritual body and Soul mind of Love to Life empowered by the Loving Spiritual Life-force of our Loving Creator, and we will be ready to enter the Heavenly World.

Our Loving Spiritual Creator is only Love.

We must become Spiritual children of

only Love on Earth.

Chapter 11
Mark

All of the important sayings in Mark that are repetitions found in Matthew have been combined with the Matthew sayings in the previous chapter. Other sayings from Mark have been placed in the appropriate early chapters regarding specific topics. The following are those sayings not mentioned in Matthew or earlier.

Crowds Follow Jesus

Mark 3:7-12 Jesus withdrew with His disciples to the sea. And a great multitude from Galilee followed Him, and from Judea and Jerusalem and Idumea and beyond the Jordan; and those from Trye and Sidon, when they heard how many great works He was doing and came to Him. So, He told His disciples that a small boat should be kept ready for Him because of the multitude lest they should crush Him. For He healed many, so that as many that had afflictions pressed about Him to touch Him.

And the unclean spirits, whenever they saw Him, fell down before Him and cried out saying, "You are a Spiritual child of the Loving Spiritual Creator." But He sternly warned them that they should not make Him known.

Author: As Jesus became well known He faced the problem of being mobbed by people so they may be healed. We often see that He retreated into the countryside with the disciples to get a break from the demanding crowds and to be closer to our Loving Creator without being disturbed. Today we should also leave the busy cities and go out to nature to find a peaceful place to contemplate our Spiritual life and become closer to our Loving Spiritual Creator in Heaven. Some may call this praying while others call it meditation or contemplation on Heavenly existence. It is a good practice to do whenever you have the chance.

The Growing Seed

Mark 4:26-29 Jesus said, "The Heavenly Spiritual World is like a man who scatters seed on the soil, and sleeps by night and rises by day while the seed sprouts and grows but he himself knows not how. For the earth yields crops by itself; first the blade, then the head and after that the full grain in the head. But when the grain ripens, immediately he puts in the sickle for the crop is ready to harvest."

Author: Spiritual awakening occurs in stages after hearing the Spiritual words or seeds planted in our earthly minds. And as they grow, they begin to provide all the necessary foundations and building blocks for us to build our Spiritual home, until finally they culminate in transforming our earthly identity into our Spiritual identity.

Then we will also be awakened Spiritual children of our Loving Spiritual Creator just as Jesus was, and ready to leave our dead body of flesh behind and enter into the Eternal Heavenly Spiritual World beyond all suffering.

Man Casts Out Demons in Jesus' Name

Mark 9:38-40, Luke 9:49-50 John said to Jesus, "Teacher, we saw someone who is not with us casting out demons in your name, and we ordered him to stop because he is not one of us." Jesus said, "Do not forbid him, for no one who works a miracle in My name can suddenly speak evil of Me. For he who is not against you is for you. For whoever gives you even a cup of water to drink in My name because you follow Me, I say to you, there is no way that he will lose his reward."

Author: Already the disciples were beginning to be exclusive in their treatment of other followers of Jesus just like the Jews who thought wrongly that they were the only children on Earth who knew who God was making them the only children of their two headed distorted God Yahweh.

Jesus has to guide the disciples out of that thinking to see the Universal understanding of what He was really teaching them. We are all potential Spiritual children of Love and Non-violence of our Loving Spiritual Creator in the Heavenly Spiritual World if we just follow His Way and Teachings and awaken into our True Spiritual identity. The choice is ours to accept our Spiritual Life or reject it.

Forgive Before Praying

Mark 11:25-26 Jesus said, "And whenever you stand praying, if you have anything against anyone, forgive them and pray for them so your Loving Spiritual Creator in the Heavenly Spiritual World can also forgive you your wrongdoings."

Widow's Two Mites

Mark 12:41-44, Luke 21:1-4 Now Jesus was sitting opposite the temple treasury and watched how people were putting money into the treasury. And many who were rich put in much. Then one poor widow came and threw in two small coins, which was only worth one quarter of a copper coin. Jesus called His disciples to Him and said, "Truly I say to you this poor widow has put in more than all those who gave to the treasury. For they all put in out of their abundance, but she out of her poverty put in all that she had, her whole livelihood."

Author: The materially rich seemed to put in more but still kept plenty for themselves but the poor woman put in all the material wealth she had as an offering to their God. She trusted her whole life to their God while the rich hung on to the material security. As Spiritual children we must always remember Heaven is a real world, but it is Spiritual not material. It is the richness of our Spirits that matters at the end of our journey not how much money we leave behind in the bank.

The bulk of Mark's Gospel has already been presented in the Matthew chapter. Theological scholars tend to agree that Matthew and Luke copied most of Mark into their own Gospels and then placed in their own extra accounts.

Our Loving Spiritual Creator is only Love.

We must become Her Spiritual children of

only Love on Earth.

Chapter 12

Luke

All of the important sayings in Luke that are repetitions found in Matthew have been combined with the Matthew sayings in that chapter. Other sayings from Luke have been placed in the appropriate early chapters regarding specific topics. The following are those sayings not mentioned in Matthew or the earlier chapters.

Jesus Calls Peter

Luke 5:1-11 As Jesus stood by the lake of Gennesaret the multitude pressed around Him to hear the Spiritual Teachings of our Loving Spiritual Creator and He saw two boats standing by the shore, but the fishermen had gone to wash their nets. Then He asked Simon, one of the fishermen, if He could get into his boat and push it a little way from the shore so He could teach the crowd more easily. Simon agreed and Jesus sat in the boat and gave the crowd Spiritual Teachings.

When finished, He said to Simon, "Launch out into the deep and let down your nets for a catch." But Simon answered, "Master we have toiled all night and caught nothing; nevertheless, at your word I will let down the net." And when they had done this, they caught a great number of fish and their net was breaking. So, they signaled to their partners in the other boat to come and help them. And they came and filled both the boats, so much that they began to sink. When

Simon Peter saw this, he fell down at Jesus's knees saying, "Depart from me, for I am a sinful man O master."

For he and those with him were astonished at the catch of fish which they had taken, as were James and John the sons of Zebedee who were partners with Simon. And Jesus said to Simon, "Do not be afraid. From now on you will be catching men." And when they brought the boats ashore, they left everything and followed Him.

Women Followers of Jesus

Luke 8:1-3 The twelve were with Him as He went teaching throughout the cities and villages bringing the glad tidings of the Heavenly Spiritual World of our Loving Spiritual Creator that lies beyond this life on Earth and how to reach it. And certain women also followed with Him including Mary Magdalene, out of whom had come seven demonic spirits, and Joanna the wife of Chuza, Herod's steward, and Susanna, and many others followed who provided for Him from their own wealth.

Jesus Rebukes Disciples

Luke 9:51-56 Now it came to pass after Jesus was fully Spiritually awakened that He was determined to go up to Jerusalem. As He went, He sent messengers before Him into a Samaritan village to prepare a place to stay on the way. But they would not allow Him a place because He was only passing through and would not spend any time teaching them as He previously did after talking to the Samaritan woman at the well.

And when His disciples James and John saw this, they said to Jesus, "Teacher, do you want us to command fire to come down from Heaven and consume all the Samaritans just as Elijah did?" But Jesus turned and strongly rebuked them saying, "You do not know what manner of Spirit you are of. For the Spiritual child of our Loving Creator did not come to destroy men's lives but to save them." And they went to another village that would let them stay.

Author: This is another stunning example of the enormous difficulty Jesus faced trying to bring His disciples out of the distorted two headed God of the Jews into the singularity of the One True Loving Spiritual Creator. The two disciples were still under the heavy influence of the two headed God of the Jews with a violent, murdering, revengeful Godhead of War Yahweh 1 and a Godhead of evolving Love Yahweh 2. And they saw no problem as followers of Jesus asking their War God Yahweh 1 in Heaven to send fire down to consume and destroy all the Samaritans in the town for insulting Him.

Being heavily indoctrinated and still trapped in the Jewish misunderstanding about who God really was, they were referring to an account in the Old Wine Testament in 2 Kings 10-12. In this account Elijah states he is a follower of their two headed God Yahweh, and he calls down fire from the Heaven of this War God Yahweh 1 two times to consume two captains and their fifty men who had come to take him to their king. He did not want to go with them so murdered them all with help from the Godhead of War Yahweh 1 of the two headed Jewish God Yahweh.

Clearly, the disciples had absolutely no idea who our Loving Spiritual Creator really is and even thought Jesus was still worshipping their two headed God like they were. He must have been extremely upset at what they were inferring about Him and our Loving Spiritual Creator and amazed that they had made such little True Spiritual progress after being with Him for so long.

His words say it all when He tells them they have no idea about what kind of Spirit their Spiritual Life comes from and so how would they ever find it by still following the distorted two headed God of the Jews. He then tries to bring them out of their delusional distorted belief about the two headed God of the Jews by telling them True Spiritual children of our Loving Spiritual Creator never destroy men's lives but only save them to Heaven.

Jesus never gave up offering or teaching the Spiritual Truth to children no matter how distorted their Spiritual beliefs were. That was His work. That was His Life. That was His purpose in giving words of enlightenment and Spiritual awakening to save all our lives to Heaven.

Disciples Have Power

Luke 10:17-20 The disciples came and told Jesus how they were able to heal and expel demons from sick children using His Spiritual instructions. Jesus said, "I see satan falling like lightening from the sky. Behold, you have authority now to trample on all evil things including the power of the enemy and nothing shall harm your Spiritual bodies and Souls. Nevertheless, do not rejoice in this power you now have and that the enemy must obey you but rather rejoice because your Spiritual names and identities are established now in the Heavenly Spiritual World of Love."

Author: Jesus was at one with our Loving Spiritual Creator and Her Loving Spiritual Life-force filled His awakened Spiritual body and Soul. This is how He healed the sick and drove out demons by passing this Spiritual Life-force from Heaven within His Spiritual body into the physical body of flesh of the other child who needed healing. Because our Loving Spiritual Creator is only Truth, Life and Pure Love She can only heal, restore and give us True Spiritual Life.

Jesus had to first teach His disciples about Her and remove their connection to the dualistic two headed God Yahweh of the Jews to enable them to awaken also into becoming Spiritual children of our Loving Creator filled with only Her Loving Spiritual Life-force just as He was. Then they could do the same healings as He did as He said in **John 14:12**, "Truly I say to you, he who believes in Me and My Spiritual Teachings, the works that I do he will do also; and greater works than these he will do."

The reason these miraculous healings may have died out in the Jewish/ Christian churches is because 1700 years ago they mixed the New Wine of Jesus and our Loving Spiritual Creator back in with the Old Wine of the Jews and their two headed God Yahweh. This has poisoned the connection with our Loving Spiritual Creator, and we need to cut all ties with the two Headed God Yahweh of the Jews for this Spiritual connection to open again and come alive in True followers of Jesus as Spiritual children of only our Loving Spiritual Creator. Then we may see Spiritual healings become common again through the power of Her Loving Spiritual Life-force flowing into Her True Spiritual children of Love then flowing out of them to those children in need.

The Good Samaritan

Luke 10:25-37 A lawyer came to test Jesus saying, "Teacher, what shall I do to inherit Eternal Life?" He said to him, "What is written in your law? What do you understand of it?" He answered saying, "You shall Love the Lord your God with all your heart, with all your Soul, with all your strength and with all your mind and your neighbour as yourself."

Jesus said to him, "You have answered rightly, do this and you will have Life." But wanting to make sure he was right in his practice he asked Jesus, "Who then is my neighbour?" Then Jesus spoke this parable. "A certain man went down from Jerusalem to Jericho and was set upon by thieves who stripped him of his clothing, wounded him and departed leaving him to die. Now by chance a certain priest came down that road. And when he saw him, he passed by on the other side. Likewise, a Levite, when he arrived at the place, came and had a look but also passed by on the other side.

But a certain Samaritan, as he journeyed came to where he lay. And when he saw him, he had compassion. So, he went to him and bandaged his wounds, pouring on oil and wine; and set him on his own animal, brought him to an inn and took care of him. On the next day, when he departed, he took out two denarii, gave them to the innkeeper and said to him, 'Take care of him and whatever more you need to spend when I come back, I will repay you.' So, which of these three do you think was a neighbour to him who was fell upon by thieves?" And he answered, "He who showed mercy on him." Jesus then said, "Go and do likewise."

Author: Jesus is speaking to a Jewish audience, and He knows how they despise and look down on Samaritans as being inferior to themselves not regarding them as true children of God like themselves. He deliberately chooses the despised Samaritan to be the one who shows Love and mercy to the wounded man and describes the arrogant Jews as being inferior, cold hearted and uncaring.

This would have been a very strong afront to the Jews that were listening who saw themselves as being the greatest and the only special chosen ones of God. Jesus shows anyone can be a child of our Loving Spiritual Creator empowered by Her Love no matter what religion you follow. Or even if you have no religious Spiritual beliefs but live out of Love for all others you are still Her child of Love.

Jesus knew the Jews had boxed themselves into a corner by believing only they were the chosen children of their two headed God Yahweh which created a religion of exclusion instead of inclusion. Later on, this Jewish delusion was taken and overlayed onto the Jewish/Christians who also said they were the only chosen children of our Loving Creator and Jesus is the only one who can save you.

This created another religion of exclusion instead of inclusion. Jesus swings a wrecking ball into this delusion of the Jews and modern Jewish/Christians believing only they are the chosen children of our Loving Creator by making the despised Samaritan the honourable hero in this story.

He is trying to bring them out of worshiping their two headed God Yahweh into the understanding that we are all children of the One Loving Spiritual Creator. And depending on the degree of Love you have in your Spiritual Life, to that extent you will be Her Spiritual child. The two Jews in this story had no Love for the wounded man so were not children of our Loving Creator but the Samaritan freely gave his Love to the wounded man and so was a child of our Loving Creator.

He even paid for further care for the man even though he was a stranger and had no family or cultural ties with him. Anyone who lives out of Love for others and hurts no one can enter the Heavenly Spiritual World. The Samaritan had equanimity of Love empowered by the Loving Life-force of our Loving Creator and helped the injured man who was abandoned by others. He put aside his own personal activities to give his time to the injured man.

Sometimes the most valuable thing we can give someone is our heartbeats, because all of us only have a limited amount to spend. This is self-sacrifice and the selfless Loving action of a typical Spiritual child of our Loving Creator on Earth. The two Jews were selfish and would give nothing to the wounded man in need, so no Heavenly Love could enter them or flow through them to the wounded man.

When we are selfish towards others in need, we are starving our own Spirits of nourishment instead of receiving unending Love by just sharing what we have with others. For whenever Love flows out of us to others it immediately flows in from above and we are never empty of Love. This beautiful saying of Jesus has produced many wonderful Christian charities and followers who care selflessly for those in need in this dangerous world.

Mary and Martha

Luke 10:38-42 As they went into a certain village, a woman named Martha welcomed Jesus into her house. And she had a sister called Mary, who also sat at the feet of Jesus to hear Him teach. But Martha was occupied with serving everyone and she approached Jesus and said, "Teacher, do you not care that my sister has left me to serve alone? Tell her to help me." And Jesus answered, "Martha, Martha, you are worried and troubled about many little things. But only One thing is needed, and Mary has chosen to participate in that One good thing which will not be taken away from her."

Author: In the correct Thomas Gospel parable about the fisherman who found the One good and great fish representing his Eternal Spiritual body, Soul mind of Love and True Life he let go of all the other little fish. It is being echoed here again by Jesus saying Mary has chosen the One good thing by listening to His Spiritual Teachings that awakens her Eternal Spiritual Life that we all need to enter the Heavenly Spiritual World. This is the most important thing of all compared to the many little material things Martha was concerned about.

Keep Connected to Heaven

Luke 11:5-8 Jesus said, "Which of you shall have a friend and go to him at midnight and say to him, 'Friend, lend me three loaves; for a friend of mine has come to visit on his journey and I have nothing to set before him.' And he will answer from within, 'Do not trouble me, the door is now shut, and my children are with me in bed so I cannot rise and give to you.' I say to you though he will not rise and give to him because he is a friend, yet because of his persistence he will rise and give him as many as he needs."

Author: Our Loving Spiritual Creator answers our prayers but not always in the way or time that we wish for. She sees more than us and as long as we stay facing Her in connection with Her Love, She will provide us with Spiritual help for our life on Earth. We only need ask once but the material world and circumstances can delay or alter results so we must always stay close to Her in Spirit.

Keep the Word

Luke 11:27-28 And as Jesus was speaking a certain woman from the crowd raised her voice and said to Him, "Blessed is the womb that bore You and the breasts that nursed You." But Jesus replied, "No, rather blessed are those who hear the word of our Loving Spiritual Creator and keep it."

Material Wealth Vs Spiritual Wealth

Luke 12:13-21, Thomas 72, 63 One from the crowd said to Jesus, "Teacher, tell my brother to divide the inheritance with me." But He replied to him, "Man, who made Me a judge or partitioner over you?" And He said to them, "Take heed and be on guard against avarice and greed, for one's True life does not consist in the abundance of the material things he possesses."

Then He told them a parable, "The ground of a certain rich man yielded plentifully. And he thought within himself, saying, 'What shall I do since I have no room to store my crops?' So, he said, 'I will pull down my barns and build greater ones and there I will store up all my grain and my goods. And I will say to my Soul, 'Soul, you have many goods laid up for many years now; take it easy, eat drink and be merry.' But our Loving Spiritual Creator said to him, 'Mindless one, this night you will die and your Soul will be called then who's will those things be which you have stored up?' This is the one who lays up material treasures for his temporary physical life but is not Spiritually enriched by using the Loving Spiritual Life-force in his Spirit to produce Eternal Spiritual fruits of Heaven."

Author: Jesus again directs us to become primarily Spiritual children filled with the Loving Spiritual Life-force of our Loving Spiritual Creator. When we pass through our death experience only our Spiritual body and Soul leave to hopefully enter the Heavenly Spiritual World. Being rich in Spiritual Love is all that matters at that important time.

Faithful Servant

Luke 12:35-38 Jesus said, "Be always ready with your lamps burning and be like men who wait to join their master after his wedding so that when he calls, you may open your door and go to him immediately. Blessed are those servants who are watching out for him when he calls. Truly I say to you, he will be ready to receive them and have them sit down to eat with him and serve them himself. He may call you to come in the second watch or the third watch and blessed are those ready and waiting to hear his call."

Author: Jesus reminds us that we will all pass through our death experience at some time unknown to us. Therefore, He tells us to always keep our Spiritual Light of Love burning brightly so we are ready to die to the flesh and be called into the Heavenly Spiritual World in our Living Spiritual body where He now is with our Loving Spiritual Creator. And He will be there to greet us home.

Barren Fig Tree

Luke 13:6-9 Jesus spoke this parable, "A certain man had a fig tree planted in his vineyard, and he came seeking fruit on it and found none. Then he said to the keeper of his vineyard, 'Look, for three years I have come seeking fruit on this fig tree and find none. Cut it down, for it is a waste of ground.' But he answered, 'Sir let it be for this year also until I dig around it and fertilise it with manure. Then if it bears fruit all will be well. But if not, after that you can cut it down.'"

Author: For things to grow they need nourishment. Our Spirits grow through receiving the Spiritual words that help awaken our Spiritual body and Soul mind of Love which are then further nourished by the Loving Spiritual Life-force from the Heavenly Spiritual World of our Loving Creator.

Be Humble

Luke 14:7-14 Jesus noticed that those invited to a dinner chose the best places first. He then said to them, "When you are invited by anyone to a feast, do not sit down in the best place for one more honourable than you may also have been invited. And the host may come to you and say, 'Give up your place to this man' and then in embarrassment you take a lower place.

But instead, when you are invited go and sit down in the lowest place and then if the host comes to you, he may invite you to sit in a higher place. Then you will be honoured in the presence of those who sit at table with you. For whoever exalts himself will be humbled and he who humbles himself will be exalted."

And He continued, "When you give a dinner or supper do not ask your friends, your brothers, your relatives, nor rich neighbours who may invite you back and you will be repaid. But when you give a feast, invite the poor, the maimed, the lame and the blind and you will be blessed, because they cannot repay you. For you shall receive your blessing when you rise in Spirit from your body of flesh."

Author: Those who are lowly and humble treat all others with respect and are happy to remain a simple child of our Loving Spiritual Creator. They are content within themselves, have Loving equanimity towards all and need no special recognition or special treatment. Whereas arrogant and egotistical children need to feel superior and more important, so they look down on others treating them as being inferior, less deserving and demand privileged treatment.

They do not realise our Loving Spiritual Creator Loves all Her children with the same Love, and we are all equally important and valuable in Her eyes. Those with their feet on the ground who are level with all other children are stable and cannot fall but those who live in high ivory towers of arrogance above other children, will one day fall and come back down to earth.

Jesus inspires us as Spiritual children to care for those who cannot easily care for themselves or repay us in any way for the care and Love we give to them. The Love we give to these special children of our Loving Creator who are in need will be waiting in the Heavenly Spiritual World for us to receive back from our Loving Creator after our body of flesh dies. Reap as we sow. Karma.

Letting Go to Follow Jesus

Luke 14:25-33 Jesus spoke to those following Him, "For anyone wishing to be My disciple, they must love their father and mother, wife and children, brothers and sisters and even their own life less than My Spiritual Way. And whoever does not carry the cross of their body of flesh and follow Me in Spirit cannot be My disciple.

For which of you intending to build a tower does not first sit down and count the cost and whether he has enough to finish it? For if he has laid the foundation and is not able to finish, all who see it will mock him saying, 'This man began to build and was not able to finish.' Or what King going to make war against another King does not sit down first and consider whether he is able with ten thousand to meet him who comes against him with twenty thousand? Or while the other is still a great way off, he sends a delegation and asks for conditions of peace. So also, any of you who cannot commit all that exists of Himself cannot be My disciple."

Author: Full Spiritual commitment could make us a full time Shepherd like Jesus, teaching the Spiritual Truths of Life about Heaven and how to prepare to enter the Heavenly Spiritual World after we pass through our death experience. These are the leaders of Spiritual congregations supported by the congregation for all their material needs just as Jesus and the disciples were.

But we can all be Shepherd disciples to some degree within our own family, circle of friends, neighbours, workmates or even with the homeless children on the streets. As long as we are fully committed to living a Spiritual Life of Love and Non-violence guided by the Way that Jesus taught, we are all His disciples. Our Spiritual commitment to the Way of Love provides us with the ability to prioritise the important Spiritual practices we must do in our life over the mundane, less important material things. His Way is our Way.

The Lost Coin

Luke 15:8-10 Jesus said, "What woman having ten silver coins, if she loses one coin, does not light a lamp, sweep the house and search carefully until she finds it? And when she has found it, she calls her friends and neighbours together, saying, 'Rejoice with me for I have found the piece that was lost!' Likewise, I say to you, there is joy in the presence of the Angels of our Loving Creator over one sinner who changes their ways."

Author: Our Loving Spiritual Creator can never hurt or condemn us. She never gives up on us and always sees us in our True Spiritual identity. Even if we move out of our True Spiritual identity and become a false, dark shadow identity and commit evil, we can always change back and ask Her to forgive us. And with great joy She pours Her Loving Life-force back into our Spiritual body and Soul for we are Her children. But the Spiritual Law of Reaping as We Sow is always in existence and we can create our own Hell if we are not careful. She does not do it to us; we do it to ourselves.

Lost Son Parable

Luke 15:11-32 Jesus spoke this parable, "There was a man who had two sons. The younger of them said to his father, 'Father, give me the portion of goods that is my inheritance.' So, he divided between them his possessions. And not many days after the younger son gathered all his things together and journeyed to a far country, and there wasted his possessions and substance through riotous living.

But when he had spent all he had, there arose a severe famine in that land and he was destitute. So, he went and kept company with a citizen of that country, who sent him into his fields to feed pigs. And he would gladly have filled his stomach with the pods that the pigs were eating, and no one gave him anything.

But when he fully realised his situation, he thought of all the servants of his father who have enough bread and more to spare while he perishes with hunger? And He said to Himself, 'I will arise and go to my father, and I will say to him Father, I have sinned against Heaven and in your sight and I am no longer worthy to be called your son. Make me like one of your hired servants.'

And he arose and came to his father. But when he was still a great way off his father saw him and had compassion and ran and fell upon his neck and kissed him. And the son said to him, 'Father, I have sinned against Heaven and in your sight and am no longer worthy to be called your son.' But the father said to his servants, 'Bring the best robe and put it on him put a ring on his hand and sandals on his feet. And bring the fattened calf and kill it and let us eat and be joyful; for this my son was dead and is alive again; lost and is found.' And they began to celebrate.

Now his older son was in the field. And as he came near to the house, he heard music and dancing. So, he called one of the servants and asked what these things meant. And he said to him, 'Your brother has returned, and your father has killed the fattened calf, because he has received him safe and sound.' But the brother was angry and would not go in.

Therefore, his father came out and pleaded with him. And he said to his father, 'Look, I have served you for many years and never transgressed your commandments at any time and you never even gave me a young goat, that I might celebrate with my friends. But as soon as this son of yours came, who has devoured your livelihood with prostitutes, you killed the fattened calf for him.' He said, 'Son, you are always with me, and all that I have is yours. It was right that we should celebrate and be glad, for your brother was dead and is alive again, and was lost and is found.'"

Author: Another beautiful Loving saying of Jesus. If we leave our True Spiritual identity that connects us to the Heavenly world to become a false, dark shadow identity to indulge in evil we can bring about our own ruin and be empty of Spiritual Love and Life. But we can also realise our mistake and regret it, feeling remorseful for the dark things we did and want to be Spiritually healed and well again.

Once we sincerely feel that deep remorse, acknowledge the wrong things we have done and never want to indulge in them again, we only have to say sorry to our Loving Spiritual Creator for abusing this beautiful Spiritual gift of Life She has given to us and ask Her forgiveness. And with these preliminary stages all correctly completed She forgives us, washes our sins away from our Souls and embraces us with Her never-ending Love once again. And we can then return to be Her Spiritual child, a little wiser but still on the path to Heaven once again.

Some Jewish/Christians teach that it is the blood of Jesus on the cross that cleanses you of your sins which is a false Teaching. Here and elsewhere in His Teachings, we see Jesus giving us a clear path to follow involving certain necessary stages we must go through for our sins to be cleansed from our Souls by our Loving Spiritual Creator.

His Spiritual instructions involving acknowledging our wrongs, sincere remorse, no longer sinning and asking our Loving Creator to forgive us for damaging Her beautiful gift of Spiritual Life She gave to us to live out of, are like a wellspring of Spiritual Water and Truth to help us wash away our sins and change our ways to be blessed by our Loving Creator once again. The dialogue with the jealous older brother is a direction from Jesus to always welcome those who have gone astray back into our own Love.

Unjust Steward

Luke 16:1-13 Jesus then said, "There was a certain rich man who had a steward and an accusation was brought to him that this man was wasting his goods. So, he called him and said to him, 'What is this I hear about you? Give an account of your stewardship, for you can no longer be steward.' Then the steward said to himself, 'What shall I do? For my master is now taking the stewardship away from me. I cannot dig and I am ashamed to beg. I know what I will do, so that when I am put out of the stewardship they may receive me into their houses.'

So, he called his master's debtors and said to the first, 'How much do you owe my master?' And he said, 'A hundred measures of oil.' So, he said to him, 'Take your bill and sit down quickly and write fifty.' Then he said to another, 'And how much do you owe?' He said, 'A hundred measures of wheat.' And he said, 'Take your bill and write eighty.'

The master admired the wrongdoing of the steward because he had acted so cunningly. For the children of this world are more conceited than the children of Light in their world. And I say to you, make friends away from the unrighteous mammon for it will fail, so you will be received into an everlasting home. He who is faithful in what is least is faithful also in much; and he who is unjust in what is least is unjust also in much.

Therefore, if you have not been faithful in the unrighteous mammon, who will commit to your trust the True riches? And if you have not been faithful in what is another man's, who will give you what is your own? No servant can serve two masters; for he either hates the one and loves the other or else he will be loyal to one and despise the other. You cannot serve material wealth and our Loving Spiritual Creator at the same time."

Author: Jesus is pointing out that if you waste your Spiritual goodness, it will be of no use to put your trust in material wealth of your own or others. For all material mammon is temporary and will fail in the end. It is better to have Spiritual friends who are not involved in relying on such things as they and you will have Eternal homes in Heaven. The dependence on material wealth can lead to corruption through the desire to gain more of it. So, you can no longer be trusted in anything else. But those who are honest like the children of Light can be trusted in all things.

And if we cannot be trusted with material wealth, how can we be given the True Heavenly wealth of our Spiritual Life? Material things and possessions of wealth are not who we really are. And if we are misusing or attached to them, how can we possibly receive our own Higher Spiritual Life and identity of Truth, Goodness and Love empowered by the Loving Spiritual Life-force of our Loving Creator who is perfect.

Rich Man and Lazarus

Luke 16:19-31 Jesus told this parable, "There was a certain rich man who was clothed in purple and fine linen and ate sumptuously every day. But there was a certain beggar named Lazarus full of sores, who laid at his gate desiring to be fed with the crumbs that fell from the rich man's table. Moreover, the dogs came and licked his sores. The beggar died and was then carried by the Angels to be with Abraham. The rich man also died and was buried but was in torment in Hell and lifted up his eyes and saw Abraham far off with Lazarus there with him.

Then he cried out, 'Father Abraham, have mercy on me and send Lazarus that he may dip the tip of his finger in water and cool my tongue; for I am tormented in this flame.' But Abraham said, 'Son, remember that in your lifetime you received your good things and likewise Lazarus evil things; but now he is comforted and you are tormented. And besides all this, between you and us there is a great gulf fixed in place so that those who want to pass from here to you cannot, nor can those from there pass to us.'

Then he said, 'I beg you father, that you would send him to my father's house, for I have five brothers, that he may testify to them lest they also come to this place of torment.'

Abraham said to him, 'They have Moses and the prophets; let them hear them.' And he said, 'No father Abraham; but if one goes to them from the dead, they will repent.' But he replied, 'If they do not hear Moses and the prophets, neither will they be persuaded though one rise from the dead.'"

Author: Jesus was always teaching that after we die to the flesh and our Spiritual body leaves, we shall all reap as we have sown. The rich selfish one who indulged in a material life of plenty and gave no love to Lazarus who was in great need, ended up experiencing tormented sufferings or burning realisations about his own failings after he died. Lazarus who was sick and poor in this material world had no wealth to be selfish with and ended up in the Heavenly Spiritual World of Love.

All Spiritual followers of Jesus should share from any material abundance they may have with the other children of our Loving Spiritual Creator who have been struck down and are in need for whatever reason. All material things are eventually just dust, only our Spiritual body and Soul travel on and they must be enlivened with the Loving Life-force of our Spiritual Creator in Heaven to have True Life. To have no Loving Spiritual Life-force in you and flowing through you to others is to be dead to the Spirit.

Do Your Duty Well

Luke 17:7-10 Jesus then said, "When a servant is doing the tasks given to him to perform, it is enough for him to take joy in completing the tasks well for the one who asked him to do them. You also must be like this when you perform your Spiritual tasks that our Loving Spiritual Creator gives to you to do."

Author: The joy of Spiritual children of our Loving Spiritual Creator is to partake in sharing the Loving Life-force of our Loving Creator in their Spiritual lives with other children in whatever way it needs to be shared with them. Whether the task is small or large we can all be thankful for the opportunity to consolidate our Spiritual Life of Love through helping others in need. They are the jewels in our life that provide us with the way to enrich our own Spirits through sharing Heaven's Love in us with them.

Heaven is Within You

Luke 17:20-21 The Pharisees asked Jesus when the Kingdom of our Creator would come. Jesus replied, "The Kingdom of our Loving Spiritual Creator does not come with observation; nor will they say, 'See, here it is,' or 'See, there it is.' For indeed the Kingdom of our Loving Spiritual Creator is within you."

Thomas 113 His disciples asked Jesus, "When will the Kingdom come?" Jesus said, "Her kingdom will not come by waiting for it, nor by saying, 'Behold, it is over there,' or 'Behold it is that one there.' Rather, our Loving Spiritual Creator is spreading Her Kingdom out upon the earth, but men do not look to see it."

Thomas 3 Jesus said, "If your leaders say to you, 'Behold, the Kingdom of our Loving Creator is in the sky,' then the birds in the sky will get there before you. If they say to you, 'It is in the sea,' then the fish will get there before you. Rather, the Kingdom of our Loving Spiritual Creator is inside you and outside you. When you know yourselves, then you will be known and will understand that you are children of our Living Spiritual Creator. But if you do not know yourselves then you live in poverty and embody that poverty."

Thomas 51 His disciples asked Him, "When will the final rest for the dead take place, and when will the new world come?" He said to them, "What you look for has already come but you do not know it."

Thomas 18 The disciples said to Jesus, "Teacher, tell us about the end." Jesus replied, "Have you already discovered the beginning, that now you seek after the end? For where the beginning is, the end will be also. Blessed is the one who stands at the beginning; that one will know the end and will not taste death."

Thomas 19 Jesus said, "Blessed is one who came to Life before coming to Life."

Author: Jesus is telling us that we all have a Living Spiritual connection to the Heavenly Spiritual World of our Loving Spiritual Creator within us right now. It is not a new material Jerusalem coming out of the sky at the Apocalypse as some Jewish/Christians wrongly teach or Jesus coming back on the clouds to establish an Earthly Kingdom after being a catalyst for causing massive sufferings.

If we listen to the words of Jesus and follow them, we will awaken into our Eternal Spiritual body and Soul mind of Love identity that is with us right now but may still be dormant. That would be like staying in poverty. But if we do wake up, are born again or arise into Spirit, it will mean we have reached the end of our identity based on the body of temporary flesh and begun our True Heavenly identity as Spiritual children of our Loving Creator in the Heavenly Spiritual World while still in the flesh.

At the ending of one life, we find the beginning of the other as Jesus said. And Spirit goes to Spirt as earth goes to earth at the time of our death. By becoming Spiritual now, we are bringing Heaven to Earth through the Loving Spiritual Life-force that sustains our Eternal Spiritual bodies and Soul minds of Love which we then share with all other children. This is how Her Heavenly World of Love is spread out upon the earth, through our own Spiritual awakening.

Then, "It will be inside and outside you." But many do not see or know about this Spiritual reality and keep looking for a material answer and material Kingdom. Jesus tells the disciples the new Spiritual awakening and Heavenly World already exist, but children do not know it. And that is why Jesus and Buddha taught the Spiritual path of Love and Non-violence to awaken our Spirits that connect us to the Heavenly World or Nirvana to be ready to leave this dualistic, material world of suffering when our body of flesh dies to enter the Heavenly Spiritual World of Peace and Love.

Pharisee and Tax Collector

Luke 18:9-14 Jesus spoke this parable to some gathered there who had convinced themselves that they were more righteous than others, and who looked down on them and despised them. "Two men went into the temple to pray; one was a Pharisee and the other a tax collector. The Pharisee stood and prayed to our Loving Creator saying, 'God, I thank You that I am not like other men; extortioners, unjust, adulterers or even this tax collector. I fast twice a week and give contributions from all that I possess'

The tax collector standing a way off, would not so much as raise his eyes to Heaven, but beat his breast saying, 'My Loving Spiritual Creator, be merciful to me a sinner!' I tell you; this man went down to his house justified rather than the other; for everyone that exalts himself will be humbled, and he who humbles himself will be exalted."

Author: By remembering that none of us are perfect all the time, we can feel a sense of oneness with all other children and never act in a superior way towards anyone else. This is an aspect of Love in Equanimity towards all. And we must always be in communication with our Loving Creator with our life on full display before Her and always acknowledge our mistakes and ask for Her understanding and forgiveness.

Zacchaeus' House

Luke 19:1-9 And Jesus passed through Jericho. And behold there was a man named Zacchaeus, who was the chief tax collector and he was rich. And he sought to see Jesus but could not because of the crowd, for he was of short stature. So, he ran ahead and climbed into a Sycamore tree to be able to see Jesus as he passed by.

And when Jesus came to the tree, He looked up and saw Zacchaeus and said to him, "Zacchaeus, make haste and come down, for today I must stay at your house." So, he quickly climbed down and welcomed Jesus joyfully. But when the crowd saw this, some complained saying, "He has gone to be a guest to eat with a man who is a sinner."

Then Zacchaeus stood and said to Jesus, "Teacher, I will give half my goods to the poor; and if I have taken anything from anyone falsely, I will pay back fourfold." And Jesus said, "Today salvation has come to this house, because he is also a child of our Loving Creator, for I have come to seek and to save that which was lost."

Author: The Spiritual impact that Jesus had on many children and still does to this day is to transform them into good Spiritual children inspiring them to turn away from wrongdoing. Again, Jesus clearly states He and our Loving Spiritual Creator do not condemn anyone but only try to save them to Heaven.

Many Jewish/Christians teach a slanderous notion that Jesus and our Loving Creator will destroy Her children who are lost. They are unwittingly worshiping and teaching about the violent Yahweh 1 War God of the Jews not our Loving Spiritual Creator who is more like the evolving Yahweh 2 God of the Jews who says to Love your neighbour as yourself.

Jesus is Sad for the Jews

Luke 19:41-44 As Jesus drew near to the city of Jerusalem, He wept tears and said, "If only you had known the things that would have brought you to peace. But now they are hidden from your eyes. For days will come upon you when your enemies will build an embankment around you, surround you and hem you in from every side. And they will level you and your children within you to the ground, and they will not leave one stone upon another because you did not know the time of your investigation."

Author: Although the Spiritual Teachings of Jesus are Universal, He first tried to bring His own Jewish people out of their dualistic religion worshiping the two headed God Yahweh and bring them to our Loving Spiritual Creator who is only Love. But they rejected Him which naturally would have saddened Him. He predicted that they would receive the same type of brutal War God treatment to themselves that they gave to others like the people of Jericho. As we sow, so shall we reap.

Advice for Disciples

Luke 22:35-36, 38 Jesus said to His disciples, "When I last sent you without money bag, knapsack and sandals did you lack anything?" They said, "Nothing." Then He said, "But now, he who has a money bag let him take it with him and likewise a knapsack and he who has no garment let him sell his sword and buy one." Then they said, "Teacher, look, here are two swords." Jesus then said, "That is ample!"

Author: When the disciples were first sent out to share the new Spiritual Way and Teachings of Love and Non-violence with the common Jews that Jesus taught, they received much local support and provisions along the way. But as the Jewish authorities started attacking Jesus and His new

Teachings and threatened Jews with being expelled from the synagogue if they acknowledge Jesus or His followers, it was more dangerous to be seen with them. So, naturally they would need their own provisions as they would not be getting as much support on the road as they did earlier on.

All modern Gospel translations say Jesus said to sell your garment to buy a sword. But just later on that very night after the last supper as Jesus was being taken captive and a follower cut the ear off one of the crowd, He famously said, "Put your sword back into its place. For all those who take hold of the sword shall perish by the sword." The words sword and garment have most likely been either accidentally switched in early translations or deliberately to pervert the pacifist Teaching of Jesus to allow Christians to take up the sword in battle.

I wouldn't be surprised if this switch occurred around the time of Emperor Constantine by the corrupt Christian leaders to allow Roman soldiers to go to war and kill with the sword but still be Christians. The disciple's response may have been more correctly, simply offering two swords to donate towards buying cloaks for those who had none.

Our Loving Spiritual Creator is only Love.

We must be Her Spiritual children of

only Love on Earth.

Chapter 13
John

All of the important sayings in John that are repetitions found in Matthew have been combined with the Matthew sayings in that chapter. Other sayings have been placed in the appropriate early chapters regarding specific topics. The following are those sayings in John that are not mentioned in the Matthew chapter or the earlier chapters.

Destroy This House

John 2:18-22 Jesus drove the money lenders out of the temple. The Jews asked Jesus, "What sign will You show us to explain why You are doing these things?" Jesus said, "Destroy this temple and I will raise it up." The Jews said, "It has taken forty-six years to build this temple, how will you raise it up by yourself?" But Jesus was talking about the temple of His body that contained His Spiritual body within it. Therefore, when He had risen from His dead body of flesh in His Spiritual body the disciples remembered He said this would happen.

Thomas 71 Jesus said, "I will destroy this house, and no one will be able to rebuild it."

Author: The Gospels have been altered to falsely lead followers of Jesus into believing our bodies of dead flesh rise again. But the Thomas Gospel saying is the accurate one. Jesus is saying He is going to voluntarily allow His body of flesh to be killed and destroyed and it does not come back to life. As Jesus taught, our dead bodies of flesh are just food for the vultures. Only our Spiritual body travels on to reap as we have sown. He knew He had a fully awakened Spiritual body within His body of flesh that does not die.

Jesus is a Child of our Loving Creator

John 3:13-21 No one has ascended into the Heavenly Spiritual world through awakening except the Spiritual child who has awakened and come forth into this world. And as Moses lifted up the serpent in the wilderness, even so must the Spiritual child of humanity be lifted up, that whoever believes in Him and His Spiritual Way should not perish but find Eternal Spiritual Life. For our Loving Spiritual Creator so loves the whole world that when one of Her Spiritual children awakens, She inspires them to help others to also awaken to become Her Spiritual children as well. For our Loving Creator does not awaken Her Spiritual children to condemn the world but to help save it.

When Her children of Light awaken and appear in this world, by their own Spiritual existence of Love, they stand out in contrast and expose those who love evil and darkness more than the Spiritual Light. For everyone practicing evil hates the Spiritual Light and avoids coming to the Light for it is Truth and Love and exposes their evil deeds. But those who are in Spiritual Truth and Love come to the Light so their deeds may reflect the Love of our Loving Spiritual Creator in them."

Author: Jesus was an awakened Spiritual child of our Loving Spiritual Creator in the Heavenly Spiritual World of Love. Once He awakened, He realised how important this Spiritual enlightenment is to be able to have Spiritual Life after the death of the body of flesh. So, He dedicated His life to teach others how to experience this Spiritual awakening as He Knew we all have the same potential to realise it. Then they would have a new Spiritual Life in Heaven after the death of their body of flesh so never really die. Children who have become dark shadow figures of evil hate the Light and the children of Light.

Samaritan Woman at the Well Teaching

John 4:1-26 When Jesus knew that the Pharisees had been told that He was baptising and attracting more disciples than John, He left Judea and departed into Galilee. And as He passed through Samaria, He came to a city which is called Sychar near the plot of ground Jacob gave to his son Joseph.

Jesus was weary from His journey and stopped to rest at the well of Jacob and it was about the sixth hour. A Samaritan woman came to the well to draw water. Jesus asked her, "Can you give Me a drink?" For His disciples had gone into the city to buy food.

The Samaritan woman asked Jesus, "How is it that You, a Jew, ask for a drink from me a Samaritan woman? The Jews have no dealings with Samaritans." Jesus answered her, "If you knew the gift offered by our Loving Spiritual Creator, and who it is who says to you, 'Give Me a drink,' you would have asked Me and I would have given you the Living Spiritual water of Life."

The woman said to Him, "Sir, you have nothing to draw the water up with, and the well is deep. Where will you get this Living water of Life? Are you greater than our father Jacob who gave us this well and drank from it himself as well as his sons and their livestock?" Jesus said to her, "Whoever drinks of this Earthly water shall thirst again, but whoever drinks of the Living Spiritual Water that I shall give them shall never thirst again. And that water shall become in them a wellspring of Living Spiritual water lifting them up into everlasting Life."

The woman said to Jesus, "Sir, give me this water you speak of so I may never thirst or have to come to this well to draw up water." Jesus said to her, "Go, call your husband and come here." The woman answered Jesus that she had no husband. Jesus said to her, "You have rightly stated that you have no husband, for you have had five husbands and the one you are with now is not your husband either, you have spoken the truth."

The woman said to Him, "Sir, I can see that you are a prophet. Our fathers worshiped on this mountain but you Jews say that only Jerusalem is the place where one should worship." Jesus said to her, "Woman believe Me, the time is coming when neither on this mountain nor in Jerusalem, will you worship the Loving Spiritual Creator.

The time is coming and is now here, when all Spiritual children of our Loving Creator will express their Love Truly in Spirit for Her. For the Loving Creator is waiting for children to awaken and join Her and be filled with Her Loving Life-force. Our Loving Creator is Spirit and those who wish to Love Her, must come to Her in Spirit and in Truth."

The woman said, "I believe the Messiah will come and when He does, He will reveal all truths." Jesus said to her, "I who speak to you am He." The disciples returned and marveled to find Jesus talking to the woman, but no one asked why He was talking with her. The woman then left her water pot and went into the city and told everyone, "Come and see a man who told me all things that I ever did. Could this man be the Messiah?" So, they all went out to see Jesus.

The disciples offered Jesus something to eat, saying, "Teacher eat some food." But He said, "I have nourishment which you do not know about." So, the disciples said to one another, "Has someone already brought Him something to eat?" Jesus explained to them, "My nourishment comes through performing the Spiritual works shown to Me by our

Loving Creator and bringing them to Spiritual perfection for all children on earth to see and follow.

Do you not say, 'There are still four months and then the harvest comes?' Behold I say to you, lift up your sight and look upon the countryside for the Spiritual children of the Light are ready to be awakened and harvested. And he who reaps receives Spiritual reward through leading the children to Eternal life, so that He who sows and he who reaps may rejoice together. For this saying is true, 'One sows and another reaps.' I send you forth to reap those for whom you have not labored, others before you have labored and now you join in with their labors."

Many Samaritans in that city believed in Jesus because of the testimony of the woman who said, "He is a prophet and told me all I ever did." When the Samaritans had come to see Him, they urged Him to stay with them, and He stayed there for two days. And many more believed in Jesus after hearing His Teachings. Then they said to the woman, "We also believe, not because of what you told us but because we ourselves have heard His Teachings. And we now know He really is a Spiritual child of the Loving Creator, the anointed one, who delivers us from the delusions and evil of this material world."

Thomas 74 Jesus said, "There are many standing around their fountain and well, but no one is in their water."

Author: Once again, Jesus draws a contrast between our temporary physical body of flesh and its needs which have to be continually replenished by earthly elements to have life, or it will die. As opposed to our Spiritual body and Soul which once it is connected to the Loving Spiritual Life-force or Living waters of our Loving Spiritual Creator, it comes to Life and will be sustained Eternally from within from a perpetual Spiritual wellspring.

This is the nourishment Jesus was referring to that the disciples had yet connected with. And as Eternal Life is in the Heavenly Spiritual World, not the Earth world, we need this Living Spiritual water now to bring our Spiritual body alive to be able to enter the Heavenly Spiritual World.

The water Jesus refers to is given to us through hearing His words and understanding them which awakens our Spirit to receive the Loving Spiritual Life-force of our Loving Creator that empowers our Spirit and Soul mind of Love. We must drink His words in and be awakened by them Spiritually. We then arise into our True Spiritual identity and will begin to realise who we really are as Spiritual children of our Loving Creator in the Heavenly World, and we will be just like Jesus Himself.

The Thomas Gospel saying points out how many children have potential to awaken and be Spiritual, but they have none of the Loving Spiritual Life-force or Living water, from Heaven in them to empower their Spirits. It is like being the vase instead of the water in the vase.

Clearly the Samaritan woman could only think in terms of the earthly water without the Spiritual awakening given by Jesus. Just as Nicodemus could not conceive of being born again in a Spiritual body and was also stuck only in earthly realities of birth. Jesus helps us all to awaken from the body of flesh to realise we have another body of Spirit with us right now and then guides us to open our Spirit up by following His Teachings and Spiritual Way of Love and Non-violence. Then we are prepared to fully receive and live out of the Loving Spiritual Life-force from our Loving Creator in the Heavenly Spiritual World. And as Jesus said, we then come to be with Her in Spirit and in the Truth of who we really are as Her Spiritual children of Love.

Jesus with the Loving Creator

John 5:16-47 The Jews pursued Jesus and sought to kill Him, because He had done these works of healing on the

Sabbath. But Jesus answered them, "My Loving Spiritual Creator has been working until now and I am also working as Her child."

The Jews now wanted to kill Him even more, because He not only broke the Sabbath but said He is a child of the Loving Creator making Himself similar to the Loving Creator. Jesus said to them, "Truly, I say to you, that the child can do nothing out of himself except what He understands His Loving Creator does, for whatever She does Her child does in the same way.

The Loving Creator loves Her child and shows him all things that She Herself does and will show Her Spiritual child even greater things than these, so that you may be amazed. For just as the Loving Spiritual Creator awakens those dead to their Spirit by giving Spiritual Life to them even so, the child of the Loving Creator can also give Spiritual Life to whomever wishes to receive it.

For the Loving Spiritual Creator judges no one, but all judgment is received through the child of the Loving Creator. For all who honour the Spiritual child of the Loving Creator honour the Loving Creator as well. But he who does not honour the child of the Loving Creator does not honour the Loving Creator or Her Way of Love as well.

Most assuredly I say to you, he who hears My words and understands them and believes in our Loving Spiritual Creator who sent Me and Her Way has Eternal Spiritual life. And he shall not come into judgment but shall pass from physical death into Spiritual life. I say to you truly, now is the time when those who are dead to the Spirit and asleep will hear the voice of the Spiritual child of the Loving Creator and awaken. And anyone who hears and understands His words will have Spiritual life.

The Loving Creator has life in Herself, and She gives Her Loving Spiritual Life-force to Her Spiritual children to have life within themselves. And all those who have done good go on to the Spiritual resurrection and True Eternal Life, and all those who have done evil go on to receive the consequences of their evil. By Myself I can do nothing. I conclude according to what I hear and My decision is just. I do not seek My own will but the will of the Loving Spiritual Creator who sent Me. If I testify about Myself My testimony is not True. John testified about Me and has spoken the Truth. He was the burning light that shone forth and you were willing for a while to rejoice in his light.

But I have a greater witness of Me than John's. For the works which the Loving Creator has given Me to perfect, these very works that I do, are a witness about Me showing I have been sent by our Loving Spiritual Creator in Heaven. So, the Loving Creator has testified about Me. You have never heard Her voice at any time nor perceived Her appearance. You do not have Her word living in you, because you do not trust or believe the one She sent to you. You examine the scriptures for in them you believe you have life eternal, but these testify about Me. But you refuse to come to Me to receive True Spiritual Life.

I do not receive glory from men. But I know you, and you do not have the Loving Spiritual Life-force of our Loving Creator in yourselves. I come in the name of the Loving Creator in Heaven, and you do not accept Me but if another comes in his own name him you will accept. How can you believe when you accept praise from one another but do not seek the glory that comes from the One True Loving Spiritual Creator."

Thomas 1 Jesus said, "Whoever discovers the interpretation of these words shall never taste death."

Author: The Jews had no correct Spiritual understanding of the One True Loving Spiritual Creator and our relationship with Her as Her Spiritual children of Love. And that all human children are equally precious to Her as everyone has a Spiritual body created by Her within them, that is

Heavenly and Eternal if it is filled with Her Loving Spiritual Life-force and we are Living out of it. Jesus had awakened to His Spiritual body and Soul mind of Love and so was Her Spiritual child and said this to the Jews. But for them that was blasphemy due to their own ignorance of this Spiritual relationship with the One True Loving Creator.

Jesus explains how all His works and Teachings come from knowing Her as Her Spiritual child and without Her He could do nothing. And She awakens those dead to their Spirit as He is also doing through His Teachings and works as Her Heavenly child on Earth.

She never judges anyone, but children choose to either believe or not believe in Her and Her Spiritual Way of Love that Jesus teaches. The choice is theirs and if they reject Jesus then they reject Her.

Jesus states that we all reap as we sow after passing through our death experience. And He just speaks the Truth as he sees things for what they really are. He says the works He does should be witness enough to show He is with our Loving Creator in Spirit. But He tells the Jews they do not have Her Loving Spiritual Life-force in them.

The Bread of Life

John 6:22-71 They asked Jesus when did He arrive there on the shore. And Jesus answered them saying, "Truly, I say to you, you seek Me not because you saw the wonders I performed but because you ate your fill of the loaves of bread. Do not labour for the food which perishes but for the food which endures to Eternal life which the Spiritual Child of Humanity will give you. For the Loving Spiritual Creator has set Her seal of approval upon Me."

And they asked Him, "What should we do, that we may do the works of the Loving Creator?" And Jesus answered them saying, "This is the work of the Loving Creator that you trust in Him whom She has sent to you." Then they asked Him, "What sign will you perform so that we may see and believe in you? What work do you do? Our ancestors ate the manner in the wilderness; as it is written, 'He gave them bread from Heaven to eat.'"

Jesus then said to them, "Truly, truly, I say to you, it was not Moses who gave you the bread of Heaven, but our Loving Spiritual Creator gives you the True bread from Heaven. For the bread of the Loving Spiritual Creator is the one who awakens and comes forth from Heaven and gives True Spiritual Life to the world."

They said, "Master, give us this Spiritual bread always." Jesus replied, "I am the Spiritual bread of life, he who comes to Me shall not hunger and he who believes in Me shall never thirst. But I said to you that you have seen Me but still do not believe. Everyone that the Loving Creator gives to Me will come to Me and anyone who comes to Me I will not cast out.

For I have come forth from the Heavenly Spiritual world not to fulfill My own personal will but the will of the Loving Spiritual Creator who sent Me. And this is the will of the Loving One who sent Me, that everyone who has been given to Me to care for I will destroy none but help them to be lifted up in Spirit on their last day.

And this is the wish of the Loving Creator who sent Me that everyone who understands the Child of Humanity and trusts in Him, may find Eternal life and be lifted up in Spirit on their last day." The Jews murmured against Him because He said, 'I am the bread which came forth from the Heavenly World.' And they said, "Isn't this Jesus, the son of Mary and Joseph whom we know? How can He say, 'He came forth from the Heavenly World?'"

Jesus said to them, "Do not grumble amongst yourselves. No one can come to Me unless the Loving Creator inspires them, and I will help to lift them up in Spirit on their last day. It is written in the prophets, 'And they shall all be taught by God.' Therefore, everyone who has listened to the Loving Creator and understood who the Loving Creator truly is, will go with Me.

Not that anyone has clearly perceived the Loving Spiritual Creator except He who is with the Loving Creator, He knows the Loving Creator. Most assuredly I say to you, he who trusts in Me and follows My Teachings has Eternal life. I am the Spiritual bread of life. Your ancestors ate the manner from Earth in the wilderness and are dead.

This is the bread which comes out from the Heavenly Spiritual World, so that anyone who takes it into themselves will not die. I am the Living Spiritual bread which comes forth from the Heavenly Spiritual World. If anyone takes this Heavenly bread inside themselves that I give to them they will be alive for ever. And the Spiritual bread that I give to you comes through the living flesh of My life, which I dedicate for the life of the world."

The Jews then quarreled among themselves saying, "How can this man give this thing to us through His flesh?" Then Jesus said, "Most assuredly I say to you, unless you take into yourselves the Spiritual food that the Child of Humanity offers to you and drink of His Loving Life-force, you will have no Spiritual life in you. He who follows My Way and lives like Me has Eternal life and will be lifted up in Spirit on his last day.

For My Way of living in Spirit is True food and drink indeed. He who follows My Teachings and lives by My Way will live in Me and I in him, and he will become like Me. Just as the Loving Spiritual Creator sent Me and I have Spiritual life because of the Loving Creator, so he that follows My Way will have Spiritual life because of Me. This is the Spiritual bread which comes forth from the Heavenly Spiritual World, not like your ancestors who ate Earthly manna and are dead. He who eats this Spiritual bread, will live forever."

These things Jesus taught in the synagogue. And many of His followers after hearing this said, "This is a hard saying, who can understand it?" When Jesus heard them grumbling about it, He said to them, "Does this saying offend you? What if you should see the Spiritual Child of Humanity ascend to the Heavenly Spiritual World?

It is the Spirit of the Loving Spiritual Creator who gives True life; the flesh profits nothing and cannot create Spiritual Life. The words that I speak to you are Spirit and they are life. But some of you do not believe Me." For He knew from the beginning those who did not believe in Him and who would turn against Him. He said, "I have told you that no one can come to Me, unless they have been inspired in Spirit by our Loving Creator."

Following these sayings, many disciples departed from Him and walked with Him no more. Then Jesus said to the twelve, "Do you also want to leave Me?" But Simon Peter answered saying, "Master, to whom shall we go? You hold the words and Teachings of Eternal life. And we have come to believe that you are the Messiah, a Spiritual child of the Loving Spiritual Creator in Heaven."

Jesus said, "I chose the twelve of you, but one of you is a devil." He spoke of Judas, one of the twelve, who would betray Him.

Thomas 108 Jesus said, "Whoever drinks from My mouth will become like Me, and I will be like him and those things that are hidden will be revealed to him."

Author: Jesus uses the analogy of earthly bread made from earthly substances to sustain our bodies of temporary flesh verses the Spiritual bread made from the Loving Spiritual Life-force of our Loving Creator and the Heavenly World that sustains our Eternal Spiritual bodies and Souls. The Jews had never understood this Spiritual Truth about us all having two different bodies in one which Jesus Himself was now displaying through the Heavenly power of His awakened Spiritual body and Soul mind of Love. Clearly even those close to Him had doubts about what He was teaching because they had not yet arisen from the flesh identity to be born again into their Spiritual identity.

He gives them the Spiritual words and Teachings from His own being to nourish their Spirits and bring them to full Life if they take them into their hearts and minds and are transformed by them. Once He became Spiritually enlightened, He was able to understand all the problems preventing Spiritual awakening and how to overcome them.

His understanding of the Heavenly Spiritual World of Love and His Spirit being connected with Heaven and our Loving Spiritual Creator allowed Him to have experiences and wisdom that others could not have until they too awakened into their True Spiritual identity.

As He said, "It is the Spirit that gives True Life, the flesh profits nothing." And those who awaken into their Spirit will have Eternal Life in the Heavenly Spiritual World after passing through the death experience of their temporary body of flesh. As Jesus said, "He who follows My Way will live in Me and I in him and he will become like Me." The caterpillar dies and the butterfly flies.

Jesus' Brothers Doubt Him

John 7:1-9 Jesus continued in Galilee for He did not want to walk in Judea, because the Jews sought to kill Him. Now the Feast of Tabernacles was at hand. His brothers said to Him, "Depart from here and go into Judea, that Your followers there may also see the works that You are doing. For no one does anything in secret while he himself seeks to be known openly. If You do these things, show Yourself to the world." For even His own brothers doubted Him.

Then, Jesus said, "My time has yet to come, but your time is always ready. The world cannot hate you, but it hates Me because I testify of it that it's works are evil. You go up to this feast. I am not yet going up for My time has not yet fully come." Jesus then remained in Galilee.

Author: Jesus was an awakened Spiritual child of our Loving Spiritual Creator. Children who worship material things and earthly power hate Spiritual children because their whole being is filled only with Love. This stark contrast of their beautiful Spiritual nature that emanates from their Spiritual body and mind of Love exposes the greed and evil of other children and makes them stand out.

Jesus at Feast of Tabernacles

John 7:10-44 His brothers left and went to the Feast. Jesus then went, but not openly. The Jews searched for Him at the Feast for there was much talk about Him among the people. Some said He was a good man, while others said He is a deceiver. But no one spoke openly about Him, for fear of the Jews. During the Feast Jesus entered the temple and taught. The Jews were amazed that such an unlearned man could teach such Spiritual Teachings.

Jesus said, "My Teaching is not mine but She who sent Me. If anyone follows Her will, he will know if My Teaching is from the Loving Spiritual Creator or whether I am just speaking on My own authority. He who speaks out of his own opinion seeks his own selfish glory; but he who seeks to glorify and honour the One who sent him is True, and in him there is no deceit or evil intent.

Moses gave you the law. Yet none of you keeps the law. Why do you seek to kill Me?" They answered saying, "You have a demon in you. Who is seeking to kill you?" Jesus replied, "I did one deed in front of you and you all marveled, but because I healed the man on the Sabbath you are angry with Me. Do not judge according to appearance, but judge with virtuous judgment." Some of them said, "Is this not He whom the Jewish leaders seek to kill? But look! He speaks boldly and they say nothing to Him. Do the rulers know indeed that this is truly the Messiah?"

However, they knew where Jesus was from, but none would know where the Messiah was from, so how can some say He is the anointed one. Jesus then proclaimed, "You both know Me and know where I am from; for I have not come of My own accord; She who sent Me is True whom you do not know. But I know Her for I am from Her and She sent Me." And they wanted to arrest Him, but no one was willing to lay a hand on Him.

Many people believed in Him saying, "When the Messiah does come will he do more miracles and signs than this man?" The Pharisees heard the crowd murmuring these things about Him, so the Pharisees and the chief priests sent officers to seize Him. Then Jesus said to them, "I shall be with you a little while longer and then I will go to Her who sent Me. You will seek Me and not find Me, and where I am you cannot come."

The Jews said among themselves, "Where does He intend to go, that we shall not find Him? Does He intend to go to the Jewish Dispersion among the Greeks and teach the Greeks? What does He mean when He said, 'You will seek Me and not find Me, and where I am you cannot come?'"

On the last day, the great day of the Feast, Jesus stood and cried out saying, "If anyone thirsts let him come to Me and drink. He who believes in Me as the scripture has said, out of his inner Spiritual being will flow rivers of Living water." Now this He said about the Loving Spiritual Life-force which those who believed in Him and His Teachings were to receive from the Loving Spiritual Creator to bring their Spirits alive.

After hearing Jesus say these things, there was division among the people about who He was. Some said He is a

Prophet, while others said He was the Messiah. But some questioned His authenticity.

Author: Jesus states His Spiritual Teachings come from the Loving Creator in the Heavenly Spiritual World. And anyone filled with Her Loving Spiritual Life-force will understand His Teachings are correct. He questions why they are attacking Him when all He does is good.

He tells them that if they follow His Spiritual Teachings and Way of Love and Non-violence, they will awaken their Spiritual Life and also receive the Loving Spiritual Life-force from the Heavenly Creator into their Spirits which can then flow out of their Spiritual bodies and minds of only Love to other children in need.

There is division amongst the Jews about Jesus with some believing in Him and others not. The Jewish authorities want Him arrested and silenced as He was taking many Jews away from worshiping their two headed God Yahweh, to only follow the One True Loving Spiritual Creator of Jesus. He also tells them He will soon be leaving in His Spiritual body to be with our Loving Spiritual Creator in Heaven, but they do not understand this.

Jesus Avoids Arrest

John 7:45-52 The officers sent to arrest Jesus returned to the chief priests and Pharisees, who said to them, "Why have you not brought Him?" They said, "No man ever spoke like this man!" Then the Pharisees said, "Are you also deceived? Have any of the Jewish rulers or Pharisees believed in Him? This crowd that does not know the law is cursed." Nicodemus said to them, "Does our law judge a man before it hears him and knows what he is doing?" They answered, "Are you also from Galilee? Search and look, for no prophet has arisen out of Galilee."

Woman Caught in Adultery

John 8: 1-12 Jesus went to the Mount of Olives. In the morning, He came into the temple and taught. And the scribes and Pharisees brought to Him a woman caught in the act of adultery. And they placed her in the midst of them, and said to Jesus, "Teacher, this woman was caught in the act of adultery. Moses in the law, commanded us that such a woman should be stoned to death. But what do you say?"

They said this to try and trap Him in blasphemy, so they might accuse Him. But Jesus stooped down and wrote on the ground with His finger, ignoring them. And as they continued asking Him, He stood up and said to them, "He who is without sin amongst you, let him throw a stone at her first." And He stooped down again and continued to write words on the ground in front of them.

Then those who heard Him say this, being convicted by their own conscience, left one by one beginning with the oldest. And Jesus was left alone with the woman in the midst of them. When Jesus stood up and saw the woman standing alone, He said to her, "Woman, where are those who accuse you? Has no one condemned you?" She said, "No one Master." Then Jesus said to her, "Neither do I condemn you. Go, but sin no more." He then said, "I am the Light of the world. He who follows Me shall not walk in darkness but have the Light of Spiritual Life."

Author: Jesus had a very difficult situation to contend with but dealt with it on a number of levels through the Loving Spiritual Life-force and wisdom that empowered His Spiritual body and Soul mind of Love. The Jews worshiped a two headed God and the Yahweh 1 Godhead of War and Death whom they loved to serve any chance they could get, was the source of this violent condemnation and potential murder of the woman. The Yahweh 2 Godhead of Love is ignored when they want to murder or steal.

Firstly, He had to save the woman's life. Then He had to do it without committing blasphemy against the two headed God of the Jews to avoid being murdered by them Himself for contradicting their two headed God Yahweh and Moses. If He openly spoke that Moses followed a false two headed God, they would have killed Him on the spot. He accomplished this in a very simple, effective and powerful way that the murderers could not easily get out of. He just wrote down many of the other rules and laws of the Jewish religion on the ground of dirt for them to see.

He knew they were all imperfect in some way and had undoubtedly broken these laws also. Once they saw these other laws that He wrote each individual realised they were guilty of transgressing a law also like this woman. And since they didn't want to be stoned to death if anyone found out, it prompted their own conscience to walk away from committing murder as Moses instructed them to do. This sought of profound wisdom can only arise through being a fully awakened Spiritual child of our Loving Spiritual Creator as Jesus had become.

At the same time as saving His and the woman's life He was helping them question their own perverted religion to help them see how brutal their Yahweh 1 Godhead of War and Death really is. They were devoid of True Spiritual Love and Life so He was directing them to find the One True Loving Spiritual Creator who can never hurt any child. And He provided them with a Living example of how a Spiritual child of our Loving Spiritual Creator in this world behaves.

Finally, He pours out His and our Loving Creator's Love over her shame to heal her of this wrongdoing and its consequences and lovingly advises her to continue on her way in this world towards Heaven by not sinning anymore. Unlike the two headed God of the Jews and its followers, He and our Loving Spiritual Creator cannot murder or kill anyone for their entire mind and being is empowered only by Her Loving Spiritual Life-force. They are single in their identity and are not divided within like the two headed God of the Jews and are full of Light and Love for all Her children and only save them to Heaven and never condemn them.

Here, Jesus gives us all a beautiful example of how to engage with any child who has committed a wrongdoing through seeing them through the eye of Love, compassion and forgiveness instead of hatred and brutal judgement.

Jesus Speaks the Truth

John 8:13-20 The Pharisees said to Jesus, "You only bear witness of yourself. Your own witness alone is not true." Jesus replied, "Even if I do bear witness of Myself, My witness is true, for I know where I came from and where I am going, but you do not know where I come from and you do not know where I am going.

You judge according to the flesh, I judge no one. Yet if I do judge My judgment is true for I am not alone, I am with My Loving Creator who sent Me to you. It is also written in your law, that the testimony of two is true. I am one who bears witness of Myself, and My Loving Creator who sent Me bears witness of Me."

They asked, "Where is your Loving Creator?" Jesus replied, "You know neither Me nor My Loving Creator. If you had known Me, you would have known My Loving Creator also." Jesus said, "I am going away and you will seek Me, but you will die in your sins. Where I go you cannot come."

The Jews then said, "Will He kill Himself, because He says, 'Where I go you cannot come?'" He said, "You are from beneath; I am from above. You are of this world; I am not of this world. So, I say to you, you will die in your sins; for if you do not believe who I am you will die in your sins."

They asked Him, "Who are you?" And Jesus replied, "I have been showing you who I am all along from the beginning. I have many things to say and judge concerning you. She who sent Me is True, and I speak to the world those things which I heard and understand from Her." They did not understand He spoke to them about the Loving Spiritual Creator. Then He said to them, "When you realise the Spiritual Child of Humanity is higher in honour, then you will know who I am and I do nothing by Myself, but I teach these things as the Loving Creator has taught Me. And She who sent Me is with Me. The Loving Creator has not left Me alone, for I always do those things that please Her." As He spoke these words many believed in Him.

Author: Jesus is accused by the Pharisees of just teaching His own opinions and understandings to children. Jesus tells them they have no idea at all about His Spiritual identity and His awakening to become a Spiritual child of our Loving Spiritual Creator in Heaven. They do not know about the True One Loving Creator.

He points out that they are still judging out of their identity of flesh whereas He judges no one in that way, as He now has a Spiritual identity and He sees things through Spiritual wisdom and Truth. And He only does the things our Loving Creator does and only teaches the True Spiritual Way of Love that She has shown Him.

He tells them He will leave in His Spiritual body to go to Heaven, but they have no idea of what He means or how to get there because they follow the two headed God Yahweh not the One True Loving Creator of the Heavenly Spiritual World of Love.

His Spiritual awakening to become a Spiritual child of our Loving Creator meant He was no longer primarily of this earth world but was now primarily from the Heavenly Spiritual World above. And He tells them that if they had only come to know Him and His Spiritual Way of Love to

Heaven then they would have come to know our Loving Spiritual Creator as well. But by refusing to leave their two headed God Yahweh they remain in Spiritual ignorance and driven by their worship of the Yahweh 1 Godhead of War, they continue to sin.

The Truth Makes You Free

John 8:31-38 Then Jesus said to the Jews who followed Him, "If you live out of My word, you are My followers indeed. And you shall know the Truth, and the Truth shall make you free." They answered Him, "We are Abraham's descendants and have never been in bondage to anyone. How can You say, 'You will be made free'?"

Jesus answered, "Most assuredly, I say to you, whoever commits sin is a slave to sin. And a slave does not live in the house forever, but a son lives there forever. Therefore, if the son makes you free you shall be free indeed. I know that you are Abraham's descendants, but you seek to kill Me because My Spiritual word has no place in you. I speak what I have seen with My Loving Spiritual Creator, and you do what you have seen with your father."

Thomas 70 Jesus said, "If you bring forth what is within you, what you have found will save you. If you do not have that within you, what you do not have cannot save you."

Author: Jesus tells them if they follow His words and understand them, they will discover the Truth. This is the Spiritual Truth Jesus taught that we all have two different bodies in one with us right now. A temporary body of flesh that dies and disintegrates and returns to the earth from which it was formed.

And an Eternal Spiritual body and Soul formed from the Loving Spiritual Life-force of our Loving Creator that leaves the body of flesh at death to return to be in the presence of our Loving Creator in the Heavenly Spiritual World. If we have lived a Spiritual life free of sin, we are then set free.

In the Thomas saying Jesus states we must all bring our inner Spiritual identity within us alive to be saved to Heaven. Once we become Spiritually awakened and live out of our Spiritual identity on Earth we can no longer sin in any way as our Spiritual Life is only empowered by the Loving Spiritual Life-force of our Loving Creator in Heaven who is only Love. Therefore, as Her awakened Spiritual children on Earth, we are only Love. It is the body of flesh that can produce a false shadow identity prone to temptation through which we can commit all evil and sin.

Satan's Children

John 8:39-47 They said to Him, "Abraham is our father." Jesus said, "If you were Abraham's children, you would do the works of Abraham. But you seek to kill Me, a man who has told you the Truth which I heard from our Loving Creator. Abraham did not do this. You do the deeds of your father."

Then they said to Him, "We were not born illegitimately; we have one Father; Yahweh." Jesus said to them, "If the Loving Spiritual Creator were your God, you would love Me, for I proceeded forth and came from the Loving Spiritual Creator. I have not come from Myself, but She sent Me.

Why do you not understand the words I teach? Because you are not able to listen to My words and perceive their meaning. You are of your father the devil, and the desires and lusts of your father you want to do. He was a murderer from the beginning and does not stand in the Truth because there is no Truth in him. When he speaks a lie, he speaks from his own self for he is a liar and the father of it.

So, because I speak the Truth you do not believe Me. Which of you convicts Me of any sin? If I tell the Truth, why do you not believe me? He who is a Spiritual child of the

Loving Spiritual Creator understands the Loving Creator's words; therefore, you do not understand because you are not Spiritual children of the Loving Spiritual Creator."

Author: Jesus knew the Jews were worshiping two different Godheads but were deceiving themselves by giving them the same name Yahweh. Yahweh had one body but two heads. A brutal, murdering, lying, thieving, revengeful Godhead of War called Yahweh 1. And another Loving, forgiving, peaceful Godhead of Love called Yahweh 2. Opposing Godheads and forces of Darkness and Light in the One temple dedicated to their two headed God Yahweh.

All War Gods are satanic by their very nature, and all followers become demonic beasts of the flesh, killing and stealing from others. Jesus tells the Jews this satanic God of War has a hold on them, and they are following him and his evil ways. This is making it impossible for them to understand His Spiritual Teachings and Way of Love and Non-violence that comes forth from the One True Loving Spiritual Creator.

Before Abraham, 'I Am' Was

John 8:48-59 The Jews answered him, "Are we not right in saying that you are a Samaritan and have a demon." Jesus answered, "I do not have a demon, but I honour My Loving Spiritual Creator while you dishonour Me. And I do not seek My own glory; there is One who seeks it and will judge it. Truly, truly I say to you, if anyone keeps and observes the words of My Teachings, he shall never see death."

Then the Jews said to Him, "Now we know that you have a demon in you! Abraham died as did the prophets; and You say, 'If anyone understands and observes the words I teach, they will never taste death.' Are you greater than our father Abraham who is dead? And the prophets also dead. Who do you make yourself out to be?" Jesus answered, "If I glorify

Myself, My honour is nothing; it is our Loving Spiritual Creator who makes Me glorious, whom you say is your God, but you do not even know Her.

But I know Her. And if I say, 'I do not know Her,' I shall be a liar like you; but I do know the Loving Spiritual Creator and I keep and observe Her word. Your father Abraham rejoiced to see My day, and he saw it and was glad." The Jews then said to Him, "You are not yet fifty years old, and have you seen Abraham?" Jesus said to them, "Truly I say to you; before Abraham our Loving Spiritual Creator was in existence, and I am Her Spiritual child." They took up stones to stone Him to death, but Jesus hid and going through the midst of them, He went out of the temple.

Author: Again, Jesus tells them they must listen to and follow His Words and Spiritual Way of Love to have Eternal Life in the Heavenly Spiritual World of the one True God, our Loving Spiritual Creator. He tells them they do not know the One True Loving Creator, but He does and She existed well before Abraham and He is an awakened Spiritual child of Hers. The Jews wanted to stone Him to death for blaspheming their beliefs and their two headed God Yahweh. Typical of all followers of a brutal, domineering, revengeful, murdering War God.

Jesus the Shepherd

John 10:1-10 Jesus said, "Truly, I say to you, he who does not enter the sheepfold by the door but climbs in another way, he is a thief and a robber. But he who enters by the door is the shepherd of the sheep. To him the doorkeeper opens and the sheep hear his voice, and he calls his own sheep by name and leads them out. And when he brings his own sheep out, he goes before them; and the sheep follow him for they know his voice. A stranger they will not follow but they will flee from him for they do not know the voice of strangers." They did not understand what He was saying.

So, Jesus spoke again saying, "Truly, truly, I say to you, that I am the door of the sheep. And whoever came before Me are thieves and robbers, but the sheep did not hear them. I am the door and the Way and if anyone enters by following My Way, he will be saved and go in and out and find Heavenly pasture. The thief comes only to steal, kill and destroy. I have come so that they may have Spiritual Life and have it beyond measure."

Author: Jesus states there have been many false Spiritual Teachers, but He has the True understanding of how to guide children who follow His Spiritual Way to the green pastures of the Heavenly Spiritual World. He can be trusted because His own life as a Living example of an awakened Spiritual child of our Loving Creator on Earth is on full display for all to see. He is not like a sneaky thief with a hidden agenda.

The Good Shepherd Gives His Life

John 10:11-21 "I am the good shepherd. The good shepherd lays down his life for the sheep. But a hired servant who is not the shepherd, one whose sheep are not his own, sees the wolf coming and abandons the sheep and flees and the wolf takes hold of the sheep and scatters them abroad. The hired servant flees because he is just a servant and does not care about the sheep.

I am the good shepherd, and I know My sheep and they know Me. Just as the Loving Spiritual Creator knows Me and I know the Loving Creator and I lay down My life for the sheep. And I have other sheep which are not from this fold, them also I must bring and they will also hear My voice, and there shall be one flock and one shepherd.

Therefore, My Loving Spiritual Creator loves Me because I lay down My physical life, so that I may take up My life again in Spirit. No one takes it from Me, but I lay it down of My own free will. I have authority to lay My flesh down and authority to take My Spiritual Life up. This direction I have received from My Loving Spiritual Creator."

A division arose among the Jews because of these sayings. Many said, "He has a demon and is mad. Why do you listen to Him?" While others said, "These are not the words of one who has a demon. Can a demon heal a blind man?"

Author: Jesus dedicates His whole life to being a Spiritual Teacher, shepherd and guide for all those who hear His words and want to follow His Spiritual Way. As an awakened Spiritual child of our Loving Spiritual Creator, He knows Her as She knows Him. His Spiritual Way is open to all children in the world. He never abandons anyone and is willing to even sacrifice His body of flesh to show His followers we all have another Spiritual body that cannot die. Some Jews rejected Him outright while others were more accepting of Him. As Jesus said, "My coming will cause division."

My Sheep Know Me

John 10:22-31 It was the feast of Dedication in Jerusalem, and it was winter. And Jesus walked in the temple, in Solomon's porch. Then the Jews surrounded Him and said to Him, "How long will you keep us in doubt? If you are the Messiah, tell us plainly."

Jesus answered, "I told you and you do not believe. The works that I do in the name of our Loving Spiritual Creator, they bear witness of Me. But you do not believe because you are not of My sheep as I said to you. My sheep hear My voice, and I know them and they follow in My Way.

And this gives them Eternal Spiritual Life and they shall never perish; neither shall anyone snatch them out of My hand. My Loving Creator, who has given them to Me, is greater than all; and no one is able to snatch them out of My Loving Creator's hand. I and My Loving Creator are as One in purpose." And the Jews took up stones again to stone Him to death for what He said.

Author: Jesus again tells them that anyone who follows His Spiritual Way to enlightenment will have Eternal Life. And the miraculous Spiritual works He performs should be enough for them to believe He is from our Loving Creator.

He then says He and our Creator are as One. The Jews think He is referring to their two headed God Yahweh which is blasphemy by saying He is at One with Yahweh so want to kill Him. When Jesus was actually referring to the One True Loving Spiritual Creator that they did not know.

We Are All Children of Our Loving Creator

John 10:32-39 But Jesus said to them, "Many good works I have shown you from My Loving Creator. For which of those works do you stone Me?" The Jews answered Him, saying, "We do not stone you for the good works but for blasphemy because you, being just a man claim to be at one with God the Creator."

Jesus answered, "Is it not written in your law, 'I said you are Gods?' If they were called Gods to whom the word of your God came, why do you say of Me whom the Loving Creator has purified in Spirit and sent into the world, 'You are blaspheming,' just because I said, 'I am a child of the Loving Spiritual Creator?'

If I do not do the works of My Loving Creator do not believe Me; but if I do, though you may not believe Me, believe the works. Then you will come to know and believe that the Loving Spiritual Life-force of our Loving Spiritual Creator is in Me, and I am in Her Loving Spiritual Life-force." The Jews tried to seize Him, but He escaped out of their hands.

Author: Jesus tries to point out to the Jews that in their tradition other men in the past have been called Gods appointed by their God Yahweh. So, why are they so shocked that He is saying that He is also appointed by the True Loving Spiritual Creator as Her child to perform Spiritual works and teach.

But the Jews do not know about the One True Loving Creator and that every single child on earth is potentially Her child, whether they know it or not. So, they have no idea about the proper relationship we can all have with Her as Her Spiritual children on Earth as Jesus taught. He was speaking Truthfully about His relationship with Her as He had become an awakened Spiritual child Himself.

Jesus Beyond Jordan

John 10:40-42 Jesus went away again beyond the Jordan to the place where John was baptising at first and there He stayed. Then many came to Him and said, "John performed no sign, but all the things that John spoke about this man were true." And many there believed in Him.

Plot to Kill Jesus

John 11:45-57 After Jesus raised Lazarus back to life, many of the Jews who were with Mary and had seen Jesus do this, believed in Him. But some went to the Pharisees and told them the things Jesus did. Then the chief priests and the Pharisees gathered a council and said, "What shall we do? For this man works many signs. If we let Him alone like this, everyone will believe in Him and He will take away both our position of power and nation."

And one of them, Caiaphas, being high priest that year said to them, "You know nothing at all, nor do you consider that it is expedient for us that one man should die for the people and not that the whole nation should perish." Now this he did not say on his own authority; but being high priest that year he was prophesising that Jesus would die for the nation. But not for their nation only, but also He would gather together in one the True Spiritual children of the Creator who were scattered abroad.

From then on, they plotted to put Him to death. Therefore, Jesus no longer walked openly amongst the Jews but went from there into the country near the wilderness to a city called Ephraim and there remained with His disciples. And the Passover of the Jews was near, and many went from the country up to Jerusalem before the Passover to purify themselves. Many sought Jesus and as they stood in the temple they spoke among themselves, "What do you think? Will He come to the Feast?" Now both the chief priests and the Pharisees had given a command that if anyone knew where He was, they should report it so they might seize Him.

Author: The longer Jesus taught about the new Spiritual understanding of the One True Loving Spiritual Creator and Her Way of Love and Non-violence, the greater the threat was to the Jewish leaders and the power they wielded over the people. And also, to their two headed God Yahweh religion. So, they wanted Jesus killed.

Jews Want to Kill Lazarus

John 12:9-11 Jesus came to Bethany and visited with Mary, Martha and Lazarus whom He had brought back to life. Many of the Jews knew that He was there and came not only to see Him but also Lazarus. But the chief priests plotted to put Lazarus to death also, because on account of him many of the Jews were leaving them and believed in Jesus.

Follow Me to Eternal Life

John 12:20-27 Now there were certain Greeks among those who came up for the Passover to worship at the Feast. And they came to Philip, who was from Bethsaida of Galilee, and asked him, "Sir, we wish to see Jesus." So, Philip came and told Andrew and they told Jesus.

Jesus answered, "The hour has come that the Spiritual child of humanity should be glorified. Most assuredly I say to you, unless a grain of wheat falls into the ground and dies it remains alone; but if it dies it will produce much grain.

He who loves his physical life will lose it but he who thinks less of his physical life in this world will keep his Eternal Spiritual Life. If anyone pays attention to Me let them follow Me; and where I am they will be there also. If anyone pays attention to Me, My Loving Spiritual Creator will also honour them as She has honoured Me."

Author: If Jesus allows the Jews to kill His body of flesh He knows He will live on in His Spiritual body and Soul mind of Love that had come alive within Him. He knew we all have this same Spiritual body and if He appeared to the disciples after His death in His Spiritual body only, they could then understand this Spiritual Truth He had been teaching them all along and teach other children about it.

That way the death of His body of temporary earthly flesh becomes like a seed placed in the earth to die. Then its death releases and reveals our True Spiritual body and Soul mind of Love and will help many believe and understand they also have a Spiritual body just like Jesus and inspire them to also awaken into it by following His Way to enter the Heavenly Spiritual World after death. From one physical death, many shall be awakened to this Spiritual Truth. If we try to hang onto our body of flesh and material life we will lose it. But if we awaken and live out of our Spiritual body and Life, we will have it for all Eternity.

Jesus Foresees His Death

John 12:27-36 Jesus said, "Now My Soul is troubled and what shall I say? Loving Spiritual Creator, please save Me from this hour. But for this purpose, I came to this hour. Loving Creator glorify your name." Then a voice came from Heaven saying, "I have both glorified it and will glorify it again." The people who stood nearby and heard it said that it had thundered. Others said, "An Angel has spoken to Him."

Jesus said, "This voice did not come because of Me but for your sake. Now is the judgement of this world; now the Spiritual child of this world will be cast out. And if I am lifted up from the earth in My Spiritual body, I will draw all children to Myself." This He said to signify the manner of His death and resurrection. The people answered Him, "We have heard from the law that the Messiah remains forever; so how can You say, 'The Spiritual child of Humanity must be lifted up?' Who is this Spiritual child of Humanity?"

Then Jesus said, "A little while longer the Spiritual Light is with you. Walk while you have the Light, lest darkness overtake you; he who walks in darkness does not know where he is going. While you have the Spiritual Light, believe in the Spiritual Light so you may become children of the Spiritual Light." Jesus then departed.

Author: Jesus was human and His physical death would be as painful as many deaths are and naturally, He was anxious about that. But He knew He had this important Spiritual task to perform as a culmination of all that He had been Teaching the disciples. His Spiritual body and Soul would be released from His dead body of flesh, and He would be lifted up to the Heavenly Spiritual World. But not before appearing briefly to His disciples in only His Spiritual body.

This vital demonstration is how He will help us all become Spiritually awakened and move into our Spiritual identity also to follow Him to the Heavenly Spiritual World after our own death. Jesus refers to Spiritual children of our Loving Spiritual Creator as children of Light who understand the Truth of who they really are and where they are going. The Heavenly Spiritual world of our Loving Creator.

I Came to Save Not Judge

John 12:42-50 Many believed in Jesus even among the rulers but because of the Pharisees they did not admit it, lest they should be put out of the synagogue; for they loved the praise of men more than the glory of our Loving Creator. Jesus said, "He who believes in Me, believes not in Me but in She who sent Me. And he who sees Me sees She who sent Me. I have come as a Spiritual Light into this world that whoever believes in Me and My Spiritual way should not live in darkness anymore.

And if anyone hears My words and does not believe, I do not judge them for I did not come to judge the world but to save the world. He who rejects Me and My Spiritual Way and Teachings and does not live by them, will receive the consequences of not following the Spiritual Way but I judge him not.

For I have not spoken on My own authority; but My Loving Spiritual Creator gave Me all that I should say. And I know that Her Spiritual Way leads to everlasting Life. Therefore, I speak just as She has told Me to speak."

Author: Jesus was an awakened Spiritual child of our Loving Spiritual Creator. A beacon of Spiritual Light and Truth in this material world that can be filled with darkness and ignorance. He knew the Way that leads to the Heavenly Spiritual World and taught it to all who would listen.

He condemned no one for not wanting to follow His Spiritual Teachings but simply offered them the Way to follow that will lead them out of this material world of suffering into the Heavenly Spiritual World of Love beyond all suffering. His life of Love and Non-violence is also the nature of our Loving Spiritual Creator. We should all be following His Way. Shut down the armaments industry and teach children the evil of war and death no more.

Jesus Washes Disciples Feet

John 13:1-17 After supper with the disciples Jesus knew He did not have long before He would be handed over to the Jewish authorities. Jesus rose and laid aside His garments, took a towel and wrapped it around Himself. And then He poured water into a basin and began to wash the disciple's feet and wipe them with the towel. When He came to Simon Peter, he said to Jesus, "Master, are you washing my feet?" Jesus answered saying, "What I am doing, you do not understand now, but you will understand after I finish." Peter said to Him, "You shall never wash my feet!"

Jesus said, "If I do not wash you, you have no destiny with Me." Simon Peter then said to Him, "Teacher, wash not only my feet but also my hands and head." Jesus said, "He who has bathed, needs only to wash his feet and is completely clean; you are clean, but not all of you." Jesus was referring to the one who would surrender Him up to the Jews.

After washing their feet, He put on His garments and sat down and said, "Do you know what I have done to you? You call Me Teacher and Master, and you are right for so I am. If then your Master and Teacher has washed your feet, you should also wash one another's feet. For I have given you an example that you should do as I have done to you.

Truly I say to you, a servant is not greater than his Master, nor is he who is sent greater than She who sent him. He who receives anyone I send receives Me, and he who receives Me, receives She who sent Me. If you know these things and do them, you will be blessed in Spirit."

Author: Jesus gives a final personal example of how His disciples should behave by being humble and serving others no matter how lowly the service may seem. As long as it is done with Love, they will be Spiritual Children of our Loving Spiritual Creator just like Himself. We must do the same.

Choosing the One to Surrender Him Up

John 13:21-30 Jesus was troubled in His Spirit and said, "One of you must surrender Me up." The disciples looked at one another uncertain of whom He was speaking about. Now, the disciple that Jesus loved was leaning on Jesus and Simon Peter motioned to him to ask Jesus who He was talking about. Then the disciple said, "Who will it be Teacher?" Jesus answered, "It will be the one to whom I give a piece of bread to after I have dipped it."

And having dipped the bread, He chose to give it to Judas Iscariot, the son of Simon. Then Jesus said to him, "What you must do, do quickly." But no one else knew why He said this to Judas, but Judas knew.

Some thought because Judas handled the money Jesus may have wanted him to buy more things for the feast or go and give something to the poor. Having received the piece of bread from Jesus he then went out immediately into the night to do as Jesus wanted.

Author: Although Judas is regarded as a secret betrayer of Jesus, it is also quite possible he was chosen by Jesus as the only disciple willing to do what Jesus asked and lead the authorities to Jesus to capture Him so He could fulfill His Spiritual destiny.

Either way Jesus clearly knew what Judas was doing and set it in motion Himself at that specific time of the Passover. As He said, "I lay my body of flesh down of my own free will. And I take My Spirit up."

Love as I Have Loved You

John 13:31-36 Jesus said, "Now the Spiritual child of humanity is honoured and our Loving Spiritual Creator is honoured through Him. If our Loving Creator is glorified through Him, She will also glorify Him in Himself at the same time. Little children I shall be with you only a little longer. Then you will seek Me; and as I said to the Jews, I now say to you, where I am going you cannot come.

A new commandment I give to you, that you love one another as I have loved you, that you may also love one another. By this everyone will know that you are My followers, if you have love for one another. Simon Peter said, "Teacher, where are you going?" Jesus answered, "Where I am going you cannot follow Me now, but you shall follow Me later."

Thomas 25 Jesus said, "Love your companion like your own life, protect such a one like the pupil of your eye."

Author: Jesus is a fully awakened and enlightened Spiritual child of our Loving Spiritual Creator. All such children can enter the Heavenly Spiritual World after they pass through the death experience of their body of flesh. Jesus practiced a very high level of Love towards everyone in whatever way they needed to be loved. He instructs His followers they must also have this high level of Spiritual Love in their own life now.

I Am the Way and the Truth

John 14:1-6 Jesus said, "Let your hearts not be troubled, but believe in our Loving Spiritual Creator and believe in Me also. In our Loving Creator's Heavenly World there are many abodes, if it were not so I would have told you. I go to prepare a place for you, and I will receive you to Myself when we meet again; so that where I am there you will be also. And you know where I go and you know I will go in the Way of the Spirit."

Thomas said, "Teacher we do not know where You go to, so how can we know the Way?" Jesus said to Him, "I am the Way, the Truth and the Spiritual Life. No one comes to the Loving Spiritual Creator except through My Spiritual Way of Life. If you had understood who I really was, then you would have known our Loving Spiritual Creator also. From now on you do know Her and have perceived Her nature of Divine Perfect Love in Me."

Philip said, "Teacher, show us the Loving Spiritual Creator, that is all we will need." Jesus said, "Have I been with you all this time, and yet you still do not know Me Philip? He who understands and knows Me understands and knows our Loving Creator, so how can you say, 'Show us the Loving Creator,' when I am standing right in front of you?

Do you not believe I am living in and out of the Loving Spiritual Life-force of our Loving Creator, and the Loving Spiritual Life-force of our Loving Creator is living in Me? The Spiritual Teachings I give to you are not mine, but they are from our Loving Spiritual Creator, whose Spiritual Life-force lives in Me, and does all the works I perform. Believe Me when I tell you, I am living in the Spiritual Life-force of our Loving Creator and Her Spiritual Life-force is living in Me. Or if you do not believe Me, then believe because you have seen the miracles and works I have done, empowered by Her Love.

I say to you, he who believes in Me and My Teachings and Spiritual Way, the works that I do he will do also and even greater works than these will he do, for I go to our Loving Creator in the Heavenly Spiritual World. And whatever you ask in My name I will do for you, so that the Loving Spiritual Creator may be glorified in His Spiritual child. Ask for anything in My name and I will do it."

Thomas 37 His disciples said, "Which day will you come forth and appear to us? And which day will we see you?" Jesus said, "When you strip yourselves naked without being ashamed and you take your garments and put them under the ground of your feet, and you trample them like children, then you will see and understand the Spiritual Child of the Living One and you will have no more fear."

Author: Jesus tells them He is about to leave and go into the Heavenly Spiritual World and will prepare a place for them there for when they arrive. The disciples are perplexed about where He is going, how to get there and who our Loving Creator is. Jesus tells them that if they see who He is as a Loving Spiritual child of our Loving Creator then they see Her.

He tells the disciples He is filled with the Loving Spiritual Life-force of our Loving Spiritual Creator which is how He is able to perform miracles. He also tells them they can also be filled with Her Loving Spiritual Life-force and do even greater miracles than He has performed.

And by following His Teachings and Spiritual Way of Love and Non-violence they will know the Way to Heaven. He tells the disciples that once He enters the Heavenly Spiritual World, they can ask for anything they need in His name and He will do it for them.

But later in John, Jesus says that they no longer need Him to intervene on their behalf with our Loving Creator for once they are awakened Spiritual children like Him, then they can ask Her directly for whatever they need and She will do it for them just as She did it for Him.

In the Thomas saying Jesus again refers to us having to become like innocent children to awaken into our True Spiritual identity to be able to understand and see Him as He really is. And then we will be like Him.

Disciples Will Receive Spirit of Truth

John 14:15-23 Jesus said, "If you love Me, you will keep My Teachings and Spiritual Way of Love and Non-violence. And I will ask our Loving Spiritual Creator to give you another support that it may abide with you forever. The Spirit of Truth, the Loving Spiritual Life-force of our Loving Creator that the material worldly ones cannot receive. For they neither see it nor know what it is, but you know of it, for it is within you and empowers your Spiritual bodies and Soul minds of Love. I will not send you forth as orphans; I will be with you in Spirit.

Soon the world will see Me no more, but you will see Me again. Because I live in Spirit, you will also come alive to your Spirit. On that day you will come to understand that I am in our Loving Creator's Spiritual life-force, and you will be as Me and I as you. And anyone who loves Me will be loved by our Loving Creator and I will love them and make myself known to them as a Spiritual child of our Loving Creator."

Judas asked, "Teacher, how is it that You will make yourself known to us and not the world?" Jesus said, "Those who love Me and My Spiritual Way follow My words and our Loving Creator will love them, and She will come to them and make a dwelling place in Heaven with them. Those who do not love Me do not follow My words, and My words come from our Loving Spiritual Creator."

Author: Jesus tells the disciples to follow His Teachings and Spiritual Way, and they will receive the Spirit of Truth, the Loving Spiritual Life-force of our Loving Creator to support and empower their Spiritual lives. Materially minded children cannot easily receive it. He predicts He will die and be out of sight for a while but will appear to them again in His Spiritual body. And once they awaken Spiritually, they will have the same Loving Spiritual Life-force that is in His Spiritual body, and they will all be alike. Then our Loving

Spiritual Creator can welcome them also into their abode in the Heavenly Spiritual World to be with Her for all Eternity.

Peace I Give to You

John 14:25-31 Jesus said, "I tell you these things while I am still with you. But the Loving Spiritual Life-force whom our Loving Creator will send into you will continue to teach you and help you recall the things I have said. Peace, I leave with you; My peace I give to you; not in the same way this material world gives do I give it to you, but in Spirit. Let your Soul not be troubled or be afraid. You have heard Me tell you that I am going away and coming back to you in Spirit. If you loved Me, you would be happy for Me, because I said I am going to be with our Loving Creator in the Heavenly Spiritual World.

And I tell you this now before it happens, so you may believe when it happens. I have little time to talk with you, for the ruler of this material world is coming and nothing of Me is in him. But our Loving Spiritual Creator has given Me a Spiritual task to fulfill, and I wish to show the world that I love our Spiritual Creator. So, rise up, and let us leave here."

Author: Jesus tells them again He is leaving them but will appear to them again in Spirit. And they should not be afraid of what will happen to Him or what they will see. He blesses them with His Spiritual peace and reminds them the Loving Spiritual Life-force of our Loving Creator will teach and guide them after He has gone. Satanic children are about to seize Him so He can fulfill His Spiritual Task.

Jesus is the Vine

John 15:1-8 Jesus said, "I am the True Spiritual vine, and our Loving Creator is the farmer who planted the vine. And every branch connected to Me that does not bear any

Spiritual fruit is taken away; and every branch that does bear Spiritual fruit is cleansed, so that it may bear more fruit. You are already Spiritually clean through receiving the Spiritual Teachings I have spoken to you, and by following them.

Remain with Me and live out of the Spirit, and I will remain with you. As the branch of the vine cannot bear fruit by itself unless connected to the vine, neither can you bear Spiritual fruits unless you are connected with Me through My Spiritual Teachings and Way. I am the vine and you are the branches. He who lives with My Spiritual Teachings within him is with Me and will bear much Spiritual fruit.

He who does not know the Way of My Spiritual Teachings can do nothing Spiritual. If anyone does not live out of the Spiritual water and Spiritual Life-force found within My Spiritual Teachings, their Spirit will dry up and wither away. If you live in Spirit with Me and My Teachings live in you, ask what you desire and it will be done for you. In this way our Loving Spiritual Creator is glorified, and by bearing much Spiritual fruit you will all be My disciples."

Thomas 40 Jesus said, "A grapevine has been planted outside of the Loving Creator's Spiritual Life-force. And because it has no Spiritual vitality, it will wither and have to be removed."

Author: Jesus is a Spiritual Teacher and understands who our Loving Spiritual Creator is in the Heavenly Spiritual World and how to reach Heaven from Earth. He teaches this to other children, and some are awakened to become Spiritual children just like Him and perform Spiritual works by following His Teachings and Way. This keeps their Spirits alive and clean and prepares them to enter the Heavenly Spiritual World after their death experience. Others are not interested in His Spiritual Teachings and Way so it is unlikely they will awaken Spiritually to perform Spiritual works to be ready to enter the Heavenly Spiritual World.

Abide in My Love

John 15:9-17 Jesus said, "As the Loving Spiritual Creator has loved Me, so have I loved you; live in My Spiritual Way of Love and with the Love of our Spiritual Creator in you. If you keep My Teachings and Spiritual Way you will live out of My Spiritual Way of Love, just as I have kept our Loving Creator's Spiritual Way and live out of Her Love. These things I have told you so My joy may remain in you, and your joy may be fulfilled in Spirit.

This is My instruction, that you love one another as I have loved you. No one has greater love than this, than to lay down his Life of flesh to establish and put into place his Spiritual life for the sake of his friends. You are My friends if you follow My Teachings and Spiritual Way. No longer do I call you servants, for a servant does not know what his master is doing; but I have called you friends for all things our Loving Spiritual Creator has told Me I have made known to you.

You did not choose Me, but rather I chose you and appointed you that you should go and bear Spiritual fruit, and that fruit that is yours will continue to exist and never perish. And whatever you ask our Loving Spiritual Creator in My name She will give you. And I say again that you must love one another."

Author: Jesus Loves in the exact same Way our Spiritual Creator Loves. She is only Love and can never hurt anyone just like Jesus. He tells us all to move into this same Spiritual Love and live out of it every day of our lives for each other to become Her Spiritual children on Earth and bring forth Spiritual works of Love for other children.

Jesus regards everyone who follows His Teachings and Spiritual Way as being equal to Himself. And He is willing to establish His Spiritual body apart from His temporary body of flesh by being murdered to show us all that we have two different bodies in one. And only our Spiritual body lives on which we must keep clean and alive with the Loving Spiritual Life-force of Heaven.

World Hates You and Me

John 15:18-27, 16:1-4 Jesus said, "If the worldly ones hate you, know they hated Me before they hated you. If you were of the material world the worldly ones would love you. But you are not of this world as I chose you out of this world to be in the Spiritual World, therefore the worldly ones hate you. Remember I told you, 'A servant is not greater than his master.' If they persecuted Me they will also persecute you. But if they followed My Teachings, they would follow yours also. All these things they will do to you because you are My followers, and because they do not know the Loving Spiritual Creator who sent Me to you.

If I had not come and spoken the Spiritual Truth to them, they would have no sin but now they have no excuse for their sin. He who hates Me, hates our Loving Creator also. If I had not performed the Spiritual works among them, which no one else could do, they would have no sin; but now they have seen these Spiritual works and hate both Me and our Loving Creator who empowers Me to perform them. But when you receive the Loving Spiritual Life-force, the Spirit of Truth, who proceeds from the Loving Spiritual Creator that I shall give to you, Her Life-force will testify about Me. And you also will bear witness because you have been with Me from the beginning and now you know Me.

I have told you these things to forewarn you, so that you remain strong in the Spiritual Way, I have taught you. They will expel you from the synagogues, and indeed the time is coming that whoever kills you will think they are doing a service to their God. All these things they will do to you, for they have not known Me or our Loving Creator. I have told you about these things in advance so you will be prepared and remember Me warning you about them. I did not need to tell you these things while I was still with you."

Author: Jesus is warning the disciples that they will face persecution for leaving the Jewish two headed God Yahweh and following Him and His Spiritual Way of Love to become awakened Spiritual children of the One Loving Spiritual Creator. The Jews were ignorant of the One Loving Spiritual Creator but had a version of Her in their Godhead Yahweh 2 who taught to Love your neighbour as yourself. While their other Godhead Yahweh 1 the God of War taught to kill your neighbour and steal their land.

By rejecting the True Spiritual Way of Life that Jesus taught they were rejecting our Loving Creator as well as the Way to Heaven. The many Spiritual miracles of healing that Jesus performed with Her Loving Spiritual Life-force in Him was proof of His True and correct understanding of who our Loving Creator really was. So, they had no excuse to not change allegiance to the One Loving Spiritual Creator. But they still hung onto their two headed God Yahweh.

Loving Spiritual Life-force Sent to You

John 16:5-15 Jesus said, "But now I go away to our Loving Spiritual Creator in the Heavenly Spiritual World, but none of you asks me, 'Where are You going?' And because I tell you this your hearts are filled with sorrow. Nevertheless, I am telling you the Truth. It is to your advantage that I go away in Spirit to Heaven, for if I do not go in Spirit to Heaven I cannot send the Loving Spiritual Life-force into you. But if I am in Spirit, I can send this Helper of our Loving Creator to you. And when it has come it will shine the Light of Truth and Love on all things, exposing all Spiritual corruptions. It will guide you into all Truth, for it will not speak on its own authority but of the Loving Creator's from whom it comes forth. It will help you see what is to come. It will glorify Me and take what is Mine and declare it to you. All things that our Loving Creator has are also Mine to have."

Author: Jesus says He has to be fully in His Spiritual body only to be able to send the Loving Spiritual Life-force of our Loving Spiritual Creator into the disciples. So, it is to their advantage that His body of flesh is killed so he can be fully in His Spiritual body after rising in Spirit from His dead body of flesh. Once filled with the Loving Spiritual Life-force they will all be guided to continue on with their own Spiritual Lives. He actually gives it to them personally when He appears briefly in the room with them in His risen Spiritual body, after His body of flesh was crucified, and He breathes on them and they receive the Loving Spiritual Life-force at that moment.

Sorrow Turned to Joy

John 16:16-22 Jesus said, "In a little while you will see Me no more, then after a little while you will see Me again in Spirit, because I must go to the Heavenly Spiritual World of our Loving Creator." Some of the disciples said among themselves, "What is He now talking about? What does He mean when He says, 'In a little while you will not see Me then a little while later you will see Me because I am going to our Loving Creator.' We do not understand any of this."

Jesus realised their confusion and said to them, "Are you wondering amongst yourselves about what I meant when I said to you, 'In a little while you will see Me no more, and then a little while later you will see Me again in Spirit?' I say to you that you will weep and lament while the worldly ones will rejoice; and you will be sorrowful, but your sorrow will soon turn to joy.

When a woman is in labour she has sorrow due to pain because her hour has come to give birth; but as soon as she gives birth to her child, she no longer remembers the anguish, for she is joyous that a child has been born into the world. Therefore, you now have sorrow; but I will see you again in Spirit, and your heart will rejoice and no one will take your joy from you."

Author: Jesus is again trying to explain to the disciples that His body of flesh is going to end but He will be born again into His full Spiritual body that does not die. So, at first, they will be sad to see His body of flesh murdered on the cross but then they will be filled with joy when He appears to them in His Living Spiritual body which we all have with us right now.

But Jesus still had trouble getting the disciples to understand this Spiritual Truth even at this final stage of being with them. But He knew that once they saw Him only in His Spiritual body, they would finally understand His main Spiritual message to us all. Get ready to leave in your Spiritual body at the time of your death by becoming a Spiritual child of Love and Non-violence right now.

Pray In the Way of Jesus

John 16:25-33 Jesus said, "I have spoken these things to you in the past in parables and sayings, but the hour has come when I no longer speak to you in parables, now I speak openly to you declaring who the One Loving Spiritual Creator really is.

And from this day you will no longer need to ask Me to intercede for you with our Loving Creator for you are now Her Spiritual children as well as I and She will love you Herself because you believe and follow My Way that comes from Her. Up until now you have not understood how to ask in the Way of Her Spiritual child as I do. You are now able to ask in Spirit, and you will receive and your joy will be full.

I was born out of the Spirit of our Loving Spiritual Creator in the Heavenly World and brought Spiritual Life into this material world through My body of flesh. And I now leave this material world and My body of flesh and go to the Heavenly Spiritual World in My Spiritual body of Light.

His disciples said, "You are speaking openly, and using no parables. Now we are sure You know all things and have no need to question You about this. We believe that You have come forth from the Loving Spiritual Creator in Heaven."

Jesus said, "Do you really believe now? Behold, the hour is coming and is here when you will all be scattered each to his own, and you will abandon Me and leave Me alone. But I am not alone, because the Loving Spiritual Creator is always with Me and Her Loving Spiritual Life-force fills My Spirit. These things I have spoken to you that through Me and My Way you may have True peace. In this world you will have trouble and suffering; but cheer up, take courage, for I have overcome the world and so can you."

Author: Jesus opens up more directly explaining who our Loving Creator really is and what their relationship is with Her as Her awakened Spiritual children on Earth. He also tells them that as Her awakened Spiritual children they can now talk directly to Her just as He does and She will respond to them in the same way She responded to Him by Loving them. He again mentions He is about to die to the flesh and rise in His Spiritual body to enter the Heavenly Spiritual World. He predicts they will abandon Him at the end of His time. He then says we can all overcome the difficulties and Spiritual dangers in this material world just as He did by following His Spiritual Way of Love and Non-violence.

Jesus Prays for His Followers

John 17: 1-26 Jesus looked up to Heaven and said, "Loving Spiritual Creator, the hour has come to glorify your Spiritual child, that your child may glorify You. You have given Him mastery over all of the flesh, so that He could give Eternal Spiritual Life to all You have brought to Him. And Eternal Spiritual Life is found through understanding who You really are, the One True Loving Spiritual Creator and through following My Teachings and Spiritual Way, you sent Me to give to them. I have glorified You on Earth and I have finished the work You gave Me to do.

Loving Creator, glorify My Spirit together with Yourself through your Loving Spiritual Life-force that existed before the world was. I have manifested who You are through My Spiritual Teachings and works, to those of this Earth world who are given to Me. They were Your children to give to Me, and they have kept Your Spiritual Teachings and Way that I gave them. And they now know all the things I gave them were from You, and believe I am your Spiritual child. I pray for them, that they glorify Me and Yourself by following the Spiritual Way you have shown Me. And all Mine are Yours and Yours are Mine.

I will no longer be in this world as I am coming to You in the Heavenly Spiritual World, but these are still in this world. Loving Creator, guard those given to Me through Your Spiritual Way I have given to them, that they may be as One in Spirit, as we are as One. I have kept them on the Spiritual path and in Your Way of Spiritual Love, while I have been with them. But now I come to You and these things I have spoken to them so they may have the same Spiritual joy I have also fulfilled in themselves.

I gave them Your Spiritual Teachings and Way of the Spirit of Love, and the worldly ones have hated them because they are no longer of this material world. Just as I am not of this material world anymore. I do not pray that You take them out of this world, but that You should guard them from the evil in it. They are no longer of this material world just as I am no longer of this material world. Purify them Spiritually through Your Truth and Love. Your Spiritual existence is the ultimate Truth. And all Your words and Ways are born from Your Truth, Love and Spirit.

As You sent Me into the world, I also have sent them into the world. And for their sakes I purify Myself in Spirit, that they may also purify themselves in Spirit by the Spiritual Truth. I also pray for those who believe in Me and My Spiritual Teachings and Way, who have received it through My followers. And they shall all be as One in Spirit, just as your Spiritual Life-force Loving Creator is in Me and I am in your Spiritual Life-force it will also be in them. Then they will know I am a Spiritual child of Yours. And we will all become your Spiritual children. And the glory of Spiritual Life you gave to Me; I have given to them that they may also be at One with You and Me and be made perfect. You Love them, as You Love Me.

Loving Creator, I ask that they who follow My Spiritual Teachings and Way of Love be also with Me in the Heavenly Spiritual World where Your Love existed before the foundation of this material world. Loving Creator, the worldly ones have not known You, but I have known You and My followers know that I am from You. I have made known to them who You really are and You Love us all. And I will make it known that your Loving Spiritual Life-force is in My Soul and Spirit and also in theirs, and we are all your Spiritual children."

Author: Jesus is talking to our Loving Spiritual Creator about His Spiritual work on Earth that He is about to complete. The disciples hear Him clearly saying they are also now Spiritual children of the One True Loving Spiritual Creator and therefore the same as He. He is explaining that Eternal Spiritual Life comes through being at one with the Loving Spiritual Life-force of the One True Loving Spiritual Creator in their own Spiritual bodies.

He is about to undergo His final transformation by having His body of flesh killed and then rising in His perfect

Spiritual body. He prays that His followers are protected from evil and are able to stay on the Spiritual path and Way of Love until they also enter the Heavenly Spiritual World and that they teach this Way to all other children. He is also more openly revealing to the disciples that the two headed God Yahweh is not the One True Loving Spiritual Creator.

The Last Instruction of Jesus

John 21:20-22 After Jesus appeared in His Spiritual body and spoke to the disciples at the sea of Tiberias He gave them this one last instruction. "Follow Me."

Author: Jesus wants us all to awaken to become Living Spiritual children of our Loving Spiritual Creator in the Heavenly Spiritual World so we may also enter that world beyond all suffering after our body of flesh dies. We only have to listen to His words, be transformed by them and 'Follow Him' there. Waiting for Him to come back as some Jewish/Christians falsely teach is a waste of precious time.

We must take hold of the reigns of our life now and set our direction for Heaven by awakening our Spiritual body and Soul mind of Love and bring Heaven's Love to all children in need. And become a True Spiritual child of Light from Heaven on Earth and a bridge for Heaven's Spiritual Loving Life-force to flow across to all the Earth, all its inhabitants, all its animals and all its natural garden. Only through this Spiritual Way of awakening do we have any hope of restoring the Peace and natural balance to this rapidly deteriorating material world called Earth.

Our Loving Spiritual Creator is only Love.

We must be Her Spiritual children of

only Love on Earth.

Chapter 14
Conclusion

This Gospel translation of the Spiritual Teachings and Way of Love and Non-violence that Jesus taught has been a work of Love for my great, lifelong friend and Spiritual Teacher Jesus of Nazareth. Although I left the Jewish/Christian Catholic church when I was sixteen years old because of the Old Testament two headed God Yahweh poisoning the identity of our Loving Spiritual Creator and Jesus, I took Jesus and His words with me.

Our Loving Spiritual Creator's entire consciousness is only Love. She gives us True Spiritual Life beyond all the suffering of this temporary, dangerous material world. Jesus explains what we must do to awaken our Spiritual Life while still in the body of flesh. We only have to listen to His words, understand them correctly and become transformed by them in our daily life.

Then we Truly become Living Spiritual children of our Loving Spiritual Creator in the Heavenly Spiritual World just waiting to be in Her presence and go home. But while we are here on Earth once we awaken, we must be the Spiritual Lights in the darkness of this material world with all of its evil. So other children can see the True Spiritual nature that is within themselves just as it is within us all.

Love your Way to Heaven
Christopher John Joseph